KENTUCKY'S STRANGE AND UNUSUAL HAUNTS

by Jacob Floyd & Jenny Floyd

Anubis Press
Louisville, KY

The Bluegrass State is home to many haunted legends. Stories of witches, ghosts, demons, monsters, "black things", "white thangs", and even headless horsemen abound across Kentucky. In this book you will read nearly a hundred of those legends taken from all across the state. From the hilltop of Western Kentucky University to the classy Seelbach Hotel, from the infamous Bobby Mackey's Music World to the notorious Waverly Hills Sanatorium, you'll read tales about hotels, schools, landmarks, graveyards, mountains, hills, tunnels, lonely roads, and many other locations including the historic Mammoth Cave. So if you're in for a good scare, sit back with the Frightening Floyds and learn all about *Kentucky's Strange and Unusual Haunts.*

Thank you for reading! If you like the book, please leave a review on Amazon and Goodreads. Reviews help authors and publishers spread the word!

To keep up with more Anubis Press news, join the Anubis Press Dynasty on Facebook.

ALSO BY THE FRIGHTENING FLOYDS:

Louisville's Strange and Unusual Haunts
Kentucky's Haunted Mansions
Haunts of Hollywood Stars and Starlets
Indiana's Strange and Unusual Haunts
Be Our Ghost
Aliens Over Kentucky
Strange and Unusual Mysteries

KENTUCKY'S STRANGE AND UNUSUAL HAUNTS

by Jacob Floyd & Jenny Floyd

This book is dedicated with love to our best friend, Snow White – aka BooBoo, who passed away while this book was being written. Thank you for always being a friend and keeping our household in line, and for always being by our sides as we worked on this collection. You will always be Mama BooBoo.

TABLE OF CONTENTS

Introduction

Graveyards...01
Roads, Tunnels, and Bridges..................................50
Schools...86
Lodging..131
Natural Spots..155
Other Buildings..199

About the Authors
Bibliography
Also Available

INTRODUCTION

This book was three years in the making. We began this quest through haunted Kentucky in February of 2018. The first draft wasn't completed until December of 2020. But it's not because we had to spend so much time picking through everything – which we did spend a lot of time combing through all the information we could find regarding Kentucky haunts – but there was just so much else going on. We had works out with other publishers we had to push. We were building Anubis Press, building Nightmare Press, and building Wild West Press. There were also other paranormal projects to work on. Jacob had some short stories to write, and he even came out with a book of poetry. Put all that on top of some major life changes and personal issues and the dumpster fire that was 2020, and *Kentucky's Strange and Unusual Haunts* has spent a lot of time on the back burner.

During that time the book sat waiting – with intermittent research and writing occurring during these years – the book went from being our third installment of the *Strange and Unusual* series to the only installment to the second installment. The first two, *Louisville's Strange and Unusual Haunts* and *Indiana's Strange and Unusual Haunts* went out-of-print as we requested back the rights for *Louisville's* and were also given back the rights to *Indiana's* prematurely so we could have them all – which was a nice move on the publisher's part. Now those two books are currently sitting in limbo waiting to be added to and revised before coming back out under Anubis Press.

That left *Kentucky's* standing alone, though unpublished at the time, we thought we would be finishing it sooner rather than later – and it turned out to be *much* later. During that time, we wrote and published *Strange and Unusual Mysteries*, making that one the current standalone in the series.

So, having already written about Louisville, we decided to cut most of the Louisville entries from this book, with the exception of a couple we thought would be good inclusions (The Seelbach Hotel because it has such a history, and Waverly because, well...obvious reasons, right? What's a Kentucky ghost book without Waverly Hills?) The new Louisville haunts we researched will be included in the revised edition of *Louisville's Strange and Unusual Haunts*, whenever that one makes its return.

As it turns out, Kentucky is quite a haunted state, according to legends. We discovered well over a hundred allegedly haunted locations. Many of which had well-documented events. Some of the trails led to near dead ends with not much to go on. It would say, "At this location, lights turn off and on by themselves and doors slam shut on their own," and that doesn't really amount to much. So we would pass those by. Other locations were reputed to be haunted, even having tours, yet not much information existed about them. So, we skipped those locations, as well. Other supposedly haunted locations were cut or passed on because even though they had haunts, they were minimal and this book kept growing and growing, so we wanted to cut it down some.

As it stands, there are nearly a hundred locations included in this book. They have been categorized accordingly, and we hope you will enjoy reading about the legends and hauntings across the Bluegrass State.

As always, our intention is not to corroborate these stories. Some of these tales are quite sensational and make more for good campfire tales than they do accounts of the paranormal – stories that are likely not to be a believed by anyone, but we included because the nature of the legend is part of what makes up stories of ghosts and spirits. Where did these legends come from? Why did someone say they saw such things? Did someone really see something and blow it out of proportion? The big question with some tales is where such a wild and elaborate story came from. That question is every bit a part of the fabric of a state's alleged haunts as the haunts themselves. So, even when a tale is completely fantastic, it's still good to include.

These are accounts taken through many hours of online and other research. The bibliography is lengthy and shows how much we read about this topic. We are simply telling the stories as they exist and never seek to prove or disprove their validity. In some chapters, we may offer alternative explanations, or corrections on factual history, but that is because we felt we would be remiss if we did not. This book is not intended to be a historical reference guide of any kind. Though we made every attempt to ensure we got the facts straight, we cannot be one-hundred percent sure as most of what we studied was the legends, and any mistake in history is unintentional. This book is merely meant for entertainment purposes for those who enjoy the odd and paranormal.

Happy haunted reading as we hope you enjoy *Kentucky's Strange and Unusual Haunts*.

---The Frightening Floyds

THE FORGOTTEN GRAVEYARD

Tucked away in the corner of First Street Park in the town of Shepherdsville, Ky. is an old graveyard that is no longer used. Many residents don't even know it's there, hidden behind the plastic white picket fence; this cemetery is called the Old Pioneer Graveyard. It was once the main attraction on the *Jacob Floyd's Shepherdsville History and Haunts Tour* we used to conduct every year. Most of our guests were intrigued by it as we guided the group through the dark, with Jacob leading by lantern light; most of them liked to snap pictures in hopes of catching a glimpse of one of the alleged ghosts that are rumored to wander the grounds. There have been a few who have captured streaks of light, strange mists, and even one who caught a peculiar outline of a man somewhere in the nearby woods. We're not telling you these are ghosts, but there has been a history of strange occurrences reported within this graveyard.

We call it the "Forgotten Graveyard" because at one time it was most certainly that. Looking to be near, or even over, two-hundred years old, this small cemetery has endured a lot of hardship through the ages. Upon entering, you can immediately tell that this tiny burial ground has suffered the wrath of time, as many stones are cracked and broken, worn and dirty. As you look about the grounds, you can see where stones used to be but are now gone. Towards the side entrance, there are hardly any tombstones at all. If you're not careful, you might step in one of the holes where a headstone used to be.

By all appearances, it seems as though this was once the only graveyard in the city. Rumors of a small settlement somewhere in the area surrounding this graveyard—dating back to the early days of Shepherdsville, or even before—have surfaced, though there is no evidence to support this. But, what we do know is that this graveyard has some of the city's most prominent past members interred.

Shepherdsville, located right next to the Salt River, has seen many floods over the last two centuries, including the Great Flood of 1937 that affected many riverside towns up and down the Ohio and other smaller rivers. The last big flood the town had seen was in 1997, which wiped out many homes (including Jenny's when she was a child) throughout the historic district. Over the decades, the old graveyard has seen a lot of flood damage. Many stones are said to have disappeared as a result, and there have been rumors of coffins and even bodies washing up. But, the latter may be nothing more than urban legend as no documentation of these incidents exists to our knowledge. We think perhaps this rumor could have grown from a hole located towards the back of the graveyard that has a crumbled, brick structure inside. There has been much speculation as to what this might be, but a possible sinkhole is one theory, and some think it may have been a grave—since a couple other graves surround it closely—and that the structure that was once inside, or perhaps on top (as if a sepulcher) was somehow destroyed and someone tried to rebuild it, only to find it taken apart again. The sepulcher theory is interesting because there is a busted up stone not far from there that looks to be a possible cover for such a burial plot. It once belonged to someone from Ireland, which was a point of interest for those who came on the tour.

The cemetery was also once the site of vandalism and neglect. For many years, people used to steal the stones and use them for sidewalks and other various purposes. The city, at one point, allegedly wanted the cemetery to disappear and so they stopped taking care of it. Over time, it was engulfed by weeds, bramble, bushes, and trees. It was so encompassed by wild shrubbery that people who lived right by it didn't even know it was there. The graveyard even became a source of local lore among children as they would sometimes go in search of it, not knowing where to look.

In the late 90s, the Bullitt County History Museum got together with a local business owner and students from Bullitt Central High School to restore the graveyard. We had some of the former students that worked on the project years ago as guests on the tour. They've confirmed to us how overgrown and busted up the place was when they started work on it. There were broken and missing stones all about the place. It was painfully obvious the town had given up on the Old Pioneer Graveyard.

Once the project was completed, the workers had managed to clear out the bramble and do as much as they could to restore the stones to their proper places. The folks at the museum dug into the archives and created a small memorial marker out front listing all the known burials. However, with the many missing, broken, and faded stones, not all interred there are accounted for.

As we were gathering information for *Jacob Floyd's Shepherdsville History and Haunts Tour*, someone had told us that the graveyard is allegedly haunted—particularly haunted by doctors who were supposedly sometimes seen at night, wandering amongst the graves. Initially, our question was how did they know the grounds were haunted by doctors? Were they dressed as doctors in white coats walking the grounds?

We did eventually hear a story about a young man named Ben Louis Crist, and his father Henry Clay Crist, who were both prominent town doctors in the late 1800s. One afternoon, Ben Crist visited a local druggist by the name of John West after he had apparently said something rude to a lady friend of Ben's. The woman remains anonymous to this day, as all that is known about her is that she was referred to as Miss F. Many think she is a woman by the name of Julia Field.

Upon entering Mr. West's shop, Crist demanded that he apologize to Miss F for whatever he said. West refused, feeling no apology was in order. This led to a heated exchange of words, finally bringing West from behind the counter. As he reached the counter's end, Crist grabbed him by the shirt collar and attempted to draw his gun. West managed to keep the pistol at bay as he grabbed his own. West fired the first shot, which hit his own leg, but then managed to squeeze off two more shots that hit Crist—one in the abdomen and the other in the back.

Ben Crist died the next day—November 16th, 1872. John West was brought up on charges and released on a $5000 bail. Four days later, he was acquitted of charges. But, what happened next compounds the mystery behind this tale.

A month after the death of his son, Henry Crist suddenly died under mysterious circumstances. Being only forty-eight-years-old himself, this led to speculation over the nature of his demise. While many believed he simply died of a broken heart over the loss of his son—with whom he shared the medical practice—others think there may have been something more sinister at work, and that Henry Crist's death was not what many thought it was.

One story was that after the verdict, Henry vowed revenge. It was said that no matter what the court decided, Henry Crist would see the druggist brought to justice. Some believe that Henry approached West and tried to make good on his revenge, but was cut down much in the same way that his son had been. Others think that after hearing this declaration of vengeance, West wasted little time in finding Henry and dispensing of him before the grieving father could take his revenge.

But, that is not all. John West vanished from town not long after this. The man was not native to the county, having apparently come from somewhere in the Georgetown area. He was on no census rolls before or after the shooting. No one knows what actually happened to him, but there are certainly rumors.

While many believed he killed Henry and left town to avoid another trial—of which he probably believed he would most certainly have been convicted this time around—there are others who think his disappearance was not of his own accord. The theory is that he did indeed kill Henry Crist, and that friends of the Crist family found West and exacted the justice upon him they believed he deserved. The Crists were well respected in the city, and West was rather popular, too. But, he was an outsider while the Crists were hometown blood. It is believed that because of this, a few men from town put West to death and disposed of his body in an unknown location.

Now, this is simply town legend—with the exception of the actual altercation between Ben and West, as that incident was well documented—but, these stories often breed scary tales. Legend has it that on the anniversary of his death, the ghost of Ben Crist can be seen walking near his grave. People have also claimed that Henry has been seen there, as well. The father and son are buried side-by-side about midway through the cemetery.

There have also been reports of a white apparition walking along the tree line between the graveyard and Frank E. Simon Park just beyond the land's boundaries. Those who have seen it or heard about it think it might be one of the doctors, since their ghosts are said to wander the grounds.

One evening, while we were stopping by Shepherdsville Pioneer Graveyard for a visit, Jacob remained in the car while Jenny stood by the fence and snapped pictures of the area. Jacob had a camera handy in the car and the sky was turning gray as a storm was rolling in. He began to take pictures of the sky because he liked how the color of the coming storm contrasted with the hue of the sunset. Later on, as Jenny looked through the sky pictures, she saw something small and white hovering near the bushes at the borderline of the park and the graveyard. When zooming it in, we thought it looked like the face of a man with a beard. What was most striking about it was that it was placed in an area that was blank and dark, without much there to create any illusion to look like this.

Immediately, we decided to return to the graveyard to try and debunk this. Upon arrival, we looked where the anomaly had been seen. We determined it was not a tombstone, as none in that area were tall enough to reach where the shape had been, and even if they were, none were nearly white enough to match the form. We then decided to walk the bush line and see if any open patches in the shrubbery could have let in any daylight to create the image— there was no such opening; and if there had been, the fact that the day was waning when the picture was taken would make it very improbable that this was the answer. One last theory we had was that it could have been a tree, bush, or some other form of shrubbery back there that gave off the impression of a man's face. There was nothing back there to support this theory. Everything in that area was dark and shadowy. Nothing white shone among the shadows. This was an officially unexplained capture.

Naturally, this left us wondering if it was indeed one of the Crists.

One day, after conducting a spirit box session there, we were on our way out. Jenny decided to stop near the marker at the front gate which listed the known burials in the graveyard. With the device still running, she ran her finger down the names and asked if anyone was there and could tell her which name she was pointing at. A voice then echoed back, "Henry," and when she looked at where her finger had stopped, it was sitting on Henry

Crist. This occurred before we had even heard the tale of the Crists, and after hearing it, we then felt that there was definitely a connection between the incidents.

While the story of Ben and Henry Crist is quite the interesting tale, it is not nearly as mysterious as the other picture we caught in the wooded area behind the graveyard.

On what was one of our first excursions into the graveyard, Jacob caught a very haunting photo. As Jenny was running the spirit box, Jacob walked about the graveyard taking pictures. As he neared the northern edge there at the back of the cemetery, he came to an area where the skeletal trees of autumn stood in the foreground of what looked to be a drainage area. One would have to walk several feet down an embankment to reach it. He found it to be a rather interesting place.

With it being so late in the year, the leaves had fallen, and any movement through there would have been easily heard on the still air. As he stood there trying to snap some scenic photos, he heard a heavy trudging noise, as of something large kicking through the leaves. He envisioned either a large dog or deer running through the leaves, or possibly a human walking briskly. The birds in the naked, skinny trees started chirping incessantly. So, just in case he might have been witnessing something unexplained, he started taking pictures. At the time, we had been told the graveyard was haunted, but we hadn't heard the details just yet.

When we went through the pictures later, Jenny found a strange form off in the distance. It looks to be a figure in gray—either with gray hair or wearing a gray hood—hunkered down off in the drainage area. We get the impression that it is a woman and her face, which appears to be looking down, is either partially veiled by hair or a shroud.

Once we discovered this image, we returned to the graveyard to debunk it. We searched the entire edge of the area, looking for this very distinct dark shape. We thought maybe there was a fallen tree with roots sticking up that created this form. Or, maybe it was a very gnarly bush, perhaps with garbage caught on it, making that appear to be a person. We also considered the possibility that there was a tall pile of rubble, debris, fallen branches, or anything similar that looked like a person. We never saw anything of the sort. We even took more pictures to try and recreate the image. Never saw it again.

Later on, as people approached us with more stories about the graveyard, that was when he heard the tale that there was a settlement back there long ago, before Shepherdsville was established. We were also told that people have heard the sounds of women's laughter at night, and sometimes soft sobbing, coming from the area beyond the graveyard. People have reported hearing her voice muttering softly in the night, and even seeing the pale apparition of a woman in a dark gown walking among the trees.

Needless to say, hearing these tales after catching that picture gave us chills, especially since we are often in that graveyard after the sun goes down, conducting our tour by lantern light.

There was one tour late in the year where a questionable picture was captured. It was a small tour as the weather was getting colder, and the days much shorter. While Jacob was telling the story of the woman in the ditch area, one of our guests said they heard someone walking through the leaves beyond the trees. He stopped the story and listened, and we heard it as well. Someone then took a picture of the area and it later revealed the image of someone wearing a hat—but, it certainly was not Jacob! The form would have been somewhere inside a cluster of trees, and the flash had captured the outline. We never actually saw anyone, and it's quite possible it could have been someone lurking about there at night, but it sure made for an interesting experience, nonetheless.

So, that's the Shepherdsville Pioneer Graveyard and just some of the interesting history and the eerie ghost tales coming out of it. As always, we're not saying that we know for certain the place is haunted, but we can safely say we have had some strange experiences in there, and so have a few of our guests.

Full shot of cemetery with white face

Close up of white face

Area behind graveyard where gray image was spotted

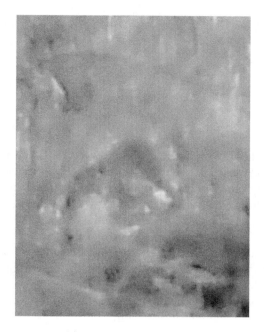

Close up of gray image

GRANDVIEW CEMETERY – "THE GATES OF HELL"

G randview Cemetery, also known as Kasey Cemetery, is a hard-to-find graveyard buried deep in the woods of Custer, Kentucky. Though many say it is in Elizabethtown, it is actually about twenty miles out of town. To find it, you must head northwest on a windy dirt path known as St. John's Road. It is very secluded, located in a rather peaceful clearing in the woods, surrounded by the ruins of a stone and iron gate. Once you find its broken remains, according to legend, you will have found the Gates of Hell.

Before Grandview had such an ominous moniker, it was simply a small town cemetery for families dating back to the 1700s, giving it a three-hundred-plus-year history in which any number of tragic events could have taken place to pin spirits to the grounds. The nickname the "Gates of Hell" has been applied to Grandview for more than thirty years, and at one point it is said that the place was known as the "killing field." There were reported signs of devil worship having been found on the premises, particularly animal sacrifices. People have reported seeing charred animal bones throughout Grandview.

In April of 2003, two members of the Kentucky Society for Ghost Research were investigating the graveyard when they came upon the scattered remains of three dogs, two cats, a deer, a calf, and a puppy. The investigators insisted that this was tied to satanic rituals and claimed that every time they visit Grandview they find black candles and occult images drawn in various places. But, after they notified the authorities, the police found nothing to tie the cruelty to anything ritualistic, finding neither black candles nor satanic markings, and the only graffiti they found were swastikas, a body outline, and an orange-yellow image of a cross, none of which are satanic. There have been reports of figures in dark robes kneeling and praying near the graveyard, which could lend credence to the claims of Satanism. But, satanic rituals or not, the graveyard has been heavily vandalized over the years and the tombstones desecrated, which could be the reason for any restless spirits that might be drifting about the Gates of Hell.

Some visitors have experienced severe car troubles after parking outside the cemetery. Batteries have died and cars have refused to start. People have even reported finding personal items inside their cars moved and rearranged.

Automobile difficulties are not the only mechanical malfunctions to occur. Investigators have had newly charged and replaced batteries in their equipment die almost instantly upon entering the graveyard. Others have reported videos with sound and no picture, and cell phones have been known to go from full life to dead in a matter of seconds. GPS devices have also been known to go haywire near the cemetery, only to return to normal once the vehicle has pulled out of the vicinity.

Investigators and those who have traveled to the Gates of Hell out of sheer curiosity have been overcome with a crushing sense of dread, as if something wicked were right upon their backs. They have said they felt as though evil eyes were upon them, watching every move they made. This feeling often becomes so overpowering that those suffering from it have felt suddenly sick and had to leave.

There is supposedly an enormous, bright-green orb that has been known to appear hovering in the graveyard. Those who have claimed to have encountered this strange anomaly say that it hovers in place for a few seconds, then races around the cemetery before rising up into the sky and vanishing, or zipping into the woods, out of sight. There have been stories where people have said they were chased by this peculiar light until they exited the cemetery. One legend tells of a time when the orb appeared over the iron gate, hovering for quite some time. Its presence is believed to have caused the iron gate to bend and break, and the stones to crumble, and this is why the gate is destroyed.

What may have given rise to the Gates of Hell claims are the shadow figures seen wandering about the cemetery. People have reported seeing them rise from behind crumbling tombstones, as well as emerging from the woods, to walk the perimeter of the grounds. Some have even been approached by fast-moving shadows, only to feel cold spots rush through them. Sometimes, it is said wails and screams can be heard before the arrival of the shadows and after their passing. Others have reported hearing these chilling cries coming from deep within the woods, even when the dark figures have not shown themselves.

There are a few other creepy accounts from the Gates of Hell. One is about a tombstone near the center of the cemetery that will glow with an unexplained light. No one knows what causes this glow, but could this be where the alleged gate opens up, if such a thing exists? Another involves the ghosts of children who have been known to go home with those who see them. One in particular—that of a little girl in a white dress—supposedly went home with a child and visited him several times in a span of a few weeks. Trees have also been said to move around the cemetery. This one is quite odd and we're not sure where it came from. Could it simply be that the wind was blowing them around, or were they supposed to be actually moving? A psychic medium did claim to have made contact with the spirit of a young man who hanged himself from a tree there sometime back in the 1980s. Maybe this has something to do with the moving tree.

Others have heard whispering voices warning them to leave the graveyard right away. Others have felt strangled by something unseen, while hearing disembodied wicked laughter nearby. One man claimed to have been scratched so badly that his arm bled heavily before he was pulled to the ground by some invisible force.

There is a legend that there was once, or still is, a former witch's cabin near the woods. If this is the case, that could explain the rumors of rituals and the screams from the darkness. It would also provide a possible lead to the origins of the Gates of Hell legend. It has also been said that there is a lone grave located somewhere beyond the cemetery. Could this be the resting place of the alleged witch, or is it just complete rubbish? There has been a woman in white witnessed there, staring at people walking through the woods. Who she is, no one knows.

If even a portion of these accounts have truth to them, then it's not hard to see why some have elected to call Grandview Cemetery the Gates of Hell. With legends of witches and Satanism abound it is not surprising that some have claimed there is a passage to the dark world somewhere inside. With that many claims, it's hard to shrug it off and think nothing has gone on there. But, could it be just a rash of urban legends run amuck? Guess there's really only one way to find out.

HI HAT CEMETERY

A town with a pretty cool name is Hi Hat – a small mining community located in the far eastern section of the state. Originally known as Fed, the post office was established in 1881 and is still open today. It was in 1943 that Fed became Hi Hat, named for the Hi Hat Elkhorn Mining Company.

The post office isn't the only spot still active in Hi Hat, and coal is not the only thing for which this unincorporated town is known. There is a small graveyard and church upon a hill overlooking the post office, and they are known to be inhabited by ghosts.

Where these ghosts come from no one really knows. There doesn't seem to be much about the history—whether documented or legend—of Hi Hat. Despite that, the alleged haunts are quite unsettling.

Those who have visited the cemetery late at night have had some frightening experiences. Passing through the cemetery, they have heard heavy footsteps running beside them in the dark. Upon turning any lights in that direction, no one has been seen. But in the distance, not far from the graveyard, is an old church, and some think the entity lurking in the graveyard resides in that building. These witnesses have often been disturbed by thumping footsteps inside the building, sounding as if someone is running back and forth across the floor. The sound of someone pounding hard on the walls also reverberates through the quiet night. Some have been so terrified by this they have quickly raced to their cars with the sounds of rapid footsteps trailing them across the grass, and gotten in only to have an unseen force slam into their vehicle and begin rocking it back and forth.

As if these occurrences are not chilling enough, the more unlucky of the visitors have bore witness to something even grimmer. Sometimes, after the sounds of footsteps have been heard in the yard, people have shined their light around only to see a large black shadow racing through the yard. They have even seen this figure rush from the church after the pounding on the walls. Apparently, it is not a shadow of a tree or some other object sliding in the passing light, either. There have been reports of people holding the light on the shadow and watching it run right towards them. According to descriptions, the figure is not human. It is large, all black, with long, spindly arms, and it moves across the ground with a loping gait.

That is quite a frightening tale. Just makes one wonder what has gone on in Hi Hat Cemetery.

GRAPEVINE CEMETERY

Grapevine Cemetery is a beautiful cemetery located on Grapevine Road in Madisonville. There is a local tale about the spirit of an anonymous young male left wandering the graveyard. Long ago, this young man met a young lady near town. This young lady, to him, was the most beautiful person he had ever seen. As he got to know her, he found that her spirit was every bit as beautiful as her outward appearance. The young man fell deeply in love with her. Some say he even became obsessive. Perhaps it was this obsession that drove her away. After a time, the young lady came to find that she just did not reciprocate the same feelings the young man had for her. Whether she needed to get away due to his clinginess, or if it was just as innocent as she didn't have those feelings for him, she left him, and it broke the young man's heart.

For a time after this, the young man slowly retreated into himself, becoming reclusive. People would hear him humming, whistling, and singing sad ballads and love songs to himself. Many speculated he had lost his mind. Finally, the immense heartache became too much for him and he took his own life. He was buried in Grapevine Cemetery. Upon his funeral, no one wondered why he had done it. Everyone had known it was the loss of his love that had driven him into the grave. There is no word as to whether or not the young lady knew of his passing.

As time passed, people began to report strange happenings in Grapevine. Visitors would hear the sounds of a young man sobbing somewhere within the shadows of the trees. Some reported a faint apparition walking the grounds. Others say that if you play a love song or a sad song near the graveyard, you will hear the broken young man begin to wail from somewhere within the cemetery.

It appears the pain this young man suffered has followed him into the afterlife, and he cannot leave the world that hurt him so deeply.

HEBRON LUTHERAN CEMETERY

The Hopeful Lutheran Church near Florence is one of the oldest congregations west of the Allegheny Mountains. Established in 1805 by immigrants from either Alsace or the Palatinate region in southwestern Germany, it was the first branch of the Hebron Evangelical Lutheran Congregation of Madison County, Virginia, located in Boone County, Kentucky.

On January 21st, 1854, the heads of sixteen of the German families that were part of the congregation met in the home of John Crigler and decided to separate from the Hopeful Lutheran Church. They then formed the Hebron Evangelical Lutheran Church, which was named after the Hebron Lutheran Church in Virginia from where they all came. The Virginian church dedicated $500 to the new congregation to assist them in raising their own house of worship. Work on the construct began in the spring with the members of the church building it from the wood of nearby trees. The work was completed in the fall and the dedication of the church was on December 3rd. Though they were separated from Hopeful, the two churches still shared twenty different ministers over the next ninety years. Hebron then became independent in 1947 and Rev. Dr. J.E. Stomberger served as their first exclusive minister. The church still operates today.

Next to this historic church lies an old graveyard known as the Hebron Lutheran Cemetery, which was established the same time as the church itself. Though its full history is not known, the original families to be interred there must have been very close, having built the church together. Though they don't seem to remain inside the church itself—perhaps out of some respect for the sanctuary—it is rumored that they, along with others, may be drifting about the cemetery.

Some who have approached the crematorium have smelled the strong aroma of something burning even when it is not in use.

There is no telling how many people have been cremated there over the years, but it is very possible a residual sensory haunt may exist. People have heard mysterious whispers among the graves while walking through the cemetery alone. This incident has often been described as sounding like several voices talking back and forth, and even simultaneously. Though witnesses report that the sound is distinctly human voices, the words themselves are usually unintelligible. Visitors have also walked through mysterious cold spots, even on hot summer days, near the older graves.

One young lady said that before her grandmother passed away, she told her that after she is gone, whenever she hears wind chimes she'll know that her grandmother is with her. The young lady would sometimes go to the graveyard and hear the sound of wind chimes, even though there are no visible chimes in the graveyard. The young lady would hear this sound even on windless days.

Perhaps members of the sixteen original families are still present in Hebron Lutheran Cemetery, watching over the grounds. It also seems like those who have been buried there in more recent years may still exist among the living. Maybe if you go there you'll hear the voices whisper to you from beyond the grave.

ASBURY CEMETERY

L ocated in Calloway County, towards the far southwestern edge of the state, about twelve miles from Murray, is the haunted Asbury Cemetery. The cemetery is surrounded by large oaks and evergreens. Without counting the unmarked graves, there are about 400 people interred at Asbury, making it pretty small by today's standards. Not so small, perhaps, by the standards of its own day, being located in such a rural area.

The oldest grave dates back to 1824, and is for a toddler who was not quite two years old. That's a pretty old stone for Calloway County considering it was founded in 1822. But there are plenty of graves for people who were born in the 1700s, including one who was born before the Colonies were free – a man by the name of Kimbrough T. Ogilvie. Ogilvie was born in 1763 and is said to have fought in the Guilford County Regiment for the North Carolina Revolution Militia during the American Revolution. This regiment was active from 1775-1783, and we couldn't find specific dates when Ogilvie participated, but that would put him in the war anytime between the ages of eleven and twenty, and we believe closer to the latter is more likely. He passed away in 1842 in Calloway County at the age of seventy-nine.

There are many more markers for people who fought in just about every American War leading up to World War II. There are also some tombstones with hand-etched lettering on them. Some very strange graves also lie within Asbury. Upon some of the concrete blocks that mark graves for those too poor to afford regular stones, there are gears. The purpose of the gears is unknown. We couldn't find an explanation for such a marker. But the gear-marked blocks are not the most interesting physical aspect about Asbury.

Scattered about the graveyard, you can find small metal pipes protruding up from the ground. At first, most people might wonder what these pipes could be used for. Those who are a tad more morbid, like us, might figure it out right away. These pipes are there in case people were buried alive – a mistake that was not uncommon in the days before medical advancements in embalming and in determining if someone was deceased. In some graveyards, bells would be placed near graves with strings tied to the corpses' fingers, so if they were buried alive and woke up, they could ring the bell. In this case, these pipes were there so the person lying in the grave could breathe and call for help.

With so many veterans buried there, and with the possibility that some folks were buried alive and never rescued, it isn't shocking that Asbury Graveyard is alleged to be haunted.

Asbury is sort of a Lover's Lane in Calloway County. Doubtless, it is due to its seclusion and being surrounded by so many trees. Through the years, couples have parked there, or wandered into the cemetery, to be alone. Some of them, however, have come back with some chilling tales to tell.

Sometime in the 1960s, a couple parked at Asbury and began to do what young couples do when they are alone in an isolated area at night. Before too long, they began to hear scratching against the car, more specifically, the back bumper. Thinking it was an animal or perhaps a small tree branch, they ignored it. After a few more minutes passed, the scratching grew louder and more intense. This time, they stopped to take a look. That's when they noticed no trees were even near them. As they sat quietly for a few more seconds, debating whether to check it out, go back to business, or just drive off, an oppressive sense of dread began to settle upon them. The car suddenly began to shake, as if something was standing on the bumper and treating the car like a seesaw. This spurred the couple into action and they quickly drove out of there.

They never did find out what had been messing around the car, so they could only speculate. It's possible a heavy animal could have done it. It wouldn't have been a person because they would have been spotted. Of course, it could have been a resident specter trying to get a better look.

Two couples who had heard the graveyard was haunted parked near Asbury on a cold dark night. The story doesn't say why they were there, but if it was because they were there to see ghosts, then they would sort of get what they came for.

As they sat in the car, they heard a strange noise outside, despite having the windows up. At first, the noise was faint, as if far away but drawing closer. In a few seconds, they heard what they thought was the sound of horse hooves galloping across the ground. They looked hard into the darkness but never saw a horse. They were then startled by the very loud and distinct sound of a horse snorting just outside the car. Still, they saw no horse.

Needless to say, this spooked them pretty good, so the driver started the car and sped off. As the car raced down the road, they could still hear the sound of hooves, only pounding harder. Still, there was no horse to be seen. It didn't take long before the galloping sound had reached the car. No matter how hard the driver pressed the accelerator, he could not shake whatever was making the noise. Again, they heard the loud snort. They drove on and on, hearing these sounds coming from what they presumed to be a ghostly horse. After a few more miles, the sounds ended.

There have also been reports of eerie shadow people moving around the graves, and near the trees around the cemetery. These figures often bring with them a deep and nearly maddening sense of fear. Witnesses have reported feeling as though they are being watched, even in daylight, then the dread would settle in. Soon after, the shadows would start to move around the graveyard.

Another incident occurred as a young man was cutting through the cemetery on his way home from work. How long ago this was, we are not sure, but we assume by the language of the story we were told that it was some time ago – perhaps early 1900s. As the man was passing beneath the shadow of the hemlock trees, he looked up and saw someone else coming his way. When the person drew nearer, he said, "How-do?" But right after she passed, he realized that he knew her face. She was a woman who had died just days before, and he had attended her funeral. Shocked by this revelation, the young man turned around to get another look – but she was gone. He then ran home, and upon entering his house he declared, "Never bury me at Asbury Cemetery. That place is haunted!"

WYNN CEMETERY

Located off Jim Wilson Road in Clay, KY near Providence, in the western portion of the state, is Wynn Cemetery. The local legend is that long ago two women were accused of witchcraft and hanged in the cemetery. Their bodies were then covered in dirt and concrete and buried above ground. Since then, visitors to Wynn have spotted their black apparitions walking the grounds. Any time anyone gets near to them, they shiver from a sudden chill that sets upon them. It is also alleged that the trees they were hanged from still stand and that on the anniversary of their deaths, the images of their bodies sometimes appear dangling from the branches from which they were hanged.

LICK CREEK CHURCH CEMETERY

Just off Lick Creek and Andy Brown Roads in Dawson Springs stands an abandoned old church with a graveyard beside it known as the Lick Creek Church and Cemetery. Spooky legends have circled the property since the 1950s. Apparently, it has long been commonplace for young boys to dare their friends to enter the graveyard and brave the paranormal entities that supposedly reside there. If the stories are true, there are many spooky sights to be seen by anyone who takes the dare.

Apparitions of women and men thought to be laid to rest in the cemetery have been seen drifting through the graveyard at night. Most have been described as wearing funeral clothes. Glowing orbs, like eyes, are said to float through the air, leaving many to believe these are possibly the eyes of the lingering apparitions, or perhaps spirits hovering above the land. Others have reported seeing figures moving through the shadows in the evening, only to vanish from sight before reappearing in another end of the graveyard.

JACOB FLOYD & JENNY FLOYD

CAMPBELL CEMETERY AND COFFIN ROCK

If you look up Campbell Cemetery in Kentucky, you're likely not to find this one without a little digging. While there are Campbell Cemeteries in the towns of Gray and Manchester, this one is actually in Busy, KY and is called Forked Mouth Campbell Cemetery due to its location off Forked Mouth Road near Forked Mouth Creek. You might also become confused if you were to go looking for this cemetery because there are a few other graveyards nearby, such as Couch Cemetery and Ivy Gap Cemetery.

Within this Campbell Cemetery is a flat rock known as Coffin Rock (not to be confused with that of the Blair Witch mythos). Many years ago, according to legend, a man was chased into the graveyard and shot. He then fell onto the rock and bled to death. Now, whenever it rains, the man's blood appears and runs down the rock.

This is not the only report of paranormal activity taking place in the graveyard. There is an older man who flags down passersby and disappears when the car stops. Is the man who was shot appearing in the last minutes of his life? Did he need a ride and flag down the wrong man? Or could he be tied to the other spirits there? Rumor has it that a transparent older woman wanders the road near the graveyard, and a little girl is often seen standing in the road and has had cars pass right through her. Perhaps all the ghosts are connected, and a family was killed there long ago. Or it could just all be coincidence?

WARFIELD CEMETERY

Off Highway 459 in Barbourville lies Warfield Cemetery. At first glance, it looks like your average small-town cemetery. But locals say that something very sinister lurks the grounds of this particular graveyard. Something that stalks you and smothers you with an intense sensation of dread.

According to the reports given by visitors and investigators, there is a malevolent spirit that follows you as you walk through Warfield. Once it has its sights upon you, it will step as you step, stop as you stop, and whisper sinister things behind you. The crunch of its footfalls can be heard just after yours. If you stop, that's when the whispers begin. Some have said they could not understand the words, but others say it whispers your name and tells you about bad things that will happen to you. Most believe this presence to be an evil one as it fills those it targets with fear and unease, and the closer it gets, the more oppressive the dread becomes.

Not everyone who is followed by this entity can see it, but some have. They have spotted it as a thick black shadow at their backs. Others claimed to have seen it following their friends or fellow investigators, describing it as something large and dark stepping in rhythm behind the person. One witness thought someone else was actually in the graveyard with them. They said the figure walked right behind another investigator. When the investigator stopped, the figure looked to lean towards them, as if whispering in their ear. When the witness shined their flashlight upon the form, it disappeared. That's when he knew he had witnessed the spirit of legend.

If this ghost does exist, it is definitely tied only to Warfield Cemetery. Anyone who has felt its presence pressing down on them states that the feeling of dread and the footsteps cease the second they step out of the cemetery. No one has ever reported the being following them out, nor have they had any complications away from the grounds after leaving. It seems that who or whatever this manifestation is, it does not take kindly to people trespassing on its burial ground.

RIDGE CEMETERY

U nion Ridge Cemetery, often called simply "Ridge" Cemetery, lies just off the roadway between the towns of Penrod and Belton in Muhlenberg County, and is the cemetery for the Union Ridge Baptist Church. While the county was established in 1798, the two small cities sprung up in the 1880s. It is not known specifically when Union Ridge Cemetery was officially created, but it was no doubt sometime in the 1880s.

This quiet, quaint cemetery surrounded by trees seems like a nice old-timey graveyard. Though it is a tad eerie when the fog catches it on a muggy morning, no one would suspect that anything out of the ordinary would or has taken place in this serene plot of land.

But they would be wrong.

Legend has it that some time in the late 1800s, two unnamed brothers were taking a stroll through the graveyard on a misty morning – perhaps visiting a relative who had past, or possibly just enjoying a fine day – when a conversation they were having took a turn for the worse. The legend does not say exactly what the topic was, but some speculate it could have been over a business arrangement, money, a recent death in the family, or even a woman, but whatever the point of interest was, it led to a heated argument.

Apparently, the two brothers had both been known as hotheads, always quick to fight, often losing their tempers. It wasn't even uncommon for them to fight amongst themselves, as it is believed they often did as children. There, in the middle of the quiet graveyard, the two men took to fighting.

The account states that according to a town resident who had witnessed the scuffle, the young men rolled in the grass, grunting, swearing, and flailing their arms upon one another. The sounds of their flesh being struck could be heard. Eventually, they tore away from one another and one of the brothers pulled a knife from his waistband and thrust it at the other brother. The brother who had been stabbed fell to his knees. The other brother, coming to his senses and realizing what he had done, suddenly dropped his weapon, put his hands on his head, and cried, "Brother!"

Now in the grips of both terror and remorse, the brother who had committed the act tried to tend to his bleeding sibling. But the dying brother would not have it. He too pulled a knife from his waistband and thrust it upwards into the abdomen of his brother, who had been standing over him. The newly-stabbed brother doubled over, wrapped his arms around is abdomen and stumbled backwards before falling on his backside. The two brothers then lay there and died on the grass of the graveyard.

The battling brothers were then buried together in graves next to or near one another. As it goes, no one in town was too surprised by this incident, yet many mourned them for they were well liked despite both men's tumultuous nature.

Now it is said that the brothers remain in the cemetery, stuck with one another as punishment for their mortal crimes. People have reported hearing them quarreling in the graveyard, saying raised angry voices could be heard when no one was around. On a misty morning, their apparitions can be seen walking through the haze and brawling near the edge of the cemetery where it is believed they died. Some claim that the blood that was spilled from that fight will appear on the grass. When and why this happens has not been determined, but some believe it happens on the anniversary of the double homicide while some think it happens when the morning is misty. Since the date of the incident is unknown, no one can be sure.

Two brothers in the midst of a disagreement so intense that they were led to kill one another, torn apart by what – jealousy, rage, betrayal – no one knows. In fact, no one even knows for sure if this incident took place. It could just be town lore. Or it could be a story given to two ghosts that roam Ridge Cemetery during the misty mornings.

THE GLOWING TOMBSTONE CEMETERY

Gibson Cemetery in Benton is said to hold a particular tombstone of legend – one that often glows. The legend of the Glowing Tombstone has led to Gibson Cemetery also being known as the Glowing Tombstone Cemetery. The tombstone has supposedly been seen glowing by several people, both day and night. There is a story behind the illumination, as well.

There was an old married couple who once lived by Gibson Cemetery, and had lived there for many years. One night, they heard some commotion outside. The husband went to check it out and could hear that it was coming from their barn out back. With rumors of cult activity taking place in the area, they feared that their property was being used for some bizarre rite or ritual. The old man was ready to run these hooligans off of his property, so he crossed the backyard and entered the barn.

A long time passed as the old woman waited in the house for her husband to return. After a while, she decided to go check on him to see what was going on. She too then exited the house and ventured to the barn. But when she stepped into the barn, she would be greeted with a ghastly sight. She looked up and saw her husband dead, hanging by his neck from the rafters. Signs of a struggle were all around her, and she then knew the rumors of the cult to be true.

The man was laid to rest in Gibson Cemetery. Now people say that his angry spirit remains in that barn, awaiting vengeance. When the old man's restless soul has its ire up, his tombstone begins to glow. This is to let his killers know that he is waiting for them to return to the barn so he can get retribution.

The house the couple once lived in is no longer there. It either fell down or was torn down some time ago. Allegedly, another couple attempted to build another house there but it collapsed each time and they never could finish the project. Perhaps the powerful, negative energy keeps knocking it down.

Whether or not this tombstone actually glows, we don't know. If it does, it very well could be foxfire, which can be found in Kentucky. Foxfire is a bioluminescent fungus that glows green. It can be found in Kentucky woods and caves, and there's no reason to think it might not be on this tombstone from time to time.

Unless it really is the old man's raging spirit seething for revenge.

FREE UNION SEPARATE BAPTIST CHURCH CEMETERY

Located on lonesome Sano Road in Columbia sits the Free Union Separate Baptist Church. The building is of average size and is located in the middle of farm country, but it has its faithful congregation. Next to it, unguarded and open to the public at all hours of the day and night is the church's graveyard. This little cemetery does not cover much land and has maybe ten full rows of neatly lined tombstones. But do not let this quaint appearance trick you. This graveyard comes with an eerie legend.

At night, somewhere along the lonely grounds walks the ghost of a man who looks to be in his fifties. Often seen moving through the rows or standing at the edge of the cemetery, this man can be seen holding an infant wrapped in a pink blanket. Though it is not known for sure who this man and child are, many believe that he is a man waiting for his wife, the mother of the infant, to die so they can be together. They say he waits there at the edge of the graveyard to see if the next funeral will be hers. Though he is only seen at night, he might also be watching during the day. It is said that there is a grave of a 54-year-old man and his infant child somewhere in the cemetery. Could this be him?

If you're ever at Free Union Separate Baptist Church and you walk the cemetery grounds, be on the lookout for a transparent man holding his infant child.

PILOT'S KNOB CEMETERY

Pilot's Knob is a small cemetery off Ford's Ferry Road in Marion. Home to a lot of greenery and time-worn tombstones, there is one grave that has gathered quite of bit of notoriety from local paranormal enthusiasts. That is the burial site of young Mary Evelyn Ford.

Mary was believed to be a child witch, daughter of a witch, and the townsfolk looked upon her and her mother with disdain and fear. What crimes the child and her mother had committed that created such a suspicion is unknown, but what is known is that, without trial, they were both deemed practitioners of the dark arts and sentenced to death by fire sometime in the 1910s. Mary, who was only about six years old at the time, would suffer the same fate as her mother.

The people in the community held a great fear that Mary Evelyn would travel to the void and, from there, begin casting spells against the town. So, they lined her grave with steel, interred her into the ground at Pilot's Knob and placed rocks upon her grave. Why they thought such precautions would keep the forces of darkness at bay is hard to say. But so is why they believed Mary Evelyn and her mother to be witches. For extra measure, they built a picket fence around the plot out of crosses that connect end-to-end; probably believing the forces of light would repel any wickedness the poor child's witchy soul would cast their way.

To take the superstitious nature of the entire tale even further, people have claimed that there is a watcher that stands sentinel by Mary's grave, attempting to get to the girl and free her supposedly sinister spirit, either to help her or so it can take her soul. However, the cross fence is believed to form a spiritual barrier that keeps the watcher from completing its duties. What this watcher is or where it comes from is not specified, but some believe it could be the soul of one of the witch's victims.

According to some, though, the girl's restless spirit is not in captivity. They say that she can be seen walking the confines of her plot, stuck between the crosses, but still able to drain anyone in the graveyard of energy in order to make herself stronger. It is believed that she entices people to pass the fence and come into her tiny prison. She does this by making faces at her prey, and when they come into her domain, she will pull them into her grave.

That's a pretty wild assertion, but there are other paranormal accounts. A group of college kids alleged to have seen tiny footprints atop Mary's grave. As they approached to get a closer look, they were chased from the area by the infamous watcher.

One couple claimed to have heard the sound of a young girl laughing in the cemetery at night. They followed the laughter to Mary's grave and claimed they saw a shadowy presence moving near the fence. Fearing it was actually a human lurking in the darkness, they left.

Other folks have reported laughter, as well. They have also alleged to hear voices in the cemetery. People interested in checking out the legend have also reported being touched on the lower back. One person said they were touched on the back and had a small, pink handprint where they felt the touch the following day. Many report an eerie feeling in the cemetery, but that could be due to the legends, as well as the seclusion of the location.

While the story of Mary and her mother is quite spooky, it is not accurate at all. According to Mary's death certificate, she died in 1916 from peritonitis and rectal impaction, not burning, and was five at the time of her death, not six. She was the daughter of Mary Rebecca Davis and James Ford. Rebecca outlived Mary, passing away in 1955. It seems as though this tale is a complete fabrication.

That, however, does not mean that the reported paranormal activity is a hoax. Perhaps the activity was experienced first, and people made up the story to explain it. The area is connected closely with the Civil War, and we know how often those locations are hotbeds of paranormal reports. If there truly is anything supernatural lingering in Pilot's Knob Cemetery, it could very well be from that.

Unless the countless times people have told the tale of young Mary the witch has caused her spirit some unrest, and she's actually back to silence the lies.

BURTONVILLE CEMETERY

The Burtonville Cemetery in Lewis County is just a few rows of tombstones next to an old white church. At a glance, there's not much to it. But there seems to be a little bit more going on that remains unseen by most.

Some folks who enter the graveyard report the sudden onset of an unexplained oppressive melancholy. This strange feeling could have something to do with the dark shadows people have reported moving about the grounds. At times, they have seen one or two; at other times, the graveyard has seemed to be full of them. While there are some trees located in the cemetery, the grounds are mostly open and there isn't much around to cast shadows, not to mention how dark the area is at night. These shadow figures have been reported as looking like black apparitions walking among the stones.

It is not only the graveyard that is reportedly haunted; the church is home to some specters as well. Lights inside the church will come on and go off on their own. People who have been inside the church when it is empty have reported the feeling of being watched by something. Others in the graveyard claim to have seen the light come on to reveal a figure standing at one of the windows just before the light goes off again. This happens when the church is locked and vacant.

Could it be someone trespassing in the church somehow? Are stragglers wandering among the graves? Or is there really some paranormal activity taking place at Burtonville Cemetery.

BAKER HOLLOW ROAD CEMETERIES

What many call the Baker Hollow Road Cemetery in Marion is actually two separate cemeteries: one known as the Baker Cemetery and the other the Phillips Cemetery. Both are located around the property of the Baker Church off Baker Hollow Road and Baker Cemetery Road.

The Baker Cemetery belongs to the Baker Church and lies off to the side of the building. The Phillips Cemetery is located on the land across the road from the church and belongs to the Phillips family. As the story goes, a man by the name of Edgar Ovel Phillips owned a farm by the Baker Church. When Baker Hollow Road was constructed, it split Phillips's land in two, leaving one section right in front of the church. In 1949, one of Edgar's cousins asked if he could bury his son, nine-year-old Major Samuel, on the land, and Phillips granted his request. From there, it became a family plot. Over the years, people have mistaken it for being part of the Baker Cemetery. In 2008, an archway indicating it as the Phillips Cemetery was raised at the graveyard's entrance.

Now, according to some superstitions, the first person interred at a cemetery is destined to be the graveyard's guardian. It is believed that this guardian will have the ability to assume different forms during the course of their duties, and some believe that Major Samuel takes the form of a black dog.

This is certainly a wild legend, to say the least. But in any event, there have been tales of a hellhound prowling the grounds. If you are driving to the cemetery from the direction of Marion, the graveyard will suddenly appear on your left when you reach the road. Other versions of the tale state that the graveyard will not be visible the first time you drive by, and that you'll have to drive to the end of Baker Hollow Road and then turn around and come back to get the graveyard to appear. Just before it comes into view, you may hear eerie music playing on the breeze, or the laughter and cries of the nearby dead. Once the graveyard does appear, you may be overwhelmed with immense sadness as soon as you see it. When that sadness sets in, that's when you will need to watch out for the hound.

The dog will appear, black as night with yellow eyes, walking along the road. Some say it will be limping, feigning injury to lure you into trying to pick it up. But do not, or it will attack, and when it attacks, it brings the malevolent spirits down on you. If you attempt to speed away, the creature will run beside your car, keeping up with you the entire way. When you make it to the fork in Baker Hollow Road, you can see the dog's shadow turn into a massive demonic beast, and the dog will vanish in the monster's shadow.

The story does not end there. In fact, it gets even creepier. Thick, eerie fog will suddenly appear on the road, and in that fog you will see ghosts of hanged criminals swinging from trees on the side of the road. Images of crashed cars will appear, and the anguished screams from the victims will ring out from inside them. The weather has been known to change to heavy rains and lightning inside the fog, bringing with it the cries of help from your own dead loved ones.

It is said that these frightening occurrences are contained within the fog, and once you drive out of it, all seems to return to normal. But beware driving into this ghostly storm because vehicles are known to die there. Some who have experienced this also claim that long after they have left the area, they have been tormented by horrendous nightmares and the visitations from wicked spirits.

Quite the tale, we would say.

JACOB FLOYD & JENNY FLOYD

LEXINGTON CEMETERY

Established in 1848, the Lexington Cemetery was initially created to help deal with the high number of bodies that needed burying due to the area's cholera epidemic. It began as 40 acres but has since expanded to 170, with more than 64,000 buried there. The cemetery has three listings on the National Register of Historic Places, including the Ladies' Confederate Memorial, the Confederate Soldier Monument, and the Lexington National Cemetery. There are also a myriad of tree species sprouting up around the land, including an American basswood which staff at the cemetery claim is the largest in the world, although the National Register of Big Trees says that the largest American basswood is in Pennsylvania.

There are a number of notable individuals buried there, including Jim Varney. There is also a mausoleum on property that is reported to be very haunted. There are countless reports of disembodied voices and footsteps, unexplainable sounds, and even shrieks coming from inside the mausoleum. On some occasions, visitors had felt themselves overcome with intense rage for no reason, just before seeing an ominous black shadow figure moving around the back of the building. They say this shadow figure runs and floats in the rear of the mausoleum, chilling witnesses. What sort of spirit this shadow is has not been decided, but signs point to it being not a very friendly presence.

MAPLE GROVE CEMETERY

If you have read our book, *Kentucky's Haunted Mansions*, then you know the tale of the Sexton House in Russellville with the image of a female bather burned into the window by a lightning bolt. The sexton of the Sexton House is the groundskeeper of the Maple Grove Cemetery located on the property. Naturally, the Sexton House is said to be haunted by the young lady who has been immortalized by lightning, but the graveyard is said to be haunted as well.

Maple Grove is an expansive, opened cemetery with long-reaching rows of stones. There are a few rumors about the grounds being haunted by people buried within as well as former residents of the Sexton House. Though, as with so many local legends, historical details are scarce.

Of course, shadows have been seen both night and day strolling about the cemetery. Unexplained orbs have been seen floating in the darkness. One man was visiting the grave of a family member one night and saw a strange streak of bluish-white light a few yards from where he stood. The wisp moved about erratically, so he went to check on the source, wondering if someone needed help. As he approached, the light dimmed out. When he came upon the spot he believed he had seen it, no one was there and the grounds were once again dark. He looked around and called to see if anyone was there, and then suddenly, a man spoke behind him, making him jump.

"Why are you here?" he said the voice spoke.

He turned to see a thin pale man with no hair, a few inches taller than he, standing just inches behind him. He told the man he was visiting someone's plot and the man said, "Go away. You're standing on my grave."

The man looked down and did see a tombstone behind him. He looked at it for a second to try to see the name and dates, but couldn't really make them out because it looked so old. When he turned around to apologize, the man was gone.

Chilled by the experience, the man left Maple Grove without looking back. Though the incident seemed rather ghostly to him, he maintains that it was probably someone who wasn't in their right mind hanging out in the graveyard, which was spooky enough for him, and is the reason he left. But, he does admit that the encounter was pretty unsettling and the man rather ghostly. He'd heard stories when he was younger about a generic man in a black suit that supposedly walks the graveyards at night, but chalks it up to coincidence. But, he has never seen the man since going back.

However, that is not the only haunted Maple Grove Cemetery in Kentucky. There is another Maple Grove Cemetery located on Taylorsville Road in the Nelson County town of Bloomfield that is allegedly haunted by Ann Coke Beauchamp. In 1825, Anne's husband, Jereboam O. Beauchamp, murdered former Kentucky attorney general Col. Solomon Sharp over a rumor that said Sharp had fathered an illegitimate son with Ann. This led to an enraged Jereboam going to Sharp's home and stabbing him to death.

Jereboam was then sentenced to swing from the gallows on July 7th, 1826. Ann was permitted to stay with her husband in his cell during his final days of life. On July 5th, the couple attempted suicide by taking laudanum. This attempt did not work. On the day Jereboam was sentenced to die, Ann convinced the guard to let them have a few minutes alone. Unbeknownst to the guard, Ann had managed to smuggle in a knife, and the both of them attempted suicide once again, this time by slitting their wrists.

When the guard returned, he found both Beauchamps bleeding out. Jereboam was quickly carried to the gallows and hanged by the neck until he died. Ann was left to die from her self-inflicted wound in the cell. The two were then allegedly buried in each other's arms at Maple Grove Cemetery.

For some reason, Ann seems to be cursed to wander the land around the graveyard. Witnesses have reported hearing her cries in the evening. Her pale apparition has been seen walking around her grave. Some say she also wanders the road in front of Maple Grove. She is often described as looking dejected, downtrodden, and eternally sad. Could this be because Jereboam has yet to forgive her for the unfaithfulness, and she remains unaccepted into the grave they share?

THE HAUNTING OF OCTAVIA HATCHER

The story of Octavia Hatcher is one of legend around Pikeville. Articles and shows have documented both her tragic death and alleged haunting. As with many urban legends, the truth gets marred with each retelling. Octavia's death and the details surrounding it have been often changed, and they have created quite a sensational campfire tale. But, despite all the grisly accounts that blur the line between fact and fiction, the real story is both tragic and poignant.

The tale begins in Pike County, famous sight of the legendary feud between the Hatfield and McCoys. In the 1880s, an eighteen-year-old James Hatcher started a warehouse business and worked to become one of the wealthiest men in the state. His fortune was substantial by the age of thirty. He met Octavia Smith, daughter of a well-to-do dry goods merchant, Jacob Smith, and his wife, Pricey. Hatcher and Smith wed in 1889, and on January 4th, 1891, had their only son, Jacob, named after Octavia's father. The child was born ill and died in a few hours. Octavia was crushed and fell into a deep depression.

It is said that Octavia fell seriously ill soon after young Jacob's death. She was bedridden in April and then slipped into a coma. Upon medical examination, doctors pronounced her dead on May 2nd, 1891, having passed from an unknown illness. She was buried in Pikeville Cemetery next to her son. In 1892, James Hatcher erected a monument in her honor, with her holding her beloved Jacob in her arms.

This is where the story gets questionable. It is said that since the summer was so hot, James Hatcher had the funeral and burial rushed so Octavia's body would not spoil. Since the process was hurried along, Octavia's body was not embalmed and she was presumably buried alive.

Not long after, others in town were afflicted by this inexplicable sleeping sickness and began to slip into comas, as well. Allegedly, doctors determined that it was the bite of the tsetse fly (a fly indigenous to Africa) that caused this disease. Once James Hatcher caught wind of this, he rushed to have the body of his late wife exhumed. When her grave was unearthed and the coffin opened, a grisly scene awaited them. The interior lining of the coffin was torn apart with claw marks, fingernails dug into the wood. Octavia's face was scratched and torn, and looked to be frozen in a scream. Her hands were found in claw-like positions, as if she had been desperately trying to dig her way out.

As it goes, James was crushed by this discovery. Already heartbroken by what he believed to be the sudden death of his beloved, to find that she met such a disturbing end made matters far worse. He then had her reburied.

As we said before, the legend evolves. People have told it so many times through the years that it is believed the true nature of Octavia's death has been dramatically sensationalized. Perhaps, even what we believed to be the original tale itself has been altered to suit a grimmer imagining. Opposing this story is the claim that there is no documentation of Octavia supposedly being buried alive. Some who debunk this story claim that if such a terrifying incident occurred in a town as small as Pikeville, it would almost undoubtedly have been recorded somewhere. Yet, no one who claims this took place has been able to cite any sources for this information. Also, there would almost certainly be record of her exhumation, yet there is none, apparently.

There is no record of the sleeping sickness, either, and it has been argued that the theory of the tsetse fly bite is unlikely, due to its African origin, and the likelihood that if such a fly had found its way over here that it would have only affected a few people. Other claims that some sort of gas from the coal mines could have caused it, but this is mere theory without any evidence to support it.

On top of this, there have been other versions of this story told through the years. One of those alterations being that Octavia died while still pregnant, which is almost certainly untrue. But, storytellers also go on to say that the mourners present at Octavia's funeral could actually hear the baby crying inside the coffin. Jacob's headstone is by Octavia's grave, and it indicates that he definitely preceded her in death, so there is practically no way this is true. We guess those who wish to cling to this version of the tale might say the stone was faked, but we find it hard to believe. Almost positively, this version of the story is complete balderdash. Perhaps, the entire "buried alive" scenario is nothing more than horror fiction, but the story exists, and it is possible that it could be true.

To help quell the spreading of false tales, a monument explaining Octavia's true demise has been placed near the grave. Also, since some unprincipled riffraff have broken the statue of the baby from Octavia's arms, a fence has been built around the monument to discourage other rabble from vandalizing it. Also, the folks who live near there are known to keep an eye on the area so no one else does something as reprehensible as this. How sad it is that there are people who would do this.

Stories of Octavia's ghost being spotted around the grave have been reported. It is said that the month of May is the best time for sightings. Those who live on the hill near the graveyard have claimed to hear a woman weeping near Octavia's grave late in the night when no one is present. Some have even said the sound of a baby crying has accompanied the weeping. Mysterious blue lights have been spotted floating around the grave, as well as swirling mist hovering at the foot of Octavia's statue. Others who have stood at her marker have been overwhelmed with the sudden onset of intense sadness or immense dread. There have also been supposed reports of a woman in black kneeling at Jacob's grave and weeping uncontrollably. Also, people claim that the statue will sometimes turn its back on the town for the disrespect of her grave. Though, this claim may very well be nothing more than a college prank, as college students were found to have turned that statue around in the past.

Those who try to debunk the story of Octavia's ghost have cited a tragic ghost story much older than Octavia's. It is said that a woman with a baby in her arms was walking along a road near Ivy Creek late at night, and as she was passing through, a large boulder fell from the hillside and landed upon her and the child, killing both. It was said that they remained buried beneath that rock and, sometimes, at night, the woman, all in black, can be spotted walking around the stone in search of her baby. Also, allegedly, on the anniversary of their death, her dying wails can be heard echoing through the darkness. Some believe that this story has actually been attached to Octavia Hatcher and that's where the legend of her spirit comes from. Even the part about the statue of Octavia holding the baby may have derived from this tale, since it has been claimed that the statue never actually held the baby, and that she actually held a parasol with an immense ring on it in her right hand. We don't know if this is the origin of Octavia Hatcher's haunting, however.

So, it is a very interesting case, this tale of Octavia Hatcher. Was she buried alive? Was there really a sleeping sickness? Was there ever a baby statue? Is it even her ghost that haunts Pikeville? The mystery just gets deeper. Nonetheless, her newborn son *did* die shortly after birth, and she followed soon after. This is a truly sad tale no matter how much of the legends are true. Either way, whether it's Octavia Hatcher or some woman near Ivy Creek, it does seem that Pikeville does possibly have at least one ghost (or ghost story) wandering about town.

ROADS, TUNNELS, AND BRIDGES

THE SLASH MONSTER AND THE HEADLESS HORSEMAN

B arren County has a few urban legends consisting of ghosts and monsters. The most notorious creature said to lurk the shadowed passes of the county is the Slash Monster, which is said to have appeared on Slash Road and the Slash Bridge, which is no longer standing.

Back in the 1940s, a mentally unstable man who stood well over six-feet tall lived in a wooded area near Old Munfordville Road and Lexington Pike. He would often wander the roads at night, lurking in the shadows of the trees and tall grass, and sometimes he would be glimpsed in the headlights of passing vehicles. His imposing and disheveled appearance led some to believe they had seen Bigfoot. Adding to the intrigue, the man would usually go barefoot and leave large footprints in the mud. These sightings led to the legends of the Slash Monster.

But, the story does not stop there. The man, who rarely spoke to anyone, went into a barber shop at the Spottswood Hotel one day in 1949 and received a haircut from a Mr. Furlong. One of the other barbers, Cloyed Cook, made a joke about the haircut just before the man left. Later, the man came back with his gun and shot Mr. Cook dead.

Now, as the story goes, his spirit wanders the woods out on Slash Road, waiting for other passersby he can grab. If someone finds themselves driving down the road, they may glimpse him moving from the shadows, as townsfolk did in the old days. Some say he will even run out in front of your car to try and stop you. If you're caught out there at night on foot, the massive man turned beastly creature may chase you through the darkness.

Another haunting from Barren County takes place just a couple of streets over on Coral Hill Road. Legend has it that one night a man was walking home down the road and stumbled upon the most fearsome sight he had ever encountered. Blocking the way before him was the pale, transparent image of a headless horseman. Frightened out of his wits, the man ran from the road and fled through the woods, running all the way home. As he ran, he heard the clopping of the ghost horse's hooves on the ground in pursuit. After a few minutes, he managed to lose the spirit, but did not stop running until he reached his house.

Upon arriving home, his wife inquired as to why he was so distraught and out of breath. Frantically, the man told her what he had witnessed. He stayed up for some time watching, but never saw the horseman.

When he woke the next morning, he found that the horseman had indeed followed him home. When he alerted his family, they all saw the spirit standing on the front lawn. Every window and door to the house was wide open. The tale ends there, and who these people were and what became of them was never said.

That is not the only tale of the Barren County Headless Horseman, however. He has apparently been spotted several times passing under what used to be the Slash Bridge. Locals say that he has been seen riding along the creek bed carrying a large axe and a bulging satchel. People believe this satchel contains the severed heads of the poor souls the horseman has taken over the years. When the bridge still stood, it was said that if you parked on the bridge and turned off your car, you could hear the thump of the hooves on the rocks echoing through the still night air. Others claim they have looked into the bed and seen sparks from the horse's hooves slapping against the rocks.

While the history behind the Slash Monster is pretty easy to explain, it is uncertain where the legend of the Headless Horsemen stems from. We think its origin is tied to another bit of town lore. Allegedly, back in the 1800s, a slave who was angry at his owners took the family's young daughter out to the bridge and chopped her head off with an axe, then threw her body into the creek. The story was that if you stopped on the bridge and listened, you could hear the sound of the axe chopping the block, followed by the splash of a body being tossed into the water.

Perhaps the sound of the axe chopping on the block and the clopping of the hooves are the same sound. What that sound is, we don't know. Maybe it's the sound of water hitting the creek bank or some other object in the water. Maybe there's a thick branch or something in the creek that is pushed against a rock by the water. Or the sound could just be that of the lapping water in the creek. The sparks could very well be water on the edge of the creek bed glistening in the moonlight. As for the images people have seen of the horsemen? Are they campfire tales, active imaginations, or is there really a headless ghost on horseback riding between Slash and Coral Hill roads? Who knows who could have lost their lives in that area in the past, or what other forms of tragedy could have happened?

In any event, these are very interesting tales that are left to the imagination. It is doubtful a monster wanders about Slash Road, but why not the ghost of the large, unstable murderer that once lived there? What if the Headless Horseman was actually one of the monster's victims? We'll just leave these questions to the yarns of urban legend.

JACOB FLOYD & JENNY FLOYD

COLVILLE COVERED BRIDGE

The secluded Colville Covered Bridge a few miles northwest of Millersburg in Bourbon County was built in 1877 and is located at the Colville Pike, crossing over the Hinkston Creek. The one-lane bridge stands twenty-eight feet above the water, stretching 128 feet in length and only about eighteen feet wide. Not many covered bridges remain in America, the majority of them having been burned during the Civil War, but at one time there was more than 400 of them in the country. All of those that remain have been listed on the National Registry of Historic Places. It is believed the covering was meant to protect the wood from weather damage, leading to a longer lifespan for the structure.

The picturesque view both of the bridge and of the remote location surrounding it have been favorites of photographers for many years. But the rustic and aged beauty of the bridge is accompanied by some very dark events said to have transpired there.

All accounts are local lore. We could not verify them through any source. But there are three mysterious incidents tied to the Colville Bridge.

The first account is said to have happened in the very early 1900s, sometime between 1901 and 1905. A man who had just lost his wife and child to some disease, likely influenza, walked to the bridge in the middle of the night. The covered bridge was a regular spot that he and his family would often stroll across in the evenings. On this night, however, just days after losing his family, the man decided he would join them. He dragged along with him a rope which he tied into a noose and proceeded to hang himself there on the bridge. His cold dead body was found the following morning.

In the 1930s, a couple who were seniors in the local high school went to one of the final dances of the school year. According to some accounts, the couple, or at least the young man driving, had snuck off to some dark corner with some friends and had a few too many drinks. Once the dance had concluded, the couple stayed out a couple more hours, even though they were told to come home directly after the event.

Once they decided it was time to head home, they were very tired and perhaps a little drunk. Realizing they were already later than they were supposed to be, the young man stepped on the gas to hurry home. As he came upon the Colville Covered Bridge, something happened. People speculate he either passed out at the wheel or was just too inebriated to see clearly. Speeding down the dark road at night, coming upon the bridge, the driver misjudged his direction and sped by the bridge, missing it entirely. The car zipped off the road, over the side of the bank, and plunged into Hinkston Creek where both of them drowned.

The final tale tells of an elderly woman who had taken a nightly stroll across the bridge ever since she was a young woman. She began walking it alone, but then the man she married would join her every night, and often times their children. After her husband passed, her children would often still walk with her, and even bring the grandchildren. Sometimes, it was just her grandchildren; other times, one of her children's families. As she aged, and as the burden of growing children began to steal more of her children's time, the lady returned to her solitary strolls, though her children wanted her to stop walking by herself. It was a lifelong tradition for her and she did not want to give it up despite her advancing age and ailing health.

One night, though she was feeling a little worse than usual, she headed out for her stroll. It was a cold winter's night, windy and dry, and she had to wrap her scarf around her nose and mouth to breathe properly. Once she got about halfway across the Colville Covered Bridge, her heart failed on her and she died. She was found by one of her family members later that night. If this story is factual, it seems rather romantic that she would die on a path that had seen all of her best days in life – almost as if she had used it to cross to the other side.

Though these tales seem to have some rather specific details for urban legends, it's hard to know if they are anything more than lore. Perhaps they began as little snippets about people from town, and they grew into these elaborate stories. Maybe they are completely true to life. We cannot say. Whether they are or not, there are ghosts tied to this bridge, and most believe they are somehow connected to at least one of these legends, if not all three.

Variations of the same few paranormal reports have been told through the years. Many of them involve shadow people walking along the bridge. Some have spotted only one, others have spotted several, strolling along, minding their own business. Many believe this is either the old woman alone, or the woman walking with various members of her family. Some have also heard the faint echoes of a woman coughing and crying for help when no one was on the bridge.

Some say they have heard the creaking of a rope above them. Others claim they have even seen the pale figure of a man hanging from the bridge. This is the least reported story. Perhaps the creaking is actually just the aged and weather-worn bridge squeaking in the breeze, or from the vibrations of someone walking across it. The pale man – well, that's a little harder to explain.

The most often repeated tale is obviously that of the young couple who plummeted to their deaths in Hinkston Creek. Some say that while you are walking along the bridge, lights will suddenly shine up at you from underneath, glowing through the cracks in the boards. The lights will shine for a few seconds or about a minute before slowly fading out. Those who have seen this occurrence believe it is the headlights from the young couple's car, floating in the creek before sinking to the bottom. We don't know how deep this creek is, but it must be deep enough to swallow a car.

Another story says that if you drive across the bridge sometime in the middle of the night, you will see headlights suddenly appear behind you, speeding towards the bridge. You'll want to hurry up as it appears the car is coming upon you quickly. However, the car will never reach you, as the lights will veer to the side and the car will sail off into the creek. Naturally, whoever witnesses this will believe a car has crashed and will want to go back to see if help is needed. But, when they get there, there will be no car as this is the phantom vehicle of the couple who drowned.

Very interesting stories, as most small town folktales are. Maybe these people really did meet their doom upon the Colville Covered Bridge, and maybe their spirits really are there, reliving their time spent crossing, or their last few seconds of life ticked away upon the bridge.

JACOB FLOYD & JENNY FLOYD

MESHACK ROAD

One Friday night in 1950, two young men on their way to a weekly dance in Glasgow spotted a pretty young woman in a party dress walking alone on Meshack Road near the small town of Tompkinsville. Not wanting to leave her stranded, the young men pulled over and offered her a ride into town and she accepted. The dress she wore looked a little old fashioned, but both men thought she looked to be dressed for a night out so they invited her to accompany them to the dance, to which she agreed.

After arriving, the young woman danced with both men, and, as the story goes, other men as well. Once the dance was over, the young men asked her if they could escort her home. Having had such a fine night with them, she gladly accepted.

Outside it had begun to rain heavily, and upon leaving the dance hall, one of the men gave the young lady his coat. After they got in the car, she led them to a small, rundown house on Meshack Road where they had found her. Before she got out, the young man told her to keep his coat and he would come back and get it another time. She thanked him and went to the house.

A few days later, the man returned to the home to retrieve his coat. After knocking on the door, he was greeted by an older lady. He explained to her the situation and said he had come to get his coat back. The woman told him that the girl he is describing sounds like her daughter, but she had been killed in an accident on Meshack Road years ago.

The young man was shocked, thinking that there had obviously been a mistake. He told the woman that he was positive the young lady had led him to this house. The woman insisted that no such woman lived there, and even told him her daughter's name and where she was buried.

After the young man left, he decided to visit the church cemetery the woman had indicated. He walked the grounds for a while and found the young lady's grave. When he did, he was greeted by a chilling sight, for he had found, draped over the tombstone, the very coat he had lent the woman.

But, the young lady returned from the grave is not the only phantom said to haunt Meshack Road. There is one presence that has been felt for decades, by both horse riders and motorcyclists. They have reported feeling a presence grasp them around their waste while riding down the road. The invisible presence will hold on for about a mile before letting go. There's not much speculation about what or who this presence could be, only that several people have reported feeling it.

Hitchhiking ghosts are a staple of so many small towns across the country, including a few around Kentucky strikingly similar to the one about the girl going to the dance hall. One even has a woman riding on the back of a motorcycle, holding the driver tight around the waist. Sounds like a combination of the two tales. Nonetheless, the stories circulate through towns to become local legends. Who knows how real these are, but there is only one way to find out: take a ride down Meshack Road, maybe you'll find a dance partner for the evening.

NADA TUNNEL

Often referred to as the Gateway to Red River Gorge, the Nada Tunnel is a massive 900-foot tunnel that lies partially hidden along KY-77 through Powell County. Covered almost entirely by overhanging trees, the historic passage is cut into the side of a mountain and springs up on you seemingly out of nowhere.

As you approach the mountain, it looks like you might just crash right into it; but if you keep driving, you'll see the large dark crevice ahead. Before you enter, know that the tunnel is only about twelve feet wide, which is not room enough for two cars, so be sure there is no one else coming before you enter, and be sure to hit your high beams so any vehicles coming from the other side know you are there beneath the shadow of the mountain. If your vehicle is close to thirteen feet high, you might want to consider another passage.

It took a lot of dynamite, steam machines, and hand tools to carve this tunnel through the thick limestone in 1910. It was built for the Dana Lumber Company to transport timber by locomotive to a Clay City sawmill about fifteen miles from there. The tunnel was completed in 1911, but the timber companies pulled out of the area not long after the deforestation was completed. The railroad tracks that had been laid were then removed and the path was made into a dirt road for pedestrian traffic.

The creation of the tunnel did not go on without incident. One worker set a frozen stick of dynamite down by a fire to thaw it. Unfortunately, the stick exploded and killed him. That isn't the only tragic story tied to the Nada Tunnel, either. A rock climber supposedly tried to scale the cliff side just above the entrance, but misjudged a step and fell to his death on the road below. While this may be nothing more than an urban legend, since there is no documented proof of this incident, that doesn't change the fact that some folks have experienced some scary moments inside.

A glowing orb is said to hover at the mouth of the tunnel, and even float along the interior pitch, casting an eerie green-and-blue illumination along the rough-hewn rocks. Those who have seen it cannot explain it, as they say it is large, perfectly round, and unmistakable. Some claim to have watched it float in one side, navigate the entire length of the tunnel, and exit through the other end. Others have seen it simply hovering in the air at one of the entrances, pulsing and bobbing slightly.

A few of those who have been brave enough to traverse the tunnel on foot claim that they can hear muffled moans coming from inside the wall of rock. None are quite sure what or who could be causing these noises, but they and the orb are attributed to either the construction worker who died, or the rock climber. Naturally, the curious would be inclined to brave the tunnel and find out for themselves, but this is ill-advised, for the tunnel is murky and narrow – as we have already stated. Going into the tunnel on foot is dangerous and could get someone killed.

RED DOG ROAD

Harlan, KY's Red Dog Road runs from Harlan Gas Road to a hollow at the edge of town. Somewhere along that road, back in the 1930s, a murder took place in the dead of night. Incidentally, it is believed that this crime left its mark behind somewhere in the darkness.

As the undocumented story goes, one of the miners that worked in town suspected his wife had been unfaithful to him. Upon arriving home, he found her with another man. This man, whom the miner barely got a look at, fled before the jealous husband could get his hands on him. It is said the miner demanded his wife tell him who the man was, but she would not.

As the miner asked around, it was told to him the man sleeping with his wife was another miner who worked in town. Though there were differing stories about who the miner was, the jealous husband believed he knew. The betrayed husband confronted the other man out on Red Dog Road. The two exchanged heated words, with the other man denying the accusation. His assertions were ignored as the enraged husband drew a gun and shot the man dead.

The husband soon found out his wife was still seeing another man, and that he had indeed shot the wrong man. Now it is believed the spirit of the falsely accused man roams the road, seeking his killer. He has been described as a large, dark entity walking the road at night, sometimes bloody, sometimes not, but always looking angry. Some say if you encounter him, he will try to harm you, thinking you are the jealous husband who shot him down.

This is not the only paranormal encounter reported on Red Dog Road. A mysterious light travels from tree to tree towards the road's end. It has been described as spherical shaped and flickering like a dying light bulb, floating from one tree to the next. Some have explained it as being some sort of flying insect, but it has been seen off and on for decades and is said to be too large and too perfectly round for that explanation to be accurate. What it could be, witnesses cannot say.

Some claim if you stop at the fork where Red Dog goes to Willard Jones Road, you will hear disembodied footsteps walking along the roads, or on a nearby hill. Some say this only happens around midnight while others claim to have heard it at different points of the day. The footsteps have been explained as wildlife, but there are those who insist they have heard the footsteps so close to them they would have seen any animal making them. If these ghostly steps exist, perhaps it is the falsely accused miner walking the road.

Red Dog Road is a dead-end road that loops around the outskirts of town. There are some sharp curves, so if you decide to visit this road in search of the miner, be sure to proceed with caution. The road is not heavily travelled, but one can never be too safe.

JACOB FLOYD & JENNY FLOYD

THE TWIN TUNNELS

Just south of Cincinnati in Ryland Heights runs twin train tunnels beneath Lamb's Ferry Road. Despite being located near a residential area, the area feels very lonely because it is located down a small hill away from the homes and there is little to no traffic that travels through the area. Combine that with the lack of lighting, and the quietude, this place can be very creepy day or night.

Certainly, this is not a recommended place to hang around, considering it's very dangerous given its proximity to the tracks, and the tight area and steep climb out. If a train came, you'd be stuck. The trains come up on the tunnels quickly and you most likely wouldn't have time to get out of the train's way. The property belongs to the CSX railroad, which means exploring down there would be trespassing, so it's best overall to steer clear of the tracks.

If none of that is enough to deter your curiosity, then there's the story of the man who appears out of nowhere near the tunnels. In the 1930s, it's alleged a man was down by the tunnels and got struck by a train, killing him instantly. Some say he was a worker, others say a drifter, and some believe he may have just been a curious person. They all agree, however, that he was killed and his ghost still lingers on.

Although we maintain staying away from the tracks is the best idea, it is said that if one happens to be around the area at ten o'clock at night, you might see the man's ghost walking the tracks. He is said to have brown hair and be wearing a white tee-shirt. Some versions state he is carrying a lantern as well, which would suggest he had a purpose down at the tracks. Usually he is walking towards the exit and will vanish into the dark mouth of the tunnel. People have said they've heard his footsteps echoing down the tunnel, but the area is said to be so quiet it is possible that sound could be anything.

Supposedly, people have taken pictures in the area where the ghostly man is said to appear and have caught some very full and bright orbs as well as misty apparitions.

We could find no record of anyone being killed by a train in the area.

AUNT NANCY'S CURSE

Eight miles north of Campbellsville stands the small town of Spurlington. Settled in the 1840s as a small farming community, Spurlington was a part of Taylor County when it separated from Green County in 1848. It was not long after this separation that the work on the railroad began. The railroad stretched for thirty-one miles, from Greensburg to Lebanon, passing through Spurlington. This created the need for the Spurlington Tunnel.

Work on the tunnel began in 1867 and concluded in 1874. The tunnel is 1900 feet, dug through the black flint and blue limestone. A shaft hole of nearly a hundred feet was carved in the middle so the train's exhaust could leave the tunnel. It would be another five years before the first train would pass through in October of 1879.

But the long stretch of underground pitch is not the only darkness that exists in this tunnel. For more than a century, the shadow of a woman named Nancy Bass has hung over the town's subterranean passage. Bass, who some people called Aunt Nancy, was believed to have been a witch, and legend has it that she was buried atop the tunnel.

Nancy Bass lived in Spurlington around 1850. She was a reclusive vagabond who wandered the streets and fields and slept in barns and haystacks. The townsfolk often claimed she was a witch because people she didn't like would fall suddenly ill or encounter other forms of bad luck and misfortune. Nancy Bass became so despised by her neighbors that they wanted to burn her to death. One day, after being threatened, she said that the only way she could die was if she was shot by a silver bullet.

In 1868, she knocked on the door of a home owned by a man named Wright. When Wright opened the door, Bass fell inside and announced that she would be dead within twenty-four hours. The woman's prediction came true, as she died in the house hours later.

The coroner later found a small silver bullet lodged in her chest while he was preparing her body for the funeral.

Now, this particular version of the story most likely does not end with her being buried on top of the tunnel. If she had been, no doubt something would be there to mark her grave. Nonetheless, people have reported taking pictures at the tunnel's entrance and finding the indistinct form of a woman standing there when the photos are developed.

There is another version of how Nancy Bass died.

It is believed that a group of train robbers robbed a passing train in Corbin, Kentucky in 1860 and then rode the line all the way from Marion County into Taylor. From this point, the story has two versions. One states that the gang came across Aunt Nancy who supposedly took care of them. The telling is very vague as to what "took care of them" actually means. If the previous accounts of her being a homeless drifter are true, she couldn't have very well housed them. But, perhaps she could have shown them the best places to sleep for the night, or the most effective ways to find food. But, this sort of generosity would not be aligned with the misanthropic nature she was said to have had. However, it is said that once the robbers decided they had lain low long enough and it was time to leave town, not wanting Aunt Nancy to tell of their exploits, they threatened to kill her if she told anyone about them. She then told them that if they did that, they would be cursed for the rest of their days. Regarding this as a threat, they killed her and buried her body under the rocks atop the Spurlington Tunnel, along with the $50,000 they had stolen. It is said that not long after, all but one of the gangsters were caught and hanged, and the remaining criminal who'd gotten away died when the L&N train bridge over the Rolling Fork River in Calvary, Kentucky collapsed, sending the train into the water.

We did find that such a wreck occurred on June 20th, 1900, and two men listed to have died in the collapse were James Houston of Pine Hills, KY and George Mullins of Mt. Vernon, KY. Was one of these men among the robbers alleged to have stopped in Campbellsville some forty years earlier? Four decades seems like a long time between the day someone had a curse cast upon them and the day they actually died, but who knows what sort of life he lived in the days between.

The second version seems likelier if the tale of Nancy Bass has any truth to it. While walking along the road above the tunnel, Aunt Nancy allegedly stumbled upon the gang of robbers burying their booty of silver and gold looted during a train robbery in the Cumberland Mountains. But, this was no ordinary gang of thieves. This was the notorious James-Younger gang, led by Frank and Jesse James and James and Cole Younger. The men saw her, and when they noticed she was watching them, they elected to eliminate the witness. Bass was murdered and buried with the treasure on top of the tunnel.

If this is to be the true story, then the 1860 timeline would not work, as the James-Younger gang didn't even exist in 1860, and hadn't conducted their first bank robbery until 1866. However, it is known that the James-Younger gang conducted several robberies across Kentucky, especially into their final years, which occurred in the 1880s, including a stagecoach near Mammoth Cave in September of 1881, and a store in Mercer in October. Their last train robbery came on September 7th, 1881 near Glendale, MO. After this, no known James-Younger gang members were caught and hanged in Kentucky, so that story does not historically add up, even though that doesn't mean every move of the entire James-Younger gang history has been documented. But, it does put the story in a better timeline with the train collapse, seeing as it would have only been twenty years from the curse instead of forty.

Maybe James Houston, one of the men to have died in the collapse, was an alias for a former member of the gang—the name 'James' combined with a city in Texas to create an assumed name? Or was George Mullins perhaps George Shepherd (AKA One-Eyed George), another former member? He fought alongside James in the war, and James, along with Jim Anderson, killed Shepherd's cousin, Ike Flannery. Shepherd later got revenge on Anderson by shooting him dead at the courthouse in Sherman, TX. Curiously, he later joined the James-Younger gang despite the bad blood, although some believe he was hired to infiltrate the gang. He later alleged to have killed Jesse James, despite the reports that Robert Ford had done so, after shooting Jim Cummings dead in Joplin, MO in 1879. It is said that Shepherd fled Joplin for Galena, Kansas, and there he proclaimed to have killed Jesse James, brandishing a bloody, severed leg as evidence. Though there was a huge shadow of doubt thrown over this claim, there were a few who believed it. Some think that maybe Shepherd incorrectly thought he had killed James and then staged his own death to avoid reprisal.

Maybe it was One-Eyed George on that train, after all. Or maybe this is just another one of the many Jesse James fairytales floating around Kentucky. The entire story of Nancy Bass is simply a local legend, right? Or is it?

Now, it is said that Bass has placed a curse upon anyone who would try to find the treasure, because to do so would disturb her grave. If anyone digs in the grounds atop the tunnel, they will be haunted by the angry, vengeful spirit of Nancy Bass. Allegedly, those who have gone in search of the treasure have been met with spells of misfortune: illnesses, financial trouble, and even death. Some have also claimed that people who have disturbed the grounds have been chased away by the dark figure of a woman as her screams echo through the tunnel. Nancy has also been known to haunt their homes and dreams, appearing to them with ominous threats.

Whether or not Aunt Nancy once existed and was a town witch, or just a victim of grave circumstances, or whether or not the James-Younger Gang ever stopped in Campbellsville, it doesn't change the fact that a lot of people are severely creeped out by the Spurlington Tunnel. If you ever decide to check it out, be very careful. If Aunt Nancy doesn't get you, there could be some unsavory characters, or wild animals, lurking in the shadows. Let the legend of Nancy Bass be a lesson to you: you never know who or what you might find alone in the dark.

NARROWS ROAD

Narrows Road winds through the north Kentucky town of Erlanger, which is part of the Cincinnati-Middletown, OH-KY-IN Metropolitan Statistical Area. Earning its name, the narrow street winds through a subdivision and into a wooded area that leads to Bullock Pen Creek. The forested end of the passage is the setting of a local legend that has been giving some residents chills for many years.

Allegedly, one night back in the 50s, an Erlanger officer made a routine traffic stop on a driver going over the speed limit. As he walked down the darkened road, another car came along and struck him, killing the officer almost instantly. Others claim that particular stretch of street was actually the site of a fatal automobile accident that took the life of a police officer. Similar stories, neither of them confirmed. Whatever the tale, this unnamed officer is said to have lost his life there that night, but he apparently never left the area.

According to the legend, if you drive down Narrows Road around midnight, you might see the flashing lights and hear the wailing siren of a police car coming up behind you. A police cruiser from the 1950s will pull in behind you and the officer will approach the car. However, before he reaches you, he will vanish into the night. Another version of the tale states that the officer will actually walk up to your window, speak with you, and then disappear as he is walking away, perhaps at the very moment he was struck down by the oncoming vehicle.

Even though there have been several people over the years who claim to have witnessed this ghostly phenomenon, it is believed that the story about a policeman losing his life on Narrows Road was completely fabricated. No official record of either accident exists, or has at least been made public. Despite this fact, people still believe in the vanishing officer of Narrows Road.

CODY ROAD RAILROAD BRIDGE

The Cody Road Railroad Bridge in Independence, Kentucky appears to be just an average nondescript railroad bridge passing over your run-of-the-mill narrow back road. Mostly, that is all it is, but there's a legend tied to this bridge that has been told in the area for many years.

That legend is of a woman who supposedly died on the tracks. The stories vary as to how this unfortunate soul met her demise on Cody Road, but they all involve this low-standing bridge. One tale states that she was fleeing from her burning home and calling for help as she wandered out onto the tracks and was hit by an oncoming train. Another story claims she either threw herself in front of a train or jumped from the bridge to the concrete below. The creek nearby is prone to overflowing during a rainstorm, and the road has a rather pronounced dip in it just below the bridge, so the area has flooded many times. Allegedly, this woman was down on the road and found herself caught beneath the waters and drowned.

Now, local lore claims that this woman's headless apparition can be seen walking across the bridge, and she is wearing white, of course. At times, the spirit is crying, and other times she is calling out for help. Perhaps ghosts do not need a head to have their voices heard. Many of the locals refer to her as Pig Face, because of the damage she suffered upon her death. This leads us to believe that there are other sightings where she still has her head.

The roaring image of a phantom train has been reported. We are not too sure what attributes distinguish the ghost train from a real train. Orbs have been spotted circling the area, passing along under the bridge at night. In many cases, reports of orbs are to be taken with a grain of salt; however, in this particular instance, we do find it to be curious. The area is pitch black at night, as there are no lights nearby. The road is hardly traveled and it is very narrow, so it isn't as if any cars could be seen passing in the distance. If there were a vehicle driving by, it would be quite obvious. If a train were passing, it's very doubtful a witness could mistake it for anything else – other than maybe a phantom train. However, if someone were witnessing a phantom train, the observation of unexplained orbs would seem pretty pale in comparison.

While there is no documentation of this woman's death, there is a historical event known by locals that can explain the root of this tale. Apparently, this area was heavy with illegal moonshine production at one point. Two of the moonshiners were said to have had a disagreement and one of them set the other's house on fire. However, no one died in the fire, only one of the pets. The woman who it is believed the legend speaks of actually escaped the blaze and ended up dying of old age in the 1980s. It is also said that it was these moonshiners who made up the stories about ghosts to keep people away from the area.

It is always quite interesting to find out how a legend possibly got started.

QUISENBERRY TUNNEL

The Quisenberry Tunnel is a graffiti-covered underpass running beneath U.S. I-64 in Montgomery County. Around that area people say that if you park in the tunnel and turn off your lights, a dreadful demon will approach your car. If you can muster the courage to chance a better look and flip the headlights on, you will see the creature fleeing the tunnel. Other stories claim the demon will leave scratch marks down your hood and even try to get into the car.

The explanation given for the presence of this creature is the age-old dark rituals. Allegedly, some teens tried a Satanic ritual inside the underpass that called this entity up from Hell. If you ever want to test this legend out, we recommend extreme caution. Not because we think any demon will come get you, but because the area is a bit secluded and the tunnel will be very dark. You might not find any demons, but you could find someone looking for trouble, or another car passing by.

HAPPY HOLLOW ROAD

Happy Hollow Road runs through a small section of Benton in the southwestern county of Marshall. Leading into a subdivision, many trees line this road that turns incredibly dark at night. Somewhere along this wooded stretch of lonely road is the home of a ghostly legend.

Rumor has it that a young lady died on this road some time ago. Whether it was in a car accident or if she was hit by a car while walking, or by some other means, this legend does not say. But it has been said that if you put your car in neutral and let it roll forward downhill, the young lady's handprints will suddenly appear on the windshield. Allegedly, she will push your car backwards.

This death is, to the best of our knowledge, strictly rumor and we found no record to corroborate it.

THE MULBERRY BLACK THING

Mulberry is a small unincorporated town in Shelby County. Though the town seems quiet and rather uneventful, there is legend of a monster stalking the roads at night. Said to show itself in different forms – such as a massive panther with monstrous claws and dark yellow eyes, a headless man with a dark body, a large black bear that also has yellow eyes and moves like a shadow; a long, thick snake with yellow eyes, or as a harrowing, black, inky void shaped like a tall, broad man with hypnotic yellow eyes – the creature always appears as a murky entity that the residents have dubbed the Mulberry Black Thing.

Many people have witnessed this beast throughout the decades, as far back as the early 1900s, and they have given different descriptions of it, which has led many to believe that the Mulberry Black Thing is a shape shifter under the control of a witch. That is why an eerie feeling always precedes it. If you are alone at night somewhere in Mulberry and the Black Thing is upon you, you will begin to fill a presence of dread and the overpowering sensation that something sinister is watching you. The air will grow dense and thick with oppression, possibly making breathing difficult. The witness may begin to choke and feel a cold chill creep down their spine. Panic will set in as the power behind the beast wraps its evil arms around you, encasing you in the black magic that controls it.

Once the Mulberry Black Thing strikes, you will be hit with a severe accident. A bear may emerge from the woods to maul you. A massive tree branch may suddenly snap and fall upon you. If you are somewhere along the road, you may find yourself straying in front of oncoming headlights and soon feel the heavy metal crash against your bones. A number of fatal accidents have been said to befall those who encounter the witch's wicked pet. In that last second, before disaster strikes, it is said you will look around you and be arrested by the flashing yellow eyes of the menacing Mulberry Black Thing.

Other legends are not quite so hideous, but still ominous. Some believe that the spirit is a manifestation of psychic energy, and it executes its initiatives depending upon a person's heart. If one is wicked in nature, they may experience one of the aforementioned gruesome deaths. Someone whose intentions are not ill could be met with a different interaction. If an innocent strays from her path and is left wandering the woods lost, the Black Thing may take the form of the serpent and lead her back to her original path. This portion of the legend ties well into the notion that the entity is controlled by a witch.

If you ever find yourself crossing through the small town of Mulberry, be aware. If you come with malice in your heart, you could have one of the most dreadful encounters of your life. However, come with good intentions, and you should make it out unscathed.

THE ALLENDALE TRAIN TUNNEL

W hat is known as the Greater Cincinnati Tri-State Area in northern Kentucky, covering several cities in northern Kentucky, southwestern Ohio, and southeastern Indiana, is home to several Kentucky haunts. Among them are the Southgate House, which we wrote about in *Kentucky's Haunted Mansions*, and Bobby Mackey's Music World, which appears later in this book, just to name a few. While those two are more widely known haunts with rich and dark histories, there is a lesser known haunted spot in the Tri-State Area that has a creepy and disturbing story.

Located just south of Cincinnati, in the small town of Elsmere, Kentucky, behind the Allendale Trailer Park, is the Allendale Train Tunnel. Despite being called a train tunnel, no train actually travels through it. The tunnel is a passage for the stream that runs beneath the railroad tracks. To find it, you must venture into the woods behind Allendale, descend a hill to find the stream, and follow the water to the tunnel. But be careful because the tunnel is said to be littered with trash and covered in graffiti murals, indicating that someone is using it for a hangout; and a dark, secluded tunnel is never a good place to find yourself in the company of strangers.

Above both entrances to the tunnel is a small hook protruding from the concrete. It is not sure what exactly these hooks were once used for—perhaps some sort of signage, maybe even lights, could be cables that once connected to something that is no longer there—but, there is a legend about what one man did use them for a long time ago. Many say that a loner in town traveled down to the tunnel one evening and hanged himself from one of those hooks.

Who the man was exactly, no one is sure, but some say he was a town drunk, others say he was just a vagrant, and there are those who believe he may have been someone who suffered from mental illness. There is even a story that the man might have lost his wife to another man and could not take the shame and heartache that came with it, so he decided to take his own life. It is also thought that the man might have been mugged and murdered. Whatever the reason, the man was found swinging one morning by some kids who went down to play in the water.

It is believed that his ghost now walks the tunnel in the night, and can be heard splashing lightly through the water and slapping his feet softly against the concrete. Voices and screams have been heard coming from the tunnel, with no one found present upon investigation. Perhaps these sounds have given rise to the belief he was murdered. But, in other stories, the residual image of his corpse can be seen sometimes dangling from the hook. Are these sightings random, or do they happen at significant times? Could it be that the man returns to relive his death, whether it was self-induced or caused by another?

This is certainly a disturbing tale, one that might be better off left uninvestigated. It is supposed to be hard to locate this tunnel, and as we previously stated, it could be the location for some illicit activities. Hopefully it's just another town legend, but what if it actually has some water behind it—or below it?

TUNNEL NUMBER NINE

Located in East Bernstadt, Tunnel Number 9 is an old train passage running through Laurel County. It is a spooky location, especially after nightfall, but there's more to be wary of there than just the atmosphere and nighttime aesthetics. There's a legend about a frightening spirit that keeps people away from the tunnel.

The townsfolk call him Caleb, and his legend stretches back to a time longer ago than any local can remember. Some say he might have been hiding in the tunnel's darkness for more than a hundred years. They say he has blazing red eyes that stare out from the pitch, eyes that have sent chills all throughout the body of anyone who has seen him.

There is a creek that runs along the railroad tunnel. One night many decades ago, a group of friends were camping out along that creek. As the day dimmed to evening and then progressed to darkness, the campers became uneasy when they heard some sounds from the tunnel. They could not quite determine what the sounds were – perhaps vocalizations of some kind, the mewling of an animal, perhaps even wind whistling rather loudly along number nine's blackened path – but they felt it was something they should investigate.

Set to enter the tunnel, they moved away from the creek towards the gaping darkness. Before they got close enough to truly peer in, they saw the fiery crimson glow of Caleb's evil eyes. As they stood in fear watching, the eyes grew wider, redder, and fiercer. The strange sounds that had prompted them to approach the tunnel grew louder, echoing off the concrete walls. Now gripped in fear, the campers began to back away. One of the men had a pistol; he quickly drew it and fired six panicked shots towards the flaming orbs. This did not stop Caleb, and his eyes seemed to grow larger, almost appearing to swirl. The peculiar sounds became sinister. The will to elude danger kicked into the campers, and so they fled.

The origins of this story, or of the alleged spirit, are not known. Though locals suspect it is a ghost of someone killed on the railroad in the early days of its operation. According to some of the older residents, untimely death was a fairly regular occurrence in Tunnel Number Nine. They believe "Caleb" may be one of those victims' ghost.

Another story suggests that Caleb may have been the victim of a train wreck in 1882. A circus train was passing through on its way to London, Kentucky when its brakes went out rounding a turn, causing the train to tip over. The accident decimated seven of the cars and killed four men, one of them being Caleb.

But the possible history of Caleb doesn't end there. There is also a story that says Caleb was a track checker, and one day he rode his horse to the tunnel to check the tracks. Little did he know that there was a panther waiting for him. The panther pounced on him, knocked him from the horse, and ate him. The horse reared back when the panther leapt again, and the massive cat was able to break the horse's neck with its mighty paws.

This version of the story states that Caleb not only walks the tunnel, but appears in three different forms: the silhouette of a man, a large mountain lion, or a Pegasus-like horse.

A resident of the nearby River Hills Community claims that her family was plagued by Caleb, that he would come to them, frighten them, and eventually chased them from the community. She described his cries like that of a woman's screams, or like a banshee, growing louder as he neared. After this incident, she was afraid to visit her family again.

Legend says that Caleb walks Tunnel Number Nine every night at midnight, singing to himself. The redness of his eyes is attributed to the notion that in life Caleb was a heavy drinker and so his eyes remained bloodshot. The singing may explain the strange sounds people have heard from him. The screaming may be the drunken ghost singing in a high-pitched voice.

One resident who lived near the railroad tracks all of her life believes firmly in Caleb. She says there were countless times she'd seen glowing red orbs moving down the street. This woman's uncle also claims that he and a group of other locals encountered

Caleb, pursued him, and cornered him in a barn but were unable to capture him. They had dogs and came at him from each side, but when they entered the barn, he was gone.

Another story is that Caleb is the spirit of a conductor who was decapitated. Every seven years he returns to search for his head. But since his head is no longer there, he is doomed to wander the tracks until it is time to return to the spirit world. This leaves the question of the red eyes. Are they just floating there without a head?

One man who has worked near the tunnel for more than thirty years does not believe in Caleb. He says he has never seen anything strange going on at the tunnel, insisting that Caleb is a cautionary story invented to steer children away from playing in the tunnel or near the tracks. According to him, anyone who has claimed to have seen Caleb only said that to scare some child from the area.

Dr. Freund, who holds a Ph. D. in folklore and is associate professor of Social and Behavioral Sciences at Union College in Barbourville, essentially agrees. He opines that the origin of Caleb may have some truth to it, but there is no doubt that his story has been altered during each retelling, which is what usually happens in such cases. He believes that this story is meant to keep people out.

There is no documentation of Caleb's existence, and seeing how anyone who would have been alive during the time of his supposed accident has long since passed, the chance of verifying the tale is unlikely. Nonetheless, his legend remains and has done so for over a hundred years, according to some accounts. Undoubtedly, it will continue on for many more.

Who will be the next one to see Caleb's crimson eyes peering out of the darkness within Tunnel Number Nine?

THE POPE LICK MONSTER

One Kentucky legend that's been floating around for decades is the one about the Goatman, or the Pope Lick Monster, that dwells beneath the Pope Lick train bridge in the Fisherville neighborhood of Louisville. According to this legend, there was a man who used to frequent the wooded area beneath the train trestles and practice devil worship. Some say it was just some drifter, others say it was a farmer in the area. One night, while sacrificing a goat to the Dark Lord, the man made a mistake and was turned into a half-man, half-goat hybrid. Some accounts say he also sacrificed a sheep and is part sheep as well as goat and man. Others say that the man died and was then resurrected with Satanic powers. Who knew goats were such a hot commodity down below?

Another version of the tale states that this man was a deformed circus freak who was mistreated. Apparently, the man who ran the circus used to beat the Goatman, and so the Goatman ran away when the circus stopped in Louisville. Since then, he vowed revenge. Though he never found his former master, he still exacts revenge on any human that crosses his path. The Pope Lick Monster despises humanity and wants to watch them die.

Now, as this silly tale goes, the Goatman is cursed to guard the train trestles for eternity, and anyone who walks across the tracks will be stopped by this creature halfway and he will charge at you. The sight of the beast is so distressing that most people jump from the tracks to avoid being caught by him.

That's just one yarn. Another even more outlandish account is that he will use hypnosis to freeze you in place, or disguise his voice as someone to lure you up on the tracks. Whichever method he supposedly uses, the end result is the same – you get hit by an oncoming train or you plummet to your death.

Here's the kicker – this tale is rubbish. It's bunk; it's ludicrous; and it's dangerous. The reason we are writing about this legend is to hopefully kill it. We despise this legend because it gets people killed. The train tracks that this absurd Pope Lick Monster guards is a hundred feet in the air and roughly 772 feet across. There is a misconception that the tracks are abandoned, but they are not. Not in the least. This stretch of the railway is a major artery into Louisville and freight trains cross over it several times daily.

Many impressionable teenagers and young adults like to go hunting this ridiculous Goatman nonsense, and many of them have died over the years doing so. In 1994, a man rode his ATV across the track. It flipped over and pinned him to the rail with a train coming along. The locomotive hit him and killed him instantly. In 2000, a teenager was on the track when the train was coming through and decided to jump to avoid being hit. The fall killed him. In 2016, a woman died hunting the monster when she was caught on the track and hit by a train. Another teen died in 2019 climbing the trestles and being caught by the train. These are just a few accounts.

When Jacob was in his early twenties, he and two other friends visited the train trestles, looking for the Goatman. Like many others, they had heard the tracks were abandoned. One of his friends wanted to climb up there, but Jacob tried to talk him out of it, insisting that he could fall to his death. After a few minutes of debate, the friend decided he would go up there, but he would only walk a little bit down the track.

He crossed the leaf-strewn area to a nearby hill leading up to the tracks. In a few seconds, they all heard the roaring of a train whistle. Jacob's friend quickly slid down the hill and joined the other two men under the track. As Jacob stood beneath the track looking up, he could see how the bridge wobbled beneath the weight of the train. Metal pieces fell from the construct, littering the ground with many other strips and squares of metal that had previously fallen. It took about five minutes for the train to pass. Afterwards, Jacob couldn't help thinking that if he wouldn't have tried to talk his friend out of going up there, he most likely would have been on the track when the train was coming through.

When we both visited there once, we saw some teens climbing up the side of the pillars holding the bridge up. We yelled for them to stop, but they either didn't hear us or they didn't care. We then called the police to let them know. Not to get them in trouble, but to hopefully save their lives. As we were leaving, we heard the train coming. We hoped the kids had gotten down. We didn't hear any news of someone being hit by the train that time, so we assume those teens did not get caught up there.

Obviously, we are all about creepy folklore and eerie urban legends. As you can tell by reading our work, we don't care if the tales are sensational, silly, and outrageous. While we're believers in the paranormal, we certainly don't believe everything we hear. We feel this is evident by our work because we often offer "more rational" explanations. And we intend to do the same here.

If there ever was a Goatman, we do believe it was a farmer. But we don't believe he was a devil-worshipping, goat-killing maniac. We think he was a farmer who had a lot of goats and children in the area, possibly adults as well, just simply referred to him as the Goatman. No doubt, funny tales about the man arose, and then grew into this stupid story about a sheep-goat-human living by the train trestles. While the story itself is fun, it's dumb because everyone in the area knows people die because of this story yet they keep insisting on it.

We really wish people would stop telling this story with such zeal. Goodness knows the Bluegrass State is full of enough paranormal legends. As is Louisville, which you will see in the upcoming re-release of our first book, *Louisville's Strange and Unusual Haunts*. There's no need to go around spreading a deadly legend to encourage kids to climb the tracks and die.

In short, there is no Goatman, no Pope Lick Monster. How many Goatman tales even exist throughout the country? At least a handful. Also, the train tracks are not abandoned, they are very much in use, and trains pass across it all the time. If you get caught up there, you *will* die, unless a miracle nothing short of divine intervention happens. If you jump, you'll die. If you get hit by the train, you'll die. If you try to hang on to the side of the rails, you'll probably die unless you are incredibly strong or agile enough to get your legs up around a beam, too. But then what? Will you be able to swing yourself back on the tracks? Don't forget how wobbly the bridge is. The force of the train passing over could shake you off like a bug. Please don't go walking across the train bridge in search of the Goatman. Too many tragedies have happened already.

JACOB FLOYD & JENNY FLOYD

SCHOOLS

THE HAUNTED HILLTOP:
KENTUCKY'S CREEPIEST COLLEGE CAMPUS

In 1876, A.W. Mell founded the privately owned Glasgow Normal School and Business College in Glasgow, Kentucky. In 1884, the facility moved to Bowling Green, which received its first bit of land in 1797, and became the Southern Normal School and Business College, owned by Henry Hardin Cherry. When the Kentucky General Assembly approved legislation for two more teacher training facilities, Cherry sold the school to the state and Western Kentucky State Normal School was born.

The school, no longer privately owned, came under control of the state with Cherry as the facility's first president. The normal school operated at that location until February of 1911 when it moved to its present day location on College Heights, also known as the Hill, where the Pleasant J. Potter College once stood. The Hill stands 125 feet above the city, overlooking downtown Bowling Green. In 1922, it was renamed Western Kentucky State Normal School and Teachers College and began programs for four-year degrees.

After merging with a private men's college, known as Ogden College, in 1927, the institution became known as the Western Kentucky State Teachers College in 1930. As the mission of the school changed over the years, it underwent another name change in 1948, becoming Western Kentucky State College. Throughout the late 50s and early 60s, major expansion and restructuring took place at the college. In June of 1963, it merged with the Bowling Green College of Commerce, which was allowed to operate as a separate institution. But, three more colleges were formed as part of Western's ever-growing campus in 1965: the Potter College of Liberal Arts; the Ogden College of Science and Technology; and the College of Education. The name of the school was changed the following year to Western Kentucky University and has continued to grow, becoming the state's third largest public college behind the University of Kentucky and the University of Louisville.

Though WKU might only be the third largest college, it seems to be the most haunted. Numerous tales of paranormal activity, ghostly encounters, and unexplained phenomena have been told from staff and students alike. These tales are so widely told that the university even embraces them and is not shy about sharing them. Among the locations said to be haunted at WKU are Barnes-Campbell Hall, Florence Schneider Hall, the Academic Complex, Greek Houses, McLean Houses, the Kentucky Museum, the Margie Helm Library, Pearce-Ford Tower, Potter Hall, Rodes-Harlin Hall, Sigma Alpha Epsilon House, Lambda Chi Alpha Fraternity, and Van Meter Hall. A plethora of articles and books have been written about the alleged hauntings, and we dug through quite a bit to gather the information.

Let's begin, shall we?

VAN METER HALL

The current Van Meter Hall sits at the top of the Hill and is one of campus's original buildings. Built in 1911, it replaced the old Vanmeter Hall, which had been built in 1901 as a replacement to the main building of the Southern Normal School & Business College which burned to the ground in 1900. The second and current building, which is on the National Registry of Historic Places, has an auditorium that is said to be haunted.

The namesake for the building is Capt. Charles J. Vanmeter, one of Bowling Green's most respected and generous philanthropists, as well as one of the town's oldest natives upon his death in 1913 at the age of 86. It was he who provided the funds for the original Vanmeter Hall to be built.

The Van Meter Auditorium is mostly used for theater, but there have been concerts and presentations held there as well. There are three different stories about the ghost that allegedly haunts there. The most accepted is that during construction a worker was on the roof and fell through the skylight to the lobby floor, dying on impact. The man was said to have possibly been distracted by a plane flying overhead, which might have been a fascinating sight to folks in those days. The man's body left behind a large puddle of blood that doesn't seem to go away. Supposedly, whenever someone washes the floor, the stain returns. It is also claimed the bloodstain glows during events. During these events, his ghost is known to appear in front of students and staff, scaring them. He also likes to cause a little mischief in the auditorium by opening and closing the stage curtain, turning the lights on and off, causing inexplicable computer malfunctions, and moving tables and music stands around the building. It is also said that the man's wife and child haunt the auditorium, wandering about, singing and talking unintelligibly.

Another version of the tale is that a member of the custodial staff was hanging lights above the stage and fell to the floor and left the unrelenting bloodstain. No matter how any times the spot where he landed was washed, the stain always came back. Eventually, a new floor had to be laid because of this. Whether it is the construction worker or custodian, people have reported seeing a phantom sitting in a seat in one of the back rows when the auditorium was otherwise empty.

The least known story is the most interesting. In this tale, there is supposed to be caverns under Van Meter Hall where a hermit once dwelt. This hermit is said to have carried a blue lantern with him through the dark passages, and after he died in the tunnels below his spirit found a path that leads into Van Meter Hall and he can now be seen wandering in the shadows carrying a blue lantern that resembles one of those blue light police cameras seen hanging off of streetlights.

POTTER HALL

One of the oldest buildings on the campus, Potter Hall was built in 1921 and named after J. Whit Potter, who was president of Potter-Matlock Trust Company and the American National Bank, and was also a regent of Western Kentucky State Normal School. The three-story residence hall was originally a women's dormitory that had a monthly rent of $8.50. During World War II, from 1942 till the end of 1943, Army Air Corps cadets stayed there. In 1949, Potter's Hall became a men's dorm until 1957 when it was changed back into a woman's dorm due to two new men's dorms having been built. As of 1994, Potter Hall has been an administration building consisting of a registrar, financial aid consulting, admissions, student counseling, and career services.

Potter Hall has a very dark and poignant legend attached to it. On April 21st, 1979, Theresa Watkins, nicknamed Tye-Dye, a student who lived in room seven on the ground floor, took a belt and hanged herself from some steam heating pipes running along the ceiling of her dorm room. It is said that there are funeral records documenting this, though we have not seen them ourselves. But, there are a few reports of paranormal activity taking place in the building.

There have been two spirits to have allegedly identified themselves, neither of which call themselves Theresa, but go by the names of Casperella and Allison instead. On separate occasions, students using a Ouija board have communicated with both spirits. Caperella confided in those she chatted with that she was a very sad spirit that likes to bother residents there by locking and unlocking doors, rattling desk drawers, and making creepy noises up and down the halls. Allison claimed she likes to take people's items and relocate and even hide them.

These incidents allegedly described by these spirits via Ouija boards have been known to transpire. Some ladies who used to live there reported hearing footsteps in the hall, followed by their name being softly spoken just outside their door. Whenever they have answered the voice or gone to check the halls, no one was there.

Some residents and faculty members describe a feeling of unease in the basement storage room where Watkins hanged herself. The usual cold spots, sense of dread, and feeling of being watched have been reported. Others say her ghost often bangs on the pipe from which she hung, but this could very well be chalked up to normal plumbing issues.

Many believe that both spirits are Theresa going by a different name. We think maybe the Casperella name was just given to the spirit by the students who called her that, and they probably didn't actually receive a name from her. Allison, though, was reportedly the name given during the other Ouija board session. Perhaps Theresa has her reasons for not wanting her true name known.

Since it has become an office building, there is a spirit that moves from room to room stealing pennies, leaving them lying around the building, and rolling them down the hall. No one knows why it does this, but because of this, people call the ghost Penny. Some faculty members have reported seeing pennies being picked up by the spirit and then carried away. One staff member in the building reported hearing the sound of coins being dropped into a vending machine when no one was out around the machines. We're not sure if this is Theresa Watkins, but Penny sure carries the tell-tale trait of mischievousness that comes with the paranormal accounts coming from Potter Hall.

FLORENCE SCHNEIDER HALL

This three-story Georgian Revival building was constructed in 1929, originally called West Hall due to its location on the Hill's western slope. A few years later it would be renamed Whitestone Hall. It was an all-women's dormitory built to house 200 young ladies. The second floor contained a large room that could be used for conferences, studies, and other general uses. On the third floor was the infirmary, complete with metal hospital furniture, a diet kitchen, and the nurses' living quarters. Just as with Potter Hall, Army Air Corps cadets were housed there during World War II.

The building became a continuing education center in 1977. This was short-lived as it was soon converted back into an all-women's dorm in 1980 due to a housing shortage. But over the next few years, enrollment of females students severely declined, leading to the closing of the hall in 1984. It was then rented out for office space and conference rooms until the first two floors became co-ed dorms in 1987. As of 2007, Florence Schneider Hall houses the Gatton Academy of Mathematics and Science in Kentucky.

Schneider Hall has quite a distinctive history. But, there is something far more sinister tied to its past.

There's a campus legend that sometime during Spring Break in the late 1940s, when the building was known as Whitestone Hall, two students had remained behind to complete a project for one of their classes. During the night, an escaped lunatic wielding an ax dragged himself up the fire escape and entered through a window on one of the upper floors. He then found the stairways and took them to the floor below. From there, he slipped into a room at the end of the hall and attacked one of the students, whose name was Judy.

The story states that Judy was studying at her desk at the time, though we don't know how that can be known for sure under the circumstances. In any event, she saw the killer and screamed, prompting him to strike her with the ax and apparently flee the scene. Severely wounded and heavily bleeding, the young lady dragged herself into the hall and scratched at the other student's door. Having heard the commotion, the other woman was too terrified to answer. The next morning, when she stepped out into the hall, she found Judy's body with the ax embedded into her head.

Though there is no documentation of this alleged murder, some residents at Schneider Hall believe it could explain the strange and spooky things they have witnessed over the years. Women have found themselves locked in the bathrooms despite leaving the doors unlocked when they went in. Doors slam shut mysteriously up and down the halls. Many students have reported hearing disembodied footsteps moving through rooms and down hallways.

Some have seen Judy sitting at windows inside, as well as standing in doorways. Others have claimed to see a pale apparition looking at them from windows while they were outside. Some say the image of a ghostly woman wanders through rooms. It appears that Judy has an affinity for electrical gadgets, such as televisions, computers, lamps, and alarm clocks, as she often turns them on and off. She is also blamed for the chairs, beds, and tables that sometimes like to move on their own.

The occurrence that seems to chill residents the most happens during Spring Break. Some of those who have stayed behind have been terrified by the sound of scratching on their doors in the middle of the night. Many believe that this is Judy trying to make her presence known, perhaps believing she is still on the run from an ax-wielding homicidal maniac.

THE HELMS LIBRARY

Originally known as the Health & Physical Education Building, the Helms Library was built in 1931 for about $250,000. Initially, it was a gymnasium referred to as the Big Red Barn. After the

Diddle Arena was built in 1963, the building was renovated into a library, which was dedicated on October 14th, 1967.

The library was named after Auburn, KY native Margie Helms. Helms was a well-educated woman who became WKU's librarian assistant in 1920, then the librarian in 1923, and finally the Director of Library Services in 1956, which she served as until her retirement in 1965. In 1950, she was awarded the Outstanding Business Woman of Bowling Green from the Business and Professional Woman's Club. The Kentucky Library Association presented her with the Outstanding College Librarian for Kentucky award in 1964.

As rumor has it, there was a student many years ago who was up on the ninth floor of the building and decided to open the window, but had some difficulty because it was stuck. After wrestling with the window, it popped open. The force pulled the student forward, and seeing as there was no screen, he fell through the opening and plummeted to his death. Now it is believed his spirit haunts the ninth floor. People have seen him standing near the window and walking the halls. Some have reported hearing the echo of his final scream as he tumbles through the open window. It is also claimed that the window will open on its own. At night, or while alone on the floor, someone will find the window open, shut it, and find it open again soon after. Many think the boy's ghost is behind this action.

THE KENTUCKY MUSEUM

When history teacher Gabriella Robertson noticed there was only one book on Kentucky in the library of the Western Kentucky State Normal School in 1914, she set out to change that. She eventually succeeded in amassing enough books on Kentucky history to warrant the requesting of a new building in which to store them. President Dr. Cherry agreed and determined that he not only wanted the library, but a museum, and he began to raise money for it through the College Heights Foundation in 1928. After the money was raised, construction of the Kentucky Building began in 1931 and was finally completed on November 16th, 1939, which was also Cherry's birthday.

The building contained the library and museum, as well as classrooms and reception areas. A number of artifacts, such as family bibles, letters from GIs to their girlfriends, children's toys, photographs, furniture, clothing, jewelry, and other items were stored in the building. The building closed in 1976 but reopened in 1980 after undergoing some major renovations.

Many people have reported strange and frightening occurrences in the Kentucky Building. These reports have led to the belief that the building is haunted, particularly in the museum where most of the haunts have been reported. Some faculty members have seen dark shapes moving in their periphery, only to turn and see no one near. Shadow figures have been spotted moving in corners and across rooms. Dark silhouettes are said to linger in doorways and stand in the halls near the museum. After spotting these forms, visitors will leave the room and hear the sounds of rapid footsteps trailing them. Many who have seen these figures claim that they are usually accompanied by sudden gusts of freezing cold air. Usually, witnesses feel the eerie sensation of someone watching them before they see the figures.

Though the museum holds the most chilling haunt in the building, the library has its own ghosts as well. Books have been thrown from shelves and tables directly onto the floor by an unseen force. Some believe this to be the ghost of a young man whose apparition was caught on film walking through the museum. A number of witnesses have spotted this young man passing through the library and they believe it to be the spirit of a former student.

MCLEAN HALL

Designed by John Wilson and Maurice Ingram, McLean Hall was built in 1947 for a cost of a half-million dollars. At the time, it was one of two female dorms on campus, the other being the Florence Schneider Hall, then known as Whitestone Hall. It housed 160 female students across 90 rooms. Other than the resident rooms, it also had laundry facilities, a social room, and a reception area.

Its namesake, Miss Mattie McLean, graduated from the State Normal School in 1902 and became secretary to then-Western president, Dr. Henry Hardin Cherry. When Cherry died in 1937, she served under the next president, Paul Garrett. She also served on the Board of Regents as well. In 1945, after forty-three years of service to the university, Miss McLean retired and moved to Mississippi, where she lived out the remainder of her life, passing away from a stroke on December 8th, 1954.

McLean Hall was quiet of any paranormal activity for many years until three students decided to pick up a Ouija board one night and see if they could make contact with her. They were compelled to do this due to hearing disembodied footsteps walking the halls at night, as well as the sounds of someone entering rooms. This led the ladies to believe that this was perhaps Miss Mattie McLean walking the halls and checking on the rooms, perhaps keeping watch over the young women staying in the hall.

According to the legend, they asked if Miss Mattie was in the room, to which the spirit replied, "Yes." They then asked her if she would be willing to materialize so they could see her, and the spirit again replied, "Yes." Next, the young ladies claim they turned off the lights in the room and a light began to glow before them. In seconds, a gray-haired woman with a gray face and wearing a gray outfit appeared. From there, they say they asked the entity questions regarding Miss Mattie's life, and when they researched the answers later, they found that the ghost had answered them correctly.

There is a portrait of Mattie McLean located in McLean Hall. Since this incident, the light beneath it will turn on and off by itself, and even glow brighter sometimes. Other reports claim that if you stare long enough at it, the image of Miss Mattie will smile at you. Maybe she feels welcome since talking to these students and wants to let them know she continues to watch over them.

BARNES-CAMPBELL HALL

Located on the south end of the campus, this nine-story men's residence hall was built in 1966 and named after Sheridan Barnes and Donald Campbell, two Board of Regents members in the 1950s.

During spring break about a year after the building's construction, a 20-year-old RA out of Leitchfield named James Wilbur Duvall stepped out of the shower and noticed that the elevator car was stuck between the 6ᵗʰ and 7ᵗʰ floors. This was apparently a regular occurrence and Duvall had fixed this issue a few times before. So, instead of walking up the stairs, he opened the door to the shaft with an elevator key with the intention of flipping the switch that would get the car moving again. Only he failed to ensure that the elevator car was not descending upon him. When he leaned into the shaft and reached for the switch, the car pinned him between the outer wall of the shaft and a steal beam, crushing him to death. Since this tragedy, it is believed his spirit still haunts the halls.

According to several eyewitness reports, sometimes, late in the evening, when the elevator stops on the fifth floor, the doors will open to reveal no passengers inside. Some have even reported a rush of cold air emitting from the empty car. Others who have rode the elevator say it will stop on the fifth floor even though no one has pressed the button. The elevator will also ride up and down with no one inside sometimes late at night. Many believe this to be Duvall's spirit riding the elevator to his floor.

During spring break, after all the students were gone, a faculty member had just finished sweeping Barnes-Campbell Hall to ensure no students were there. After finding all residents were gone, he went out for dinner. Upon returning to retrieve something from the fifth floor RA's room, he found all the water faucets and showers turned on, along with a trail of wet footprints leading from the bathroom to the RA's room. No one was found in the building.

This isn't the only incident of mysterious bathroom activity, however. Students have reported hearing the showers running late at night when everyone was supposed to be asleep. When investigating the sounds, they have found the bathroom empty with the water running. Others have even seen the wet footprints leading from the bathroom to the elevator.

It would appear that this spirit doesn't confine itself to the bathroom, elevator, and RA room only. People have entered rooms in the morning and found chairs moved around. Some chairs have even been slammed against the walls by unseen forces. Many attribute this activity to the ghost of James Wilbur Duvall.

There definitely seems to be some strange occurrences taking place in the Barnes-Campbell Hall. With such a tragedy having taken place, it seems the spirit of Mr. Duvall may still be lingering.

RODES-HARLIN HALL

Also known as Dormitory No. 4, Rodes-Harlin Hall was built in 1966 and named after John B. Rodes and Max B. Harlin. Rodes was a close friend of WKU president, Dr. Cherry, and a former Mayor of Bowling Green from 1929 to 1933 and Warren Circuit Judge in 1948. Harlin was a Tennessee native who moved to Bowling Green in 1909 to open a law practice and served as a WKU regent from 1928 to 1932.

Rodes-Harlin Hall is nine stories and houses up to 400 female students. Allegedly, a former student there elected to take her life by jumping from the roof of the building. Not long after her death, students who knew her would hear the sounds of tapping and scratching on their windows, even those on the upper floors. When they would look out to see what was causing it, only the dark, empty night was there to greet them. These reports lessened as the students living in the building when she died graduated and moved on, but even today the occasional student reports these mysterious sounds just outside their windows where there is nothing to make them.

But, the young woman's spirit did not cease her haunting. It is believed that she now returns on the anniversary of her death to scare other students. She has been heard roaming the halls of the ninth floor at night, tapping on doors. Whenever a curious student will step out into the hall to answer the knocks or investigate the footsteps, the woman will appear as a pale apparition in front of them.

On that night, she will also appear upon the roof to relive her final moments of life, and throw herself off, disappearing as she falls. This is believed to be the source of the unexplained footsteps along the roof sometimes heard.

Is she there only on the anniversary of her death, or is that just when her presence is strongest?

THE GREEK HOUSES

Known for turning boys into men, with the mission to make each member into the best version of themselves they can possibly be, the fraternities of Western Kentucky University have their own collection of creeps and specters. Steeped in urban legend and unexplained occurrences, the tales from these houses are quite interesting.

The Phi Delta Theta fraternity has been around since 1848. It came to Western Kentucky on May 6th, 1966, led by a man named Bill Hatter. Today, there are over 100 members, ranging across many WKU organizations. Not without a sense of charity, Phi Delta Theta was recently given the Clark Jackson Award for raising $17,000 between 2015 and 2016 for Lou Gehrig's disease and the ALS Association.

The house located on Alumni Avenue has often been suspected of paranormal activity. An incessant and disturbing rattling of pipes and strange groans heard in the walls have led many to believe there is a menacing supernatural force in the house. Many attribute this to very mundane plumbing problems, but no causes for these alleged problems have been found, leading others to maintain that ghosts reside in the walls.

A more peculiar tale is that of the moving stair rails. The age-worn staircase banister of the house is missing several rails, and it seems the rails that remain like to mysteriously switch places. House members have reported rails from the bottom moving to the top, and vice versa. Where there will be one missing rail in an area one day, there will be two missing there on another day, only to see one of the rails returned to its spot later on. Sometimes, when a rail in one section has magically reappeared, another rail is discovered missing in another section. A spot that was previously missing a rail will suddenly have one in its place, only to see the rail move to an entirely different area of the banister. This has been a very perplexing occurrence to some members of the house.

The Delta Tau Delta house on Chestnut Street has a more specific haunt. It seems a former member of the house is still hanging around, letting people know he is there.

The origin of this once rebellious fraternity dates back to 1858 at Bethany College in West Virginia. When those who headed an organization of poets, orators, and essayists known as the Neotrophian Literary Society fixed a prize vote, eight angry men decided to form a secret society to combat this nepotistic society.

Their goal was to take back control of this organization and return it to the student body. This organization became Delta Tau Delta, and it now has more than 170,000 members across 200 campuses nationwide.

They came to WKU in February, 1967. Their charter was suspended from the campus due to a poor academic performance and low number of members on July 22nd, 2014. But, they returned in the fall of 2018 – ghost and all.

There is a room in the house members refer to as "Billy's Room." In the 1980s, a Delt by the name of Billy Lester died mysteriously in his room, and members believe his spirit remains there. The door to the room will suddenly open and slam shut when no one is in there. Lights turn on and off and the stereo will often come on by itself, and the volume will go up full blast. It has been decided that Billy is still there in his old room, perhaps trying to get other members' attention or simply unaware he has passed away.

Lambda Chi Alpha was founded by Warren Albert Cole in the early 1900s. There are two different accounts as to how this fraternity's formation came about. One states that in November of 1909, Cole met with Clyde Nichols and Percival Morse in Boston and pledged an allegiance to this new brotherhood. This meeting was said to have been intended to reorganize a society of law students from Boston University called the Cosmopolitan Law Club, but resulted in the Lambda Chi Alpha organization instead. The laws of this new fraternity are believed to have been a mergence of the rites and regulations of a prep school fraternity known as Alpha Mu Chi, of which all men had been members, as well as a legal fraternity known as Gamma Eta Gamma and an agriculturist society known as the National Grange of the Order of Patrons of Husbandry, both of which Cole was a member.

The other story of Lambda Chi Alpha's creation states that when Cole first came to Boston University in 1909, his residence was very far from his law school. He and a few other students began renting a room at Pemberton Square where they could study between classes and work. Over time, this circle became known as the Tombs or Cosmopolitan Club. By the end of the year, he decided to move to a place on Joy Street. It was here that he shared an apartment with Charles Proctor and James McDonald who eventually joined Sigma Alpha Epsilon. Cole, however, wanted to start his own fraternity. Two years later, he moved to Hancock Street and roomed with Ralph Miles and Harold Bridge. On November 15th, along with Percival Morse, these men became the founders of Lambda Chi Alpha, basing their constitution largely on that of Gamma Eta Gamma's.

Lambda Chi Alpha came to Western Kentucky in 1965 and is housed in a building on Chestnut Street. Legend states that long before Lambda Chi Alpha moved in, a young woman was brutally murdered in that house. The story does not say who she was, but it is believed she is still there.

Past members have claimed to see the apparition of a young woman running across the lawn in distress. Whenever anyone has approached her, she disappears right in front of them. Other accounts describe young men being chased through the yard by the spirit. Does she mistake them for her killer and try to chase them away, or are the unsuspecting students simply standing in her path as she dashes across the yard?

The young lady also seems to have an affinity for fire. One member of the Lambda Chi Alpha fell asleep with a candle burning on his nightstand only to wake and find the candle at the foot of his bed. Fireplaces in the building have lit on their own. Maybe it isn't that she's attracted to fire, but simply trying to get some light because she likes to turn lights on in the house. A chandelier inexplicably turns on by itself sometimes.

Kappa Sigma is a fraternity that has origins dating back as far as 1400 when a teacher at the University of Bologna in Italy named Manuel Chrysoloras took his five best disciples and formed a secret society for protection from the city's corrupt governor, pirate Baldassare Cossa (also known as Antipope John XXIII), who often had university students beaten and robbed in the streets. The society members used secret signals and codes to protect themselves from infiltrators. Over the centuries the society grew into something more than just a protective organization, it became a brotherhood. In 1869, five students at the University of Virginia took the traditions of the Bologna order and created Kappa Sigma to carry on its legacy.

Kappa Sigma came to WKU in 1965 and their house on College Street is allegedly haunted. A group of young men who were members of Kappa Sigma were experiencing strange occurrences in the house: loud unexplained noises, doors slamming shut, disembodied footsteps, and lights turning on and off. So, they decided to get out a Ouija board to see who was causing these disturbances. According to their account, they made contact with a spirit that called itself Jim the Cowboy who laid claim to the eerie happenings in the house. There isn't any information on who Jim the Cowboy is, but some insist that he is there.

The Sigma Alpha Epsilon house that was once located on College Street may have the most notorious spirits among the WKU fraternities. SAE began on March 9th, 1856, founded by eight men at the University of Alabama in Tuscaloosa. The leader was Noble Leslie DeVotie, who chose the name, wrote the ritual, and created the grip. It spread quickly across national campuses, coming to WKU on October 2nd, 1965.

The original building on College Street burned down in 2005, forcing the fraternity to move. The current house stands on the corner of Center Street and Alumni Avenue, and as far as we know, is clear of any spooks, creeps, or spirits. But the former house was alleged to have once been a makeshift hospital during the Civil War. Former frat brothers who lived in the old house claimed they had seen some strange and spooky things: the faint image of a man appearing behind them in mirrors, and a humanly shadow that moves across walls when no one was walking by, with footsteps creaking along the floors as it passed. One evening, the ghost of a tall, skinny military man in an overcoat was seen standing on the dance floor. After spotting this manifestation, they took out a Ouija board and tried to contact him. Upon doing so, the spirit confided that his name was Kevin and he had died in the hospital and was trapped in the house.

One peculiar comment Kevin made to them was that his favorite number is seven. It was in room seven that strange incidents occurred. The most chilling happened when a couple of fraternity members were in that room and a refrigerator light suddenly went out, followed by the light in the room, and then the door slammed shut even though no one was standing near it.

During finals weeks, while the boys were in there studying, the answering machine kept coming on. No messages were left, but it just kept switching on and beeping. One brother commented that he was glad there were no messages being left at least, and the phone rang soon after. When someone answered the call, no one was on the other end.

In another room of the house, one student was getting frustrated with his roommate because he kept turning on a small fan they had sitting on a shelf. The student would get out of bed, turn the fan off, only to have it turned back on a few minutes later. After turning it off a couple more times, the next time the fan came back on, he got up to yell at his roommate but found he was alone in the room. As he stood there looking around, the fan flew from the shelf and hit the floor.

With lights burning out and fans turning on mysteriously, perhaps there were some major electrical issues taking place in the old building. If it was around during the Civil War, it no doubt had some wear and tear within its walls. Maybe that's why it eventually burned down. But, investigators were quick to discover that the fire looked to be intentionally set. They determined that arson was the cause, not age. Luckily, there were only four students inside and all were woken in time by the smoke detector, allowing them to escape unharmed. It's disappointing to think someone would set fire to a building with people inside, and as far as we know, the culprit was never caught. Perhaps it was Kevin, finally tired of being trapped there, trying to find a way out.

It's not just the boys who have ghosts in their Greek Houses. It seems the young ladies of the Kappa Delta sorority are not alone in their residence as rumors of spectral encounters are told.

Kappa Delta was founded by four young students at the State Female Normal School in Farmville, Virginia. On the rainy Saturday afternoon of October 23rd, 1897, Lenora Ashmore Blackiston, Mary Sommerville Sparks Hendrick, Sara Turner White, and Julia Gardiner Tyler Wilson sat in their small dorm room in Professional Hall and developed Kappa Delta in hopes of empowering and inspiring young women to realize their full potential. Since then, this organization has grown to 250,000 women strong nationwide. The Delta Gamma chapter settled in at Western Kentucky on March 27th, 1965.

The ghost of the woman who haunts there is believed to be a woman by the name of Ms. Norman. Apparently, Ms. Norman was a widow who resided in the house long before the sorority, and it is said that she built the house for her children and their families. Despite her intentions, she was rarely visited by the family and, saddled by the everlasting loneliness, hanged herself in the closet that is located in what is now the house mom's room.

House moms in the past have heard strange rustling and thumps coming from that closet. Other members of the house have reported the sound of moans coming from the room as well as the basement. Footsteps have been heard walking along empty rooms and hallways in the night. The disembodied sounds of a woman crying have echoed softly through the house from an undetermined location.

THE ACADEMIC COMPLEX

This building, located on the southern end of the campus, was built in 1969 and opened in 1970. It is the home of the College of Health and Human Services, one of WKU's radio stations, and their TV broadcasting station, WKYU. The land the building was built on used to be the location of Vets Village, where soldiers returning from war interested in education would stay in the 1940s and 50s. It is also said the building used to be a hospital at some point. It is also claimed that the complex is haunted.

According to the stories, disc jockeys working there in the evening tend to have paranormal experiences. They have heard voices and footsteps coming from empty rooms. Some have reported seeing a human form moving around from the corner of their eye, only to turn and find no one there. Reportedly, there is a closet somewhere in the building that has a door that will swing wide and then slam shut randomly. On one occasion, two DJs there late into the night watched in shock as a CD player began moving on its own, as well as opening and closing without being touched.

PEARCE-FORD TOWER

At twenty-seven stories tall, Pearce-Ford Tower is the largest residence hall in the state of Kentucky. When it opened in 1970, it was the largest building in southern Kentucky, standing 247 feet. It was named after William Pearce, who was director of WKU's Department of Extension and Correspondence from 1920 until 1959, and M.C. Ford who taught science and agriculture at WKU from 1913 until he passed away in 1940. Ford also served as the chair of Agricultural and Natural Sciences during his time at WKU.

The story behind the tower's alleged ghost is practically the same as the story from Barnes-Campbell Hall. A male student, who was supposedly one of the first to live there, didn't like to shower on his floor, so he went several floors up to use another shower. One evening, he went to the elevator to go back to his floor after showering, pushed the button and waited. When the doors opened, he stepped in without looking and plummeted twenty stories to his death, leaving only his wet footprints. The elevator, it seems, had become stuck on one of the floors above him.

Allegedly, on the anniversary of his death, the ghost of the young man relives his final moments. People have watched as his wet footprints appear on the floor, wandering from the shower to the elevator. Often times, when the ghostly tracks halt at the elevator, the door will open with no one inside and then close.

Another story is that a worker fell to his death down the elevator shaft during the tower's construction. His body was never found and is alleged to have become entombed somewhere in the building. Some say now when the building is closed for school breaks faculty members checking the building have witnessed the elevator running up and down the shaft, stopping at random floors, while no one is inside.

We could not find any documentation to validate these alleged deaths. But, it sounds like there is something going on with that elevator.

Well – pennies, and Ouija boards, and malfunctioning elevators; mysterious wet footprints, eerie voices in empty halls, and smiling portraits. Western Kentucky is a regular haven for haunting souls. While people often associate Kentucky's haunted locations with Waverly and Bobby Mackey's, it seems WKU outdoes them both in terms of alleged paranormal activity. There are many ghostly stories emanating from this illustrious campus. Of course, some could be the result of over-imaginative young minds, while others could have been invented to scare underclassmen. But, aren't those the types of answers skeptics give about any place alleged to be haunted? There's no reason to believe that WKU's claims are any less authentic than the more infamous super-haunts.

JACKSON CITY SCHOOL

L ocated in Jackson, in the eastern hills of Kentucky, the Jackson City School, also known as Jackson Independent School, offers pre-Kindergarten through 12th grade classes. In the 1960s, the elementary side of the school caught fire and burned to the ground, to be rebuilt soon after.

It is believed that the school is haunted by the spirit of a little girl who once attended there. This little girl, Katherine Maxine Stamper, was present during a fire, and as the alarm sounded and the children were heading down the stairs, Katherine was caught in a rushing crowd and pushed over the railing where she fell to her death.

As it turns out, this is a true story. It happened on November 23rd, 1930. Katherine was only eight years old. She is buried in the Jackson Cemetery and her story can be found on the Breathitt County Museum Facebook page, along with a photograph of her shortly before her death.

There are reports that Katherine remains at Jackson School. Young ladies who have been in the bathroom have reported that toilets would flush when no one was in the stall, and they would also hear a little girl humming when they were alone. The sound of a young girl singing "Ring around the Rosies" often echoes out in the empty hallways. The sound of a child running up and down the halls has been heard, too.

While Katherine's death is very real, who's to say if she is actually haunting the school? These reports have been going on for several decades though, so there seems to be some merit to the tale. We believe that stairs hold some significance in the paranormal world, if one does exist, and that spirits can use them as a means of conveyance, much like with hallways and doorways. That is why so often you hear about ghosts on stairs, spirits haunting hallways, and unseen forces handling doors. Perhaps dying on the stairs can get a ghost stuck, or perhaps this little girl has just decided to stay at Jackson Independent School. Is it Katherine? If the specter is truly there, it is likely she is it. Maybe she always liked it there, despite her tragedy.

MOREHEAD STATE UNIVERSITY

L ocated in Morehead, Morehead State University opened in 1887 as the Morehead Normal School, with only one student attending the first day. The original building was nothing more than a cottage. The school closed in 1922 and the Morehead State Normal School opened in 1923. The facility officially became a university in 1966.

There are rumors that a student named Penelope fell to her death from the Nunn Hall balcony in the 1970s. The legend also says that Penelope's spirit still roams the halls. Though there is no record of a Penelope falling from the balcony, but there is a likely origin for that story.

Dora Deloris Ball was a twenty-year old student who was majoring in early education at Morehead. However, she was a resident of Mignon Hall, not Nunn. On October 14th, 1971, Ball was visiting a friend at Nunn Hall and fell from an upper window and landed on the roof of Nunn Hall's lobby. She was found at 10:45pm and died in Lexington the following day from injuries.

The death of Ball is documented, and seems to be legitimate though we have not seen that actual records ourselves. However, there seems to be two other possible deaths that occurred in the area, and neither one of these are named Penelope either.

The first is of a young lady named Caroline who allegedly suffered from depression. It is said she was a loner, even though she belonged to several clubs around the college. From this point, the story basically repeats Ball's with only a slight alteration. In this tale, Caroline did not fall from an upper window, but jumped out of a ninth floor window and landed on the roof of the Nunn Hall lobby. Likely this story derived from the true story of Ball, and was slightly changed to explain the odd happenings taking place on the ninth floor.

The next story is quite sensational and sounds like the kind of tale students would make up when sitting along in the dark trying to scare one another. This one is of a young woman named Ginger who liked to get high. One night, she was rather doped up and decided to play Russian roulette. As you have no doubt guessed, she didn't win, and now her spirit allegedly lingers in Nunn Hall. We are willing to bet that this story was made up to explain the crazy laughing students claimed to hear at night, proclaiming that it's the ghost of a drug-addled young woman who inadvertently killed herself while doing something stupid, and now she is cursed to roam the halls, forever high, unaware of where she is.

The final story is about a student who became pregnant but was abandoned by the father. The night the boy walked out on her, she sat alone in her dorm room crying until she could take the sadness no longer. She went out to nearby Eagle Lake, plunged in, and allowed herself to drown. Now they say she can be heard crying in the dorm room on the anniversary of the night she killed herself. Again, as far as we know, this story is unofficial, and likely invented.

However, the story of Dora Deloris Ball is apparently corroborated by documentation. She truly did die at Nunn Hall. But is there a ghostly presence? Some say yes, and others are not so sure. Though several students have experienced the strange occurrences said to be caused by "Penelope," few believe that is a ghost. Lights will turn on and off by themselves, doors will open and close on their own, and items will be mysteriously moved sometimes, but most of those who experience these do not believe they are a result of paranormal activity.

There are those who do attribute some incidents to the ghost of "Penelope," or whomever. Some students report feeling a very creepy presence and a sense of uneasiness on the upper floors. A few students have felt an oppressive anxiety set upon them while riding the elevator towards the top.

It seems the ninth floor is where most of the spiritual disturbances happen. Students have been in their dorm rooms watching the television when it would suddenly shut off for no known reason. Some have also reported hearing the water come on in the bathroom when no one else was there. Upon investigation, they would find the sink was indeed running. At night, when the hallways are dark and quiet, residents have been awakened from their slumbers by the loud, distinct sound of female laughter flittering along the corridors.

Whether it's Dora, Penelope, Caroline, or Ginger, there seems to be a female spirit at Nunn Hall that likes to keep the students awake at night.

HALL ELEMENTARY SCHOOL

There's a legend around Hall Elementary in Harlan that a former janitor was cleaning around the furnace and managed to fall in and burn to death. When this happened and who this janitor was is unknown. Likely, this story isn't true. But it is likely that a former janitor there passed away at some point.

If one custodian there did in fact pass away, it could explain the footsteps heard walking the empty halls during classes or after the students have left. Other janitors there have found their tools and supplies missing, moved, and misplaced in strange places, like in trash cans, on top of lockers, and in classrooms on the other side of the school.

Faculty members have reported seeing the apparition of a man drifting about the school, particularly around the custodial rooms and supply closets. One custodian reported seeing a ghostly figure pass through a supply closet door.

Even if no one fell into the furnace, it seems someone's spirit still remains in the halls of Hall Elementary.

UNION COLLEGE

Founded in 1879, Union College is a private four-year liberal arts college located in the Appalachian Mountains of Barbourville. It stands in the middle of four state parks, with the Wilderness Road on the east side of the campus and the Cumberland Gap National Historic Park about thirty miles away.

Outside of its many arts and science degrees, Union College is also believed to house many ghosts. There is a legend that Union College was built upon an old burial ground and before construction could begin the bodies had to be removed from the earth and relocated. However, some say that not all the bodies were removed. This has allegedly led to many ghostly disturbances throughout the campus. There are many reports of slamming doors, loud bangs, mysterious knocking on doors and windows, and disembodied voices and footsteps all throughout the campus. There have even been reports of shadow figures seen in certain halls. These generic haunts are believed to be tied to the bodies that supposedly remain buried beneath the college. But these are not the only haunts reported at Union College.

Beyond these paranormal tidbits are a few legends of tragedy believed to be the cause of more specific paranormal incidents. They span three different residence halls: the Speed Hall Administrative Center located front and center on the campus; Pfeiffer Residence Hall, right next door to Speed; and Lakeside Residence Hall located at the back of the campus, next to the lake.

The Speed Hall Administrative Center was originally a women's residence hall that opened in the 1905-06 school year. In those days, being a woman in college was not easy. Many of the female students had to endure hardships and prejudices the males simply did not. The persecution against female students could be quite harsh, and some did not handle it well.

One young lady was encouraged to go to Union College by her father, who wanted her to achieve as much as she possibly could in her lifetime. His love and faith in her carried her through the dark days when she experienced criticism from the male students. Her father was a miner and his life was tragically taken by a mining accident. The young lady was utterly devastated for he was all she had in the world. She told some of her friends that she was going to go back home and then went to her dorm room on the third floor to pack. As she was packing, she was overwhelmed by the heartbreak and decided to take her own life. When her roommates returned to the dorm, they found her body hanging from the rafters. It is said that her body was then removed, the room cleaned out, and the third floor never used for anything other than storage.

Despite the room being padlocked and abandoned, people outside the building have reported seeing a light emanating from the room where the young lady hanged herself. When a faculty member has turned off the light, students have found it turned on soon after.

One of the coordinators of student conduct decided to debunk this story back in 1999. One night, when the lights on all three floors were left on, he began turning them all off, starting on the bottom floor. His plan was to work his way up to the third floor, flicking off all lights along the way, and then walk back down in the darkness. When he made it back down to the bottom floor, the lights were back on.

This did not surprise him, though. All the doors to the building were still open, so any student or staff member could have turned them back on. So, he decided to try his test once again. After making his way through all three floors once more, he encountered something eerie as he arrived to the middle floor. Standing at the edge of the steps was the apparition of a woman in an old-timey dress with a soft light glowing around her. He believed that this woman was not the young lady who hanged herself, though, but Fanny Speed, the namesake for the hall.

This is not the first sighting of Fanny, however. Many have reported seeing her lingering on the second floor, walking the halls and passing through closed doors. Some believe she slams doors and turns lights off and on, as well. This could explain why she was waiting for the coordinator at the bottom of the stairs. If she likes to turn the lights on and off, she might have been inquiring as to why this man was randomly messing with the lights.

That was not the end of the strange occurrences for the coordinator. After he left the building, he was approached by a student who asked him if he was closing the building for the evening. After telling her he was, she pointed out that he had missed one of the lights. He turned around and saw the light had come back on in the third floor room where the suicide took place. He decided to leave the light on for the next shift.

A tragic love story created one of the spirits in Pfeiffer Hall. A young woman residing there met a young man with whom she fell deeply in love. After dating for some time, the boy confessed to her that he did not feel as passionately for her as he once did and ended the relationship. The devastated young lady then alienated herself from the rest of her peers, spending many nights crying alone in her room. One evening, the pain became too much to bear and she allegedly ended her own life. Legend has it that just after she passed away, a cold wind swept across the floor, winding through the halls and blowing into rooms. It is said now that there are nights when a cold wind will kick up indoors, even in summer and even with the windows closed, and the sounds of her crying will echo along the corridors.

Others claim to have heard disembodied footsteps walking the halls at night when everyone is in bed. Upon investigation, no one is found out there, though the steps can still be heard. Others say closet doors will open and close on their own in certain rooms. Others claim to have seen and heard a pale woman creeping past their room when the door was open. When they get up and look out the door, no one can be seen.

One night, around four in the morning, two students were in the hall talking with a campus security officer when they heard the sound of someone running up a nearby stairway, followed by heavy footsteps racing down the hall overhead. Surprised by this strange incident, the three of them ventured upstairs and found a residential advisor chatting with a group of students. When the security officer asked who was running in the halls, the RA explained that no one had been doing so, and that these phantom footsteps occur quite often.

Also, an alleged ghost haunts room 131 at Pfeiffer Hall. Students that were staying in there started having frightening experiences after just a couple of weeks. While the students were playing video games, one of the desks allegedly rose into the air and was dropped to the floor. Not long after, more items began flying about the room. A mattress and guitar were suddenly tossed to the floor as well.

After speaking to an RA about the incidents, the RA wanted proof. So, they lined up bottles in the room and poured baby powder around them. The next day they found the bottles scattered and little swirls in the powder. Could there be a ghost playing around in the room? Or did the bottles fall and the powder swirl as a result of AC being on in the room? Even if that were the case, what about the items being tossed about the room?

Room 245 is supposed to hold the spirit of a former student, too. The student's name was James Garner (not to be confused with the famous actor), and he was a hybrid athlete, playing football and basketball. It is said that on October 30th, 1963, around midnight, Garner was attempting to close his window and somehow fell out, dying when he hit the ground. Some accounts state that there are records indicating this, but we were not sure.

Legitimate or not, it is believed that Garner's ghost (or some paranormal entity) haunts room 245. The spirit doesn't like the window to be open. If you open the window at midnight on the anniversary of Garner's death, he will slam the window shut. Others say that it doesn't have to be on the anniversary of his death. Some nights, the ghost will shut the window randomly. Aside from unexplained thumps near the window, this is the only disturbance the ghost seems to make.

The ghostly encounter at Lakeside Hall centers on the ever-present Ouija board story. In 1994, a group of male students started playing with the Ouija board and supposedly contacted a young lady named Milan, who had been murdered on campus. Milan apparently likes to run through the halls opening and closing doors. She also turns on lights in empty rooms. RAs have searched the residence hall for the culprit of these disturbances, but have never found anyone.

Milan's presence is not exclusively tied to shenanigans. She did help one male student wake up in time for his exam. He fell asleep the night before the important exam and forgot to set his clock. He suddenly woke up the next morning and saw the image of a young lady standing at the foot of his bed. When he raised his head to see her better, she faded from view. He then turned to look at the clock and saw that it was time for him to rise and get ready for the test.

It has been said that nearly every building at Union College is haunted. Some think that a few of the stories are fabrications made up for the annual ghost tour the college offers around Halloween. Many believe all tales to be true, and most of them seem to have witnesses to corroborate them. If you're ever out that way around Halloween, it might be something worth checking out.

LINDSEY WILSON COLLEGE

Founded in January 1903 as the Lindsey Wilson Training School, Lindsey Wilson College in Columbia was named after Louisville native Catherine Wilson's deceased stepson. Wilson donated $6000 to the construction of what is now the L.R. McDonald Administration Building, which is one of the campus's original buildings. Others who contributed financially to the school's creation were Columbia native Kizzie Russell, who left the school $1000 in her will, and Mrs. James Phillips of Lebanon, after whom Phillips Hall is named.

The school officially opened a year later in January 1904. During those years, the school was a normal school, preparing students to be teachers, and educated pupils in grades one through twelve. Many of the students who completed their studies there went on to Vanderbilt University for further education. The school garnered much respect and was recognized as a college-level facility in 1923 after adding a department which offered a junior college degree. A $10,000 donation was made by the citizens of Columbia to assist in Lindsey Wilson's further development. Though the training academy closed in 1934 to become solely a junior college, Lindsey Wilson did offer a Model Training School from '33 to '79.

Horton Hall, which is now part of the Horton Complex consisting of Parrot Hall and Weldon Hall, built in the 1950s, is said to be the location of some very ominous ghosts. It is said that on the second floor there are some very dark spirits that can be seen drifting about the rooms and hallways. They will float up to the ceiling and begin shaking the tiles rather violently, even to the point of causing some to fall – as the story goes. Other times, they can be seen emerging from the ceilings and crawling down the walls to wander the rooms. Those who have encountered these terrifying entities have warned others that if they see them, to remain very still and quiet, for if you are detected these grim specters will rush you and scream in your face.

Nothing is known about these shadowy forms. It is only said that they appear at night, and mostly on weekends. There is, however, rumor of a tragedy that took place in Phillips Hall in the 1930s. It is alleged that a young student hanged herself there, but we found no actual documentation of that, and that's an entirely different hall. Could there possibly be some form of dark energy hanging around the campus?

MEADE COUNTY HIGH SCHOOL

L ocated in Brandenburg, Meade County High School was originally established as Brandenburg High School in 1913, changing its name in the 1930s. On May 4th, 1974, one of the worst tornado outbreaks in the region's history ripped across many counties in the state, including Meade County. Brandenburg suffered some of the worst damage of the entire outbreak, and Meade County High was hit hard.

We were told that the gym from the school was used as an emergency morgue as the town cleaned up and found the deceased. On May 7th, there was even a funeral held there. This was a truly tragic disaster, and one that is still fresh in the minds of some of the residents of the city.

The memories, it seems, are not all that remain of that deadly spring day. Some say the echoes of disembodied voices can be heard around the gym, as well as unexplained bangs and bumps. Voices have been heard traveling up and down hallways when no one else is around, as well as footsteps walking along corridors.

This is not believed to be the only paranormal activity haunting the halls of Meade County High. The band room is another hot spot for ghostly goings-on. This is another location where a mysterious voice can be heard talking, as well as mysterious cold spots that don't seem to go away. Students and faculty have also claimed to see the figure of a boy with a tuba standing by one the room's windows. Who this boy could be is not known, but he has been seen numerous times.

During the school's construction, it is rumored a worker fell from either a ladder or platform and died. There are claims one of the school's vice principal's had a photograph of the worker's spirit bent over either working on something or inspecting the floor.

Wandering shadows and human forms are abound on the football field. Mysterious figures have been seen walking along the edges of the field as the day falls to evening. Who these specters are is also not known, but it is said there is a graveyard located behind the football field and the drifting figures could be from there.

WEST JESSAMINE HIGH SCHOOL

West Jessamine High School in rural Nicholasville, just outside of Lexington, hasn't been open all that long. In 1997, the original Jessamine County High School split into two separate schools due to the rapid growth of the county. The two schools were East Jessamine and West Jessamine. West Jessamine took the original mascot name, the Colts, and has everything any other public education facility does – academics, sports, extracurricular activities, and it also has ghosts.

Though it's only a little more than twenty years old at the time of this writing, West Jessamine seems to have quite a bit of paranormal activity reported there by both students and faculty. Witnesses have seen lockers flying open and slamming shut when no one was near them. A former teacher there said she was in the hallway heading out for the day and a locker flew open a few feet in front of her, causing her to stop. She looked at the locker for a minute and saw the lock still locked on the latch. Thinking that maybe the student hadn't closed it all the way after clicking the lock shut, she walked over to the locker to push it shut. Before she reached it, the items inside began to fall out, sliding out at first, then looking as if someone was reaching in and pulling them out aggressively. The teacher then stepped to the other side of the hall and hurried past. As she rounded the corner, she heard the locker door slam shut. Though this seems to be the most detailed and frightening account of locker shenanigans, it is not the only one. Lockers around there seem to have minds of their own.

Custodians in the school have been assaulted by flying trashcans. They have been taking out trash, or cleaning up the custodial room, and have had trashcans lift up off the floor and leap towards them, hitting them in the legs. One custodian barely dodged a spinning lid flying at his head. He heard a banging sound, looked up, and saw the lid coming at hm. He ducked just before the lid slammed against the wall behind him. But this is not the only garbage can attack. They have also tipped over and rolled towards janitors, as if someone had pushed them over and then kicked them. No one was hurt, but apparently someone did have their legs taken out from under them. It was not the same can each time, either. Perhaps the spirit of a former janitor haunts the halls and is not satisfied with her/his successors.

The lights over the football field have been known to turn on by themselves. When someone turns them off, they'll sometimes turn on again. Vehicles in the parking lot have started on their own, more than once. Members of the faculty have reported encountering an apparition of a man who walks the hallways humming a tune to himself. Perhaps he is responsible for all the banging lockers and restless trashcans.

But it seems the humming man is not the only spirit hanging around West Jessamine, and he's not the most ominous. There have been claims that three very solemn, silent women dressed in red will stalk the hallways at night. Late in the evening, those who have been there well past school hours have encountered these spirits drifting along the halls. They say the women make no sound and are quite pale, and they pass along the corridors carrying with them a very ominous air. Those who have witnessed them say they got chills and a pending sense of terror from their presence. Some have even refused to stay there late because they don't want to see these spirits again. The three women could be the cause of the temperature drops, odd feelings, and aromas of perfume some people have described

So, it seems that West Jessamine has a collection of eerie experiences taking place along its haunted halls. With the facility being relatively new, it's hard to say what could be causing these haunts. Perhaps they are connected to the land itself, or they came when the school moved. West Jessamine might have gotten the original Jessamine mascot, but it also got its school spirits.

THE RESTLESS SPIRIT OF RAFINESQUE

Though many hear the name 'Transylvania' and they automatically imagine the ominous castle secluded far atop a foggy mountain, where wolves howl and bats squeak, filled with spider webs inside its crumbling structure—the dwelling of the infamous and dreaded Count Dracula! But that is not the case here. Transylvania University in Lexington, Kentucky does not school people in the art of night-crawling, shape-shifting, or vampirism. It is actually a highly regarded liberal arts campus and the first college established in the country west of the Allegheny Mountains.

Although the Count does not live there, it is believed there is a rather riotous spirit lurking the grounds. It is said that a former professor who was disgraced and sent packing returned to exact his revenge.

Transylvania Seminary was established in 1780 after an act passed at the Virginia assembly—and act supported by then Governor Thomas Jefferson. The first classes were held near Danville, Kentucky five years later in the cabin of Reverend David Rice, who was the first chairman of the Board of Trustees. In 1793, the Board accepted an offer of land in Lexington, called College Lot, and moved their establishment there. That land is now known as the Gratz Park Historic District and is home to such notable places as the Hunt-Morgan House (which you can find in *Kentucky's Haunted Mansions*), the Carnegie Library, and the Christ Church Cathedral. There is also the Fountain of Youth, which was built with funds willed to the district by author James Lane Allen after his passing.

Upon moving to Lexington in 1799, the seminary changed its title to Transylvania University and became the first law and medical school in the western United States. Kentucky luminary, statesmen Henry Clay—who was a five time presidential candidate and former Speaker of the House—was appointed as a law professor at the school in 1805 and named to the Board of Trustees in 1807, a position he held for the remainder of his life.

The expansion of Transylvania really began in 1818 under the presidency of Horace Holley. With his connections to many significant politicians in the East, he managed to raise the national profile quite a bit. After acquiring tools and text books from Europe, Transylvania's law school was soon on par with Harvard's. This advancement soon led to the establishment of the Kappa Lambda of Hippocrates medical fraternity (the first of its kind), which soon led to the American Medical Association being founded. In 1859, however, the medical department closed.

The school experienced more expansion when it combined with Kentucky University in 1865. Over the ensuing decades, the program expanded to include the Agricultural and Mechanical College (which later became the University of Kentucky) and the College of Arts and Sciences, among others. The name was changed back to Transylvania University in 1908.

Flash forward to 1924—the year that the body of Professor Constantine Samuel Rafinesque was retrieved from its unmarked grave in Philadelphia and buried in Transylvania's Old Morrison building. Professor Rafinesque's tenure with Transylvania University was checkered, to say the least, and the controversy of his departure led many to believe in the curse his spirit left behind.

Rafinesque was born in the Constantinople suburb of Galata on October 22nd, 1783 and migrated to Philadelphia, where his father died of Yellow Fever in 1793. He soon discovered his love for botany and began collecting numerous specimens by searching the fields and woods from Pennsylvania to Virginia over the next two years.

In 1805, he went back to Europe and lived in Palermo, Sicily and served as secretary to the US consul. Rafinesque remained there for the next decade, traveling the island and collecting plants and documenting previously unrecorded fish in the local markets. He also published his first scientific books during these years.

When he returned to the United States in 1815, he lost all of his sample collections and unpublished manuscripts while shipwrecked on Long Island Sound. Later, he found work in the fields of biology and zoology. In 1819, he began his career as a professor of botany at Transylvania University. During this time, he created the binomial names for more than 6,700 species of flora and fauna without receiving any recognition for his labors. He also identified 148 pre-historic Native American sites in Kentucky.

The professor was a rather eccentric fellow, as some believed. He would sometimes skip his own classes and go for nature hikes. This did not make him very popular with the faculty, which already viewed him somewhat negatively due to his perceived peculiarities. Also, his Unitarian beliefs did not sit well. He found himself in a number of arguments with his peers. In 1826, he was forced out of the university.

But, Rafinesque did not depart quietly. As he was leaving, it is said he turned to Transylvania University President Horace Holley and declared, "Damn thee and thy school, as I place curses upon you!"

The following year, the school lost its funding. Holley was then relieved of his position, and when he decided to move to Louisiana and teach, he contracted yellow fever and died. The year after that, the school's main building burned to the ground, causing the school to move across the street. The soaring rocket that had been Transylvania University was now slowing down. Was it due to Rafinesque?

Rafinesque returned to Philadelphia and lived there until he died of stomach cancer in 1840. According to legend, Rafinesque owed quite a bit of back rent, so his landlord intended on selling his body to a local medical school for payment. Upon learning this, a few of Rafinesque's friends broke into the apartment and later had him buried in Ronaldson's Cemetery at 9th and Bainbridge, which was a graveyard created for those who did not belong to a church so they would not have to be buried in the pauper's cemetery.

In 1924, a campus organization called The Hemlock Society decided to have Rafinesque's body removed from Ronaldson's and returned to Transylvania University. He was then placed in a tomb located in the Old Morrison building, which was designed by famed architect, Gideon Shryock, and built in 1834. On the crypt is inscribed the word, "Honor to Whom Honor is Overdue." Although this gesture was obviously well-meant, the organization did make quite the blunder, it would seem. Ronaldson's Cemetery would often have as many as six people interred in one space, and it seems that when the organization pulled the body from the ground, they did not unearth Rafinesque's, but the body of Mary Ann Passamore. Tests conducted on the body's remains have proven that it is indeed one of the others who were buried alongside Rafinesque.

Perhaps this mistake angered Rafinesque even more. In 1969, a raging conflagration engulfed the building, leaving only the exterior walls standing in its wake. Inside, there was but one thing left untouched by the blaze: the crypt of Rafinesque (Passamore). On top of that, firefighters claimed that during the fire, they saw the figure of a man standing in the doorway to the crypt, laughing as the inferno raged around him.

Old Morrison was restored and re-opened in 1973. It is said that the curse still lingers and strange things occur at Transylvania University. A security guard has reported being tripped by something while he was alone in the dark halls of Old Morrison. Every year, for a week around Halloween, Transylvania dedicates a week to trying to ward off Rafinesque's alleged curse. At least they're finding a way to embrace the legend.

We can't really say whether or not Transylvania is haunted by Rafinesque's curse, or if he even cursed the place at all. But, one question that does linger is why, after discovering who actually lay in the crypt intended for Rafinesque, has no one returned the body and brought back the real Rafinesque? If they did, perhaps that would lift the curse.

EASTERN KENTUCKY UNIVERSITY

Central University opened in Richmond in 1874. Over the years, it did not do too well. By 1901, it was struggling financially and had very few students, and so it consolidated with Centre College located in Danville. It became Eastern State Normal School No. 1 in 1906, and was changed to the Eastern Kentucky State Normal School and Teachers College in 1922, and by 1930 it was known simply as Eastern Kentucky State Teachers College. Normal schools and teachers colleges, of course, helped train students to become effective teachers. In 1935, graduate studies were added to the curriculum, and in 1948, the Kentucky General Assembly dropped the word "Teachers" from the name. In 1966, the facility officially became Eastern Kentucky University.

If you have read our book, *Kentucky's Haunted Mansions,* you might recall the ghost of Emma Watts, who loathed EKU and did not want her family home to be owned by the college. When they acquired her old home, her ghost began causing mischief in the house.

Emma Watts is not the only spirit, though, said to cause a little trouble at Eastern Kentucky. Many spirits are alleged to roam the halls of the historic campus.

THE BLUE LADY

The spirit known as the Blue Lady is said to haunt the Pearl Buchanan Theatre as well as the Keen Johnson Ballroom in the Keen Johnson Building. Her origins are hazy, and there are different stories about why she is there. Some say she hanged herself in the clock tower where she used to memorize her lines. They say she did it out of love for the art (whatever that means) or that she did it out of madness. Others say she killed herself because of lost love. There are even tales that she may have been murdered. Some believe she may have died normally and her spirit decided to return to the school.

Whatever the reason for her presence, reports of her ghost date back to the 1950s. People have been reporting a blue mist swirling around the clock tower. Others have reported seeing the apparition of a woman in blue on top of the building. She has also been seen walking across the stage in the Pearl Buchanan Theatre. She can also be found dancing in the Keen Johnson Ballroom. Witnesses have described a transparent woman wrapped in a soft blue light twirling to unheard music in the middle of the room. If you don't see her, you might be able to hear her melodic voice echoing through the theatre. Witnesses claim to have heard a woman singing when the theatre was empty. Most believe this is the Blue Lady.

DISTURBANCES IN KEENE HALL

It is alleged that a student hanged himself upon the sixteenth floor of Keene Hall, even though there is no official record of this. However, students have reported watching doorknobs turn on their own when no one was on either side of the door. Sometimes, the door will also swing open.

Another peculiar occurrence is the sound of music coming from inside the walls. Whenever this is heard, students often believe it is coming from a neighboring dorm room. But, whenever they ask the other students to turn down their music, they find that the phantom tunes are not coming from any of the rooms. As they investigate, they have discovered that the music is actually coming from inside the wall.

MOZART THE DOG

According to a campus grave marker, Mozart was a black dog that lived from October 15th, 1947 until August 14th, 1964. He got his name due to his love of music and would often sit through music classes. He was so beloved by the student body that they had a portrait painted of him, have given him two gravestones, and even mentioned him in various articles regarding EKU history.

Perhaps the love students had for Mozart keeps drawing him back. Sightings of his ghost wandering around his grave have been reported. Some say he runs across campus and disappears in front of people. Disembodied barks have been reported in hallways. Maybe these events are tired to actual dogs wandering on campus, or maybe Mozart is still making his rounds at EKU.

THE NAKED GHOST

A woman who roams the halls naked allegedly haunts the Moore Building, formerly home to the science classes. Most accounts state that you'll be walking down the hall and when you come around a corner, there will be a naked woman standing right in front of you. Some have said they think she just got out of the shower because she appears to be wet. When you run into her, she'll look at you in surprise and then disappear. Others claim that she has walked into their rooms, only for her to be surprised to find she is not alone in the room and then vanish.

IS IT EMMA WATTS?

In 1969, a former chairman of the mass communications department, Ron Wolfe, lived in the basement of the building and worked upstairs. The downstairs telephone rang one day while he was working. He went downstairs and answered it, and when he returned to his office he found the drapes had been pulled open, even though they were drawn when he left the room. Wolfe then closed the curtains and went back downstairs to make a phone call. When he came back upstairs, the curtains were open once again.

This incident apparently occurred a few times. Allegedly, there have been other instances, like doors closing on their own, lights coming on and turning off, and footsteps walking the halls. No one is sure who haunts the building. It's been suggested that the ghost is the aforementioned Emma Watts, who lived next door to the campus in Elmwood Mansion. Some think she is there looking for her cats. If she is there, we believe she is there to cause a disruption since she hated EKU.

VICTORIA

Sullivan Hall was built in 1912 and is now used as the Honors dormitory. There are rumors that the building was once used as a mortuary. Other tales say it was used as a makeshift hospital during the Civil War, which would insinuate that it was actually built on a site that was used as a hospital since the Civil War ended long before 1912. Whether or not either of those stories is true, it does seem there is a ghost present. However, it has nothing to do with the mortuary or the Civil War.

Sometime in the 1970s, a nursing student named Victoria allegedly hanged herself in what is now room 425 on the fourth floor (other tales suggest room 419). Her apparition is often seen in the room and others state they have looked into the room and seen her hanging shadow on the wall. Other students claim to have seen claw marks form, and they believe they are from her tormented spirit trying to get out of the room.

People also hear loud bangs and cries from the room, and objects, such as chairs, tables, and pens, move on their own. One student said she had a hairbrush picked up and flung across the room. Others say the closet door will swing open by itself in the middle of the night. Is Victoria still present in Sullivan Hall?

There certainly are some spooky stories coming out of Eastern Kentucky University. In a state full of haunted campuses, EKU is not backing down.

LODGING

THE SEELBACH HOTEL

When it comes to Louisville hotels, none have a richer history than the Seelbach. Built by the Seelbach brothers, it opened in 1905 with a French Renaissance design intended to resemble the popular European hotels of the time. Almost instantly, it was considered one of the finest lodgings in the United States. It was thought to be so grand in style for the age that legendary author F. Scott Fitzgerald used it as a basis for a hotel in his classic novel *The Great Gatsby,* hence the name of the hotel restaurant being "Gatsby's on 4th."

Many former United States presidents have stayed there as well as numerous entertainers, ranging from the Rolling Stones to Elvis Presley and Russell Crowe. The most notorious guests would have to be the 1920s gangsters like Lucky Luciano, Dutch Shultz, and most notably, Al Capone.

Capone had a secret room that contained a hidden escape route leading to tunnels under the city. As the mobsters would operate their speakeasies and card games, their lookouts would alert them if law enforcement was closing in. The door to Capone's secret room would slide shut and blend in with the walls of the outlying Oak Room. From there, he would take several flights of stairs hidden inside the walls down to the tunnels and make his getaway.

Over time, the hotel came under different ownerships and was renamed before it fell into disrepair and was boarded up like many other forgotten buildings on that side of the city during the time period of Louisville's urban blight, ranging from the 60s to the early 90s. When it was renovated and reopened, the new owner returned the Seelbach name to it. Now, it is once again a grand hotel that attracts many visitors throughout the year.

But, with all that history comes legends, and the Seelbach has quite a few.

There is a story of the infamous Lady in Blue, who was said to have died falling down an elevator shaft back in the early 1900s. Due to an illicit affair she was having with another man, some think she may have been murdered, but no one has ever substantiated this claim.

Murdered or not, her ghost is said to still roam the halls, wearing her blue dress and lingering in the elevator where she died. People have reported seeing her, but we believe we caught a picture of her.

During one of our impromptu investigations, we walked into the lobby, took some pictures and went up to the elevator where the Lady in Blue fell to her demise. Jenny started trying to speak to any spirits that were around, hoping to capture something as she snapped the photographs. At one point, we were going to go up to the Grand Ballroom on the 10th floor in hopes of seeing some of the ghosts that have been reported there, but for some reason Jenny decided not to and stepped out of the elevator and snapped our picture in the mirror on the elevator wall before the doors closed. We then continued on our way, did some spirit box sessions outside and went home.

Upon reviewing the pictures later, Jenny found something chilling in the photo from the elevator. When she blew up the picture, she saw what we believe to be the Lady in Blue reflected in the mirror between us. She appears to be behind us, at a distance, but no one else was up there, and her placement is perfectly centered between us. We think she was actually appearing in the mirror.

Jacob remained slightly skeptical because the Lady in Blue is supposed to have grayish skin. This possible ghost was full color and looked very much alive. So, we took this picture to a fellow ghost hunter and tour operator, who goes by the moniker of Mr. Ghost Walker, who is an expert on the Seelbach haunts; he viewed the picture and said that he believed we caught a ghost. His assessment was that it is very unlikely that someone would just happen to run out there and place themselves directly in the center of our reflections just in time for the picture to be taken. While not impossible, it certainly isn't likely, especially when you take into consideration that she is, in fact, a woman in a blue dress who appeared in a picture taken inside the elevator shaft where the

Lady in Blue is said to have died. Could this be a residual spirit hanging around?

But, while that is the most physical experience we had there, it certainly is not the only one.

When we finally rented a room there one night, we were conducting an EVP session with the digital recorder and Jenny started asking random questions that pertained to the stories of the Seelbach's past. After some of the questions, a loud bump would come from the corner behind the TV. At first, we thought this was just the sound of the television settling, but it kept happening, coinciding with Jenny's questions. A couple of times, the noise was so loud that it was clearly audible on the digital recorder.

Though that was all that occurred in our room, we weren't denied more excitement that night. We took a nap in the evening and woke up around three in the morning and decided to finally make our way up to the 10th floor. Of course the ballroom was closed at that hour, but while we were up there, our EMF meter started going off in the corner by one of the doors. A very dark feeling came over us. Jenny stepped away, but Jacob kept feeling the presence. He thought he saw a shadow quickly slip across the wall back towards the elevators, so he followed it.

As he traced its path back down the hall, the heavy feeling kept getting stronger, and the meter went from yellow to red. Jacob began to feel woozy, but was determined to see where this energy was coming from. So, he checked his weariness off as a result of having just woken up not too long ago and kept going.

Suddenly, halfway down the hall, the feeling dissipated and the meter went back to green. Jacob stood there for a second and looked around. Whatever had been there was gone. Jacob returned to the ballroom area where Jenny was and stopped when he heard a noise down the hall by the elevators. We looked at each other, both aware of the sound, so Jacob turned on his video camera and headed down there, hoping to catch the shadow on film. When he reached the end of the hallway, there was a man in a suit with some papers in his hand. He looked busy and wore a Seelbach nametag. When he saw Jacob, he greeted him and Jacob said hello and turned to go back to the space in front of the ballroom doors.

The man followed and asked if we were ghost hunters. We told him we were and he became very interested. It turns out he was head of security and one of the managers at the Seelbach—and, he was a firm believer in ghosts and was willing to give us the grand tour.

Out of respect for his knowledge of the hotel and ambition to one day write the definitive paranormal compilation on the Seelbach, we will not go into great details, but keep it brief and stick to our own personal experiences. He was kind enough to show us around and impart his stories to us and since he's been roaming those halls and offices for almost twenty years, mingling with the spirits, we believe he's earned the right to claim the Seelbach's ghost stories and we will not steal them from him.

He led us into the spacious ballroom so we could take pictures while he told us some fascinating tales, from fireplace ghosts to blue lights near the windows. He also showed us some interesting pictures he caught of apparitions and faces in the room. From our own experience in the ballroom, we did catch what we believe was a faint image of the Lady in Blue in a mirror over the fireplace. Jacob also heard footsteps underneath one of the majestic chandeliers, so he went and stood beneath it while Jenny and the manager continued conversing, and heard the footsteps walk a circle around him before traveling away. The whole time we were in there, the manager kept saying the spirits were around and he could really feel them that night. We believe he was correct.

After telling us more creepy stories from the Seelbach, he agreed to meet us downstairs and show us Al Capone's secret room, he just had to deliver some room bills first. While we waited for him, we went into a dining room and bar in the lower level known as the Rathskeller, which is another name for a restaurant or beer joint in a basement. We had been in there once before and found the place fascinating, with its dark, gothic decor, the many colorful columns throughout the room, and the overall underworld atmosphere that prevailed.

Our first time in the Rathskeller, Jacob insisted there was strong energy down there. This time, we both felt and heard it. There was a faint conversation taking place somewhere around the room, but we could never find its source. We walked the entire circumference of the Rathskeller and the voices never got louder. Jacob pressed his ear against the kitchen door and never heard anything. He then placed himself in a corner by the kitchen and felt the electricity of a nearby presence. He told Jenny to take a picture; when she did, she caught a mysterious orb above his head. Usually, we pay little attention to orbs, but when there is something peculiar going on and a full one shows up in a picture, it's worth considering.

Before we went back to the lobby, Jacob detoured to a small flight of stairs to the right of the Rathskeller. Last time we had been there, he went up into the small office above to take some pictures, but didn't catch anything. This time he wanted to try the same thing. When he got up there, he heard a low hiss coming from the darkness. He chalked it up to overactive imagination and went back down to join Jenny in the lobby.

When we reached the reception area, the night manager was waiting for us, and he introduced us to some of the clerks and began telling us about the paintings above the doorways. He then led us to the Oak Room and had us wait while he opened another door leading to the Al Capone Room.

We got the lowdown on the Oak Room and how the gangsters often used it for their meetings and parties. After we walked around and took some pictures, he took us into the secret chamber of the nation's most savage mobster. The room is small with a massive two-way mirror on the wall. He closed the sliding door and told us some of the stories he knew of Capone's many escapes. He also pointed out the escape route the notorious gangster would use, and then told us the engaging information we shared at the beginning of this chapter.

After we had our fun, he took out his phone and showed us some ghostly pictures he caught in the room of figures standing around people sitting in Capone's old seat at the head of the table. Before we left, he told us most of the other guys that work there never want to deliver the room bills to the 10th floor because it scares them, and that's why we ran into him. The reason, he said, the other workers refuse to go up there is because there's something evil roaming the floor. I recalled the experience I had earlier with the shadow and asked him what the evil entity did. He said it was a black creature that often ran across the wall and hissed at people. After what had happened to me by the Rathskeller, I asked him if anyone had ever seen it down there too, but he said he had not heard of anyone experiencing such an entity in that location.

We were very fortunate to have run into the night manager. He has vast knowledge about the Seelbach and a lot of scary stories to tell. When we told someone else we ran into him, they became excited and said we were lucky because they've tried to find him several times. His tour was well worth the trip and it was an amazing experience for us.

The Seelbach is a great place with breathtaking urban views and small but luxurious suites set at a pretty fair price. If you stay there, look for the night manager who gives the ghost tours and he'll tell you some amazing stories about the grand hotel. Also, order the breakfast buffet. You will not be disappointed in either.

Full shot of the elevator and the Lady

Close up of the Lady in Blue

THE RAMADA INN

Paintsville's Ramada Inn appears to have a range of specters haunting its halls. For many years now, staff and guests alike have mentioned strange encounters and unexplained incidents taking place in the building. Some just laugh them off, while others believe wholeheartedly the inn is truly haunted.

Of the ghostly reports coming from the establishment, none seem to be more prevalent than the mystery woman in high heels. People have heard her footsteps haunting the hallways, lingering in the lobby, and echoing in the atrium. Some say she can even be heard mysteriously clacking up the stairwell late in the evenings. There are a few claims that her faint apparition has been seen crossing the lobby.

But the woman in high heels is not the only soul who has remained at the Ramada after death. There is also an unidentified man seen walking up and down the stairs, coming in and out of elevators, and walking along the corridors of each floor. With him appearing in so many different areas throughout the inn, some believe he is the spirit of someone who once worked there. Unlike the woman, he cannot be heard.

There also seems to be another energetic presence existing at the Ramada, specifically in room 216. Staff members and a few guests have heard a woman laughing in that room when no one else was in there. Her laugh has been described as loud and rather hearty, and some say it's almost manic. We could find no history tied to that particular room, so we cannot say who this spirit is and what it finds so hilarious.

Guests have reported walking in the halls, or lying down in their rooms at night, and hearing people talking nearby. Some have even thought the people were right outside their door. Others claim someone spoke to them from behind while in the halls.

At least one, if not more, of the ghosts at the Ramada Inn like to play with various items throughout the building. Objects in rooms, in the lobby, and in the halls have been spotted levitating. Most often, the items will only rise for a second before falling. Though there have been reports of the objects hovering, then moving across the room before falling.

According to staff, the kitchen is a place of very disturbing activity. Whatever spirit likes to frequent that area has a tendency to throw things. Objects have been lifted from tables, sinks, and even where they hang on walls or set in cabinets and been flung through the air. Sometimes they smash into walls, other times they skid along the floor, and there have even been instances where they appear to have been thrown at workers. Needless to say, this has spooked many employees.

It seems to us that the Ramada Inn is a rather rowdy joint in the afterlife. We could not gather stories, legends, or historic information regarding any event that happened in the past that could have caused this paranormal activity. It's hard to chalk it all up to active imaginations, misinterpretations, or outright fabrications when there have been many reports from different people over a long period of time.

THE CAMPBELL HOUSE CURIO COLLECTION

Now known as the Campbell House Curio, a Collection by Hilton, this hotel has been a significant Lexington landmark since it opened. Construction began in 1949 and took two years. In 1951, it opened as the Motor Inn, had only 99 rooms, and remained that way for twenty years. Between the years of 1972 and 1986, the inn expanded to 229 rooms and added a pool, a dining room, and a meeting area. A fire broke out in '86 and the inn had to close for remodeling. During this time, another wing was added. From 2002 to 2006, it was the Crown Plaza. A large banquet area and a few more rooms were added in 2007, and a couple of years later the hotel experienced severe wind damage. It was in 2015 that it became the Campbell House Curio.

Other than its history of expansion and natural disaster, a dark past allegedly clings to this hotel. Legends of two undocumented murders occurring there are thought to be the cause of some unexplained activity that has been witnessed by guests through the years. Although the tales of the murders are vague and unverified, people have been telling them for many years.

The first story is that of a woman who was on the stairs having a heated discussion with her lover. What they were arguing about is unknown, but it is said the argument turned physical. The man put his hands on the woman and she pushed him away. When he advanced on her again, she smacked him. This enraged the man further, and so he pulled out a knife and stabbed her several times. As she fell, he continued stabbing her. When she hit the floor, he stabbed her some more before leaving her for dead.

The other murder story is of a woman who was in her room on the second floor. There are different versions of this story. Some say a robber entered her room in the middle of the night and shot her while she lay in bed. Others say she was coming out of the shower and the burglar became alarmed and shot her. Some say she had an argument with her husband and went to the inn. In a fit of rage, her husband found her and shot her after another argument. Whichever of these accounts, if any, are true, it is believed a woman was shot to death in a second floor room.

Though the murder stories are not connected, it seems both women haunt the inn. The blood of the woman stabbed on the stairs stills appears on the carpet from time to time. Witnesses claim to have seen it appear from seemingly out of nowhere, accompanied by a sudden drop in temperature and the unexplained aroma of women's perfume. Meanwhile, the door to the room where the other woman was shot bangs open and slams shut on its own. Guests staying in the room have been woken in the middle of the night by the sound of the door crashing against the wall, only to sit up and watch it slam closed. People have also spotted apparitions of women walking on the stairs and in the halls.

Though there are no records of these murders, guests at the Campbell House Curio have been experiencing chilling incidents for many years. If there were no murders, there still seem to be some spirits. No matter how many times they change the name, the ghosts keep hanging around.

THE SHERMAN TAVERN

The Sherman Tavern in rural Dry Ridge dates back to 1812 and is the last documented inn built on the Covington-Lexington Turnpike. At 180 years old, it is among the oldest buildings left standing in all of Grant County. It was originally a stage stop for cattlemen, soldiers, and Native Americans travelling from Cincinnati, Ohio to Lexington, Kentucky before the Cason family bought it around 1850 and added a bourbon bar for the passersby. The bourbon was free, so the tavern became quite a popular spot. There is a Cason family cemetery on the land, which is now part of the Sherman Elementary School campus. Some believe there are forgotten graves located under the school.

In 2011 through 2012, restoration was completed on the building. Legend has it that some workers had heard a woman scream, "Get out!" on several occasions. Ghosts of children were heard playing in the halls and seen running by windows outside. Others who have visited the building have claimed to see these children, as well as the ghosts of Native Americans camping on the land as they did back in the tavern's early days. Many times, they have been seen walking or sitting near the tavern only to be gone a few seconds later.

Unexplained footsteps have been heard travelling across the porch and the front room, also near where the bar used to be. Some have attributed these steps to the spirits of Confederate soldiers or slaves seen in the building from time to time. The soldiers are often seen lounging around the house having drinks and the slaves can be seen moving about various rooms. Doors that suddenly swing open and then slam shut are blamed on these spirits, as well.

Others have reported hearing phantom music playing in empty rooms. None are sure the origin of this music, but many have distinctly heard it. They have also heard disturbing series of rapid knocks and loud bangs coming from inside the walls. These knocks have been described as sounding like fists and not the usual critters that can get inside the walls of a house.

The tavern has allowed ghost hunts in the building, and people have captured EVPs answering their questions. Ghostly images and unexplained moving shadows have been recording on video and in photographs. Investigators have also reported very strong readings on meters.

A few witnesses believe that the Cason family is still in the house since some of this chilling activity has taken place in the graveyard. Dark silhouettes have been spotted moving around the stones, only to be gone when someone shines a light in their direction. Voices have also been heard talking over in the cemetery when it was empty.

By these accounts, it sounds as though the Sherman Tavern is still alive with travelers. Only now, they are passing through into the land beyond instead of Lexington or Cincinnati. We wonder if the spirits are enjoying the other kind of spirits once offered at the tavern.

DOE RUN INN

L ocated in the small, working class town of Brandenburg is the historic Doe Run Inn. Built upon a former Native American settlement, the inn sits near the Doe Run Creek, so named by Squire Boone when he noticed the unusual amount of deer in the area. Surrounding by woods, the building was originally used for timber cutting and was called Stevenson's Mill. The mill ceased operations and the building sat empty, used as a barn until it became the Sulfur Wells Hotel in 1901. The presence of a nearby water spring dug up old Native American legends about healing powers within the water. Since Brandenburg stands next to the Ohio River, people from all around came to test the myth.

In 1958, the building came under new ownership after being closed for a while. The new owners added a restaurant and renamed the establishment the Doe Run Inn. Since then, a long list of reported paranormal activity has amassed. Though that might sound very ominous to some, there has never been anything oppressive, violent, or dangerous reported there. It is not believed that any demons or malicious souls haunt the location. Instead, it appears that what is witnessed is leftover from the hundreds of individuals who have passed through the building over the centuries.

There is a rocking chair in room twelve that has been reported by many to rock back and forth on its own. Some have even claimed that the apparition of an elderly gentleman has appeared in the chair, rocking it while dozing in the room. No one is sure who this is, but with the inn's lengthy history, the possibilities are many.

Room twenty has some activity of its own – both inside and out. The occurrences have not been pinned down to any specific time or pattern, but the voices and laughter of children have been heard coming from within the room, as well as flittering in the nearby hallway. It sounds as if many children are playing in and around the room. This is not a far-fetched possibility considering the room used to be a children's playroom.

Not all of the haunts at the Doe Run Inn are confined to a specific room. In fact, there is one that has appeared in several rooms, as well as areas that are not reserved for quartering guests. The mirrors all around the inn have reflected the spirit of a young lady staring back at those who look into the glass. Others have seen her passing behind them in the mirror, only to turn and find no one is there. Unfortunately, we could find no legend attached to this spirit. Is she a sad trapped soul, or just residual energy?

That leads us to another story, this one involving an entity seen outside the inn. Groundskeepers have reported seeing the ghost of a woman dressed in white walking slowly along the edge of the creek. They say she looks to be searching for something. We wonder if she is connected to the young lady in the mirrors. We could not find any record of a drowning having taken place there, but it certainly doesn't mean one never did. In such a rural place as Brandenburg, it's easy to imagine records were not always kept in the olden days.

Previously, we stated there were no malicious souls lingering at the Doe Run Inn. Well, that might not be entirely accurate. It seems there is a jokester that likes to play pranks with people's shoelaces. Many believe it to be the spirit of a young Confederate soldier who has manifested in the inn on numerous occasions. People say this spirit will untie your shoelaces and quickly tie them together, so when you stand up and take a step, you'll fall down. How the connection was made between him and these incidents, we are not sure. We assume he was spotted in the area not long before guests found themselves face down on the inn floor.

A serene southern setting, life on the river, and a whole hatful of ghosts – what other reason would one need to stay at the Doe Run Inn? However, it appears this location is closed at the time of this writing. Well, it sure isn't the first time the building has been abandoned. With all the history, it's not unlikely someone will repurpose it soon. When they do, they better wear slip-on shoes.

THE HILTON SIRE HOTEL

The Hilton Sire Hotel, formerly known as the Gratz Park Inn, is located in the Gratz Park Historic District in Lexington. The district is bound by West Third and West Second on the north and south end, and Market and Mill streets on the eastern and western borders. In 1916, the architectural firm of Frankel & Curtis built the two-story colonial revival structure on North Upper Street and the one-story wing facing West Second for Dr. Waller O. Bullock, Dr. David Barrow, and his son, Dr. David Woolfold Barrow.

In 1920, the three doctors, along with six others, opened the Mayo-Clinic-inspired Lexington Clinic. The practice did very well, with people all over the city bringing their aches and pains to be treated. The basement of the building served as Lexington's first morgue. In 1958, the practice moved to Harrodsburg Road and the building was then occupied by the Fuller Engineering Company until 1976. The place then sat vacant for the next eleven years.

In 1987, the building was renovated and converted into the luxurious Gratz Park Inn, which was a well-reviewed establishment for thirty years. Now, it is part of the Hilton Tapestry Collection and known as the Sire Hotel. The owners, who graduated from Transylvania University not far away, jumped at the opportunity to purchase the old hotel and give it new life. A lot of the interior was gutted and given an entirely new look, of which most reviews have been positive.

While many have positive things to say about this historic location's new look, the legends of paranormal encounters remain. The website, *This Old House*, featured Gratz Park Inn in an article titled, "Historic Haunted Homes," mentioning the little girl named Lizzie that often disturbs guests at the inn. It is said that she likes to run around the building opening and slamming doors and tugging on people's sleeves. It's also been said that Lizzie can be seen playing jacks on the third floor. She is also blamed for the sounds of children playing and running through the halls at night, keeping guests awake. It is said that Lizzie has crawled into bed with guests and fallen asleep.

Another ghost child seen in the building is a girl called Little Anne. Little Anne is believed to have been a patient at the clinic long ago who possibly passed away there. She is sometimes seen quietly playing with her doll in the hallways on the third floor. Due to her being seen on the third floor, some think Little Anne is also the ghost known as Lizzie, though that has not been confirmed. Others think she is a separate entity, which would make sense since Lizzie is usually rambunctious. Also, with the claims that people have heard 'children' playing in the halls, it seems possible that Little Anne and Lizzie may be friends who run about the inn getting into mischief. Maybe quiet Little Anne isn't so quiet when Lizzie's around.

There is also the spirit of a man named John that has been seen around the inn. He is said to be spotted wearing a plaid shirt and holding his hands over his face. Allegedly, according to a journal found in the basement, the clinic's first patient was a man named John (who fits the apparition's description) who came in to be treated for a gunshot wound. He is often blamed for startling housekeepers by turning lights, televisions, and other electrical items on and off throughout the inn.

Of course a large, haunted, historic building would not be complete without its resident Lady-in-Some-Colored-Outfit spirit. Many haunted locations seem to have a ghost called the Lady in Black, the Lady in Blue, the Lady in Grey, or, in the case of the Sire Hotel, the Lady in White. Nothing is known about her except that she often appears throughout the building dressed in her white dress and matching hat. Those who have seen her say she seems lost and in search of something.

There have also been talks of "drunken partygoer" spirits wandering about the place. It is said that these intoxicated specters are known for being rowdy and partying through the halls. According to the claims, they can be heard hollering, holding loud conversations, tinkling glasses about, stomping along the floors, and banging against the walls. Whenever guests or staff members investigate these disturbances, they find the halls empty of any obnoxious merrymakers.

The halls of the Sire Hotel seem to be very active paranormal hotspots. With the massive renovations that recently took place, we wonder if that stirred up anymore activity, as they often do. Will the ghosts remain now that so much has changed, or have they moved on?

JACOB FLOYD & JENNY FLOYD

DITTO HOUSE INN

The Ditto House Inn in West Point, Kentucky was built in 1823 by a boat merchant named Abraham Ditto, and his brother-in-law Samuel Lansdale. Originally, the two-story Federal-style brick home was an inn for weary river travelers, later becoming Ditto's private residence. It later became known as the Riverview House.

In 1861-1862, still as the Riverview House, it served as a hospital for the Union soldiers that built Fort Duffield during the Civil War. A measles epidemic struck during these years, causing many soldiers to develop respiratory disorders. Even though local women tended to the soldiers, despite these women's husbands, fathers, and sons being Confederates, many of the soldiers died from the ailments. General William T. Sherman, who ordered the construction of Fort Duffield, also used it as his barracks during the war.

After the war, the Riverview House continued normal operations until it closed in 1870. The building then briefly became the Reed Place Hotel before being sold to Dr. J.V. Prewitt in 1905. The house then served as both Prewitt's home and office. The home also served as a canteen for the Camp Knox troops during World War I. It has also served as a ticket agency, a primitive bank, and a boarding house. After once again serving as a private residence, the house was restored in 1985 and made into the Ditto House Inn Bed and Breakfast.

Over the years, guests and residents of the Ditto House have found remnants of the Civil War scattered randomly about the property. Such items as buttons, buckles, and coins dating back to the war are among those found. They are believed to have been left behind by the many troops who had lived and died there.

But, according to legend, these relatively inconsequential articles are not the only remains the past has left. The Ditto House

Inn is reputed to be haunted. Guests and investigators who have stayed there over the years have captured evidence and had unusual experiences that have left them chilled.

Disembodied footsteps have been heard roaming the halls. In these same halls, the pale apparitions of Civil War soldiers have reportedly been spotted. Those who have witnessed these specters walking the empty corridors encounter them after investigating the footsteps. These manifestations are described as fading in and out before vanishing altogether.

Other guests claim to have felt hands on their backs, or touching their shoulders, only to turn and find no one near. Some have even carried on conversations with strangers in the halls or rooms only to have them disappear during the conversation. Ghostly figures have also been seen lingering in windows.

If this bed and breakfast is indeed haunted, then undoubtedly many of the spirits would be the soldiers who died during the days it was a part of Fort Duffield. Perhaps even Camp Knox troops linger in the old construct. Are these spirits also attracted there by the items they left behind? Perhaps it is Ditto or Lansdale themselves that have been touching the guests and carrying on conversations with them. If not, it could be any number of former residents or workers that have passed through the house over time. One can't be sure. But, it does seem something eerie is taking place at the Ditto House Inn.

MOTEL 80

Roadside motels have a tendency to appear shady and creepy, especially if you pull into their lots at night. Oftentimes, there is minimal lighting, signs flickering, and barely any cars visible. This scene normally reminds passersby of the opening moments of a low-budget horror flick, which is probably why they keep driving by.

In actuality, these locations are usually safe and one can stay there without incident. But, there is a place in the town of Emmalena that is alleged to have been the site of such an atrocity.

That location used to be Motel 80, just off highway 80. The story is that a man came home one night to find his wife gone. After having suspected her of infidelity, he armed himself with a shotgun and went looking for her. Naturally, he checked the local motel and, sure enough, found her there with another man. Enraged with jealousy, he shot his wife and the man she was with, leaving the room a bloody mess.

We were unable to uncover any official record of this double murder, but there are stories of the deceased lovers' ghosts still haunting the room they died in. Some who have stayed there claim they could hear a woman screaming from the room. Others say that the man who was killed there manifests and walks about the room, sometimes turning the lights on. Others say his ghost ventures out into the hallway.

It appears this hotel truly is a shady place, even if the murders never happened. Some years back, it was seized by the government because of drug activity and then auctioned off. It is some sort of commercial building now, located behind the Hindman Double Kwik. Seeing as there was illicit activity taking place, it isn't farfetched to believe there has been a murder there, or death of some kind. If the ghosts there are not the victims of a double murder, they may be there because of something else.

BENHAM SCHOOLHOUSE INN

Harlan County, Kentucky is best known for the television show *Justified* and the 1976 Academy-Award-winning documentary, *Harlan County, USA*, about the "Brookside Strike" of 1973, an incident which saw 180 coal miners and their wives protest the Eastover Coal Company's Brookside Mine and Prep Plant. But, there are also some alleged ghosts hanging around the small community of Benham, in an inn that was once the town's schoolhouse.

Benham, Kentucky was founded in 1909 as a coal camp town by International Harvester's Wisconsin Steel Company out of Chicago, IL. The company purchased several thousand acres of Harlan County wilderness with the intentions to mine coal from the land and move it to their steel mill in Chicago. By 1911, the L&N Railroad moved through town, expanding rail services from Lowell, Ky. to Benham, which was essential for coal distribution. In 1912, the entire town was laid out around a central park with homes, a fire hall, a post office, a theatre, churches, a city hall, and the Benham Coal Camp Schoolhouse.

Over the ensuing decades, their venture was a great success and the community grew. By the end of the First World War, Benham employed thousands of miners. Benham was incorporated sometime in the late 50s and then turned over to the residents in 1961.

The Benham Schoolhouse was built in 1926. All faculty members were paid by International Harvesters, as they desired to employ the best educators around. The school was initially K-12, but after 1961, it was reduced to K-8 until 1992 when it closed for good.

In 1994, it was reopened as the Benham Schoolhouse Inn. The original lockers still line the hallways on both floors, the original hardwood floors still remain, and room numbers commemorate

152

past graduating classes. The inn is currently operated by the Southeastern Kentucky Community and Technical College, and students of the school's Hospitality Management program intern at the inn to gain the necessary experience, which also provides a good work-study environment. The gymnasium is still used for various local events.

But, the lockers and hardwood floors are not the only pieces of the past that remain at the Benham Schoolhouse Inn. There are numerous stories about past students haunting the building. People have reported hearing disembodied whisperings and conversations, phantom laughter, and the sounds of footsteps running about at different times, day or night. Visitors have also seen apparitions of children dressed in 1920s-era clothing standing and walking about the place. Lights have been known to flick on and off on their own, doors open and slam shut without anyone near them. There is a story about a guest who was in the bathroom when the shower turned on by itself and soaked them. A transparent man carrying a suitcase has been seen walking down the hall, only to disappear from sight.

There is a rumor that the Benham Schoolhouse was built atop a graveyard and that a full skeleton was excavated from the ground and used in the school's anatomy class. Whether or not any of this is true, we do not know. We have not found or heard any official reports confirming this, so most likely, it is an urban legend. But, if it is true, we wonder if that would be the man with the suitcase wandering around.

Nonetheless, ghosts or unmarked graveyards or not, the Benham Schoolhouse Inn is a unique place to stay. It's a significant part of the region's history and the people who operate it seem to take that status with pride. Whether you like the paranormal or not, you should check the place out.

NATURAL SPOTS

DANCER IN THE PARK

Nearly two centuries ago, before Young Park was established in Harrodsburg, there stood a hotel on the land called the Harrodsburg Springs. All that remains of this long-gone hotel are the remnants of a wall and springhouse near where there mineral waters used to run. In its time it is reputed to have been a rather resplendent establishment, full of music, laughter, and other forms of merriment. One day, a young woman came to the hotel and made a big impression—an impression that has left an enduring tale told countless times through the decades.

The identity of the young woman has been debated among the storytellers for quite some time. Many say she would tell no one her name, but that she was the daughter of a prominent judge who would be arriving soon after her. Also, though most tales proclaim the incident to have happened at the Harrodsburg Springs Hotel, that claim may not be entirely accurate. The date of the young lady's arrival has been unspecified. The date ranges from mid to late 1800s, depending on who's telling the tale. There have been different hotels to stand on the grounds that now make up Young Park, and depending on which section of the timeline the tale falls, the hotel could have been something other than the Harrodsburg Springs Hotel.

In the early 1800s, there were actually two lodging establishments on the land: the Sutton Spring was opened in 1807 by Captain David Sutton. Though it was called Sutton Springs at first, it soon became known as Harrodsburg Springs. Greenville Springs was opened around this time, as well. Dr. Christopher Graham purchased Greenville Springs in the summer of 1827 and the Harrodsburg Springs in November of 1828. These two establishments were then combined to become the Graham Springs. However, they were still referred to as the Harrodsburg Springs by some. Through the years, Dr. Graham made vast expansions to the resort, including a new brick hotel built in the early 1840s called the Saloon Spring. Due to these massive renovations, the resort became renowned for being a high-end establishment.

Graham sold the property to the US government in 1853 and it became an asylum for disabled military veteran soon after. Fire destroyed the main buildings in 1859 and the land was purchased by Captain Philip Thompson in 1861. Thompson planned to return the property into a health spa similar to the former Graham Springs, but was unable to do so thanks to the Civil War, which caused the burning of most of the remaining buildings. After the war, the land became pastures until a man by the name of Edward Gaither bought it in 1887. He then sold it in 1888 to the Kentucky Real Estate and Improvement Association, and a man by the name of John Lewis Cassell had a brick home built on the land. Some years later, Cassell passed his home on to a Ben Allin, who then reopened Graham Springs in 1911 and kept it operational until the Great Depression took it down in 1934. From then, it passed through several more owners before becoming the park it is today.

So, the historical accounts of ownership may muddle some of the urban legend. But, even though some of the tale doesn't coincide with the actual history of the land, that could simply be a result of misinformation passed down by the storytellers. It does not in any way refute the story's validity, as it could have very well happened, just not at the times claimed. So, despite all the minute and mundane details to squabble over, the tale is very poignant and definitely very peculiar.

Soon after her arrival, the young lady checked in and was taken to her room, and there she stayed until later that evening when the Grand Ballroom was opened. As soon as the music began, the young lady quickly came down the stairs and entered the ballroom to join the first dance. Once that dance was done, she joined the second, and then the third, and all that followed. She captivated the men in attendance and they lined up to dance with her.

The woman danced through the evening, never sitting down. With each new song, there came a new dance and a new partner to share it with. At the onset of dawn, with the sun rising in the sky, she expressed to a young man just how happy she was to be there; and, as the music faded and the party died out, the anonymous dancer collapsed at the young man's feet and died on the ballroom floor. Some versions of the tale say she found a favorite among the men at Harrodsburg Spring that evening and danced with him through the night out by an elm tree, and this is where she fell dead. Regardless of which variation is true, the young woman did dance herself to death at the Harrodsburg Spring Hotel.

The owners awaited the arrival of the young lady's father—the alleged judge—so that he could claim the body. A week passed and there was no sign of the man. Over the next few days, the hotel staff attempted to uncover the young lady's identity so as to contact family and inform them of her tragic death. They searched her room in hopes of finding some telling evidence, but the lady had only arrived with a trunk containing the dress she died in. They found no journal, no diary, no writing of any kind to lend a clue as to who she was. At last, they gave up the search.

Having no other ideas about how to remember her and respect her body, they decided to carry her out to an elm tree (perhaps the very tree that one version of the story had her dying under) and bury her there in a grave marked, "Unknown." Beneath the ominously anonymous marking declaring the woman's identity a mystery there was etched a cryptic epitaph: "Hallowed and Hushed be the place of the dead; step softly and bow head." It could be that this is a message remembering the lady's final night on Earth—the night that brought her so much joy before she died.

Though she was initially referred to by monikers such as the "Unknown Lady" and the "Lady who Danced Herself to Death," because it was said that she would tell no one her name, other versions say that she told people her name was Virginia Stafford. Since she did supposedly say she was the daughter of a judge, local historians searched for a Judge Stafford; they found that such a man did exist at the time, but he did not have a daughter named Virginia. This led them to believe this name to be false. However, after a while, a new lead emerged.

Some sixty years after the strange legend was said to have taken place, Joseph W. Adams of Lexington relayed the story to a man by the name of James Rupp. Rupp, surprised that the incident had become enshrouded in such mystery and scandal, said that he knew exactly who that woman was. He then claimed that when he was ten-years-old, a man named Joe Sewell, who was around forty, of Tazewell, Tennessee told him that his second wife, whose maiden name was Molly Black, had "danced herself to death" at a hotel in Harrodsburg. Sewell's family was wealthy and he had a travelling bone back then, so at the time of the dancing lady's death, Mr. Sewell was out on the road and he and Molly were estranged.

Mr. Rupp went on to claim that Sewell said Molly had been living with his mother at the time because of his travels. He and Molly had a son together who was subsequently raised with the woman's family in Laurel County under his wife's maiden name. There has allegedly been an investigation conducted by curious parties to seek out the history of Molly Black, but one has not been found, which has led the investigator(s) to assume the tale is nothing more than a ghost story.

However, a stamp collector by the name of Patricia Kaufman purchased an old Confederate cover that was addressed to a Miss Mollie S. Sewell of Tazewell, East Tennessee. Inside, there was a clipping from an old Harrodsburg newspaper from the early 1900s talking about the lady who danced herself to death, and it had the incident occurring some time before the Civil War. There was a Joseph W. Sewell, age forty-five, listed as a lawyer in Tazewell, TN in 1880, and he had a wife named Nancy who was twenty-four. Though this information is intriguing, it only succeeds in making the mystery more confusing because the timelines don't match up. So, none of it is even close to conclusive. Nonetheless, it is believed by some that the young lady lying in the grave in Young Park is Molly Black.

But, no matter who the woman laid to rest in the grave is, she is believed to haunt the park where her body remains.

The dancer's tale was nearly forgotten in the early 1900s, until a woman walking near the unmarked grave found herself approached by a distressed young lady who explained to her that she had been dancing at the Harrodsburg Spring Hotel and lost her way. She then asked the woman if she could help her find her way back to the hotel. The woman replied that the Harrodsburg Spring burned down many years ago. The young lady began to weep. When the woman tried to console her, the young lady disappeared.

Others have claimed that late at night, when the wind starts to blow through the leaves, you can hear the faint sound of the ballroom music floating on the air. If you stay long enough, you will see the woman's image appear in the moonlight and begin to dance to the mysterious music.

Some who have walked through the park at night have found their attention drawn to a strange blue light shimmering near the grave. It has been described as a flickering light that moves about in a smooth, fluid motion. When people have approached it out of curiosity, they find that it is the transparent form of a young lady dancing to music that seemingly only she can hear. Whenever anyone has tried to speak to her, she ignores them. If they get too close, she suddenly vanishes from sight, emitting a rush of cold air.

Has the dancer accepted her fate and chosen to remain forever twirling to the music that made her so happy? Or are these sightings residual imprints left from her tragic demise? Though there are a lot of questions left unanswered within this enigmatic story, it is no question that grave is there and that a young lady did come to one of the hotels sometime in the 1800s and danced until she died. Whether she was Virginia Stafford or Molly Black or someone else entirely, the story is poignantly romantic. Let us hope that if her ghost truly is there, it dances in the perpetual state of happiness she felt during her final night of life.

CUMBERLAND FALLS

Cumberland Falls is located in the Daniel Boone Forest at Cumberland State Park in eastern Kentucky near the small town of Corbin. At one-hundred-and-twenty-five feet wide with more than a sixty foot drop, it is the second largest waterfall in North America and has been dubbed the "Niagara of the South." The magnificent natural landmark has been featured in three different Hollywood films: *The Kentuckian* (1955), starring Burt Lancaster; *Raintree County* (1957), starring Elizabeth Taylor and Montgomery Clift; and *Fire Down Below* (1997), starring Steven Segal.

It is believed that Cumberland Falls has been attracting visitors since prehistoric times. The rock that creates the fall is estimated to be around 250 million years old, according to geologists, and evidence of Native American settlements supposedly dates back to nearly ten-thousand years. Though early Natives called the river the Shawnee, Dr. Thomas Walker named it after the Duke of Cumberland during his exploration of Kentucky in 1750.

The first record of ownership of the land dates back to 1800 when Matthew Walton and Adam Shepard were granted two-hundred acres from the Commonwealth of Kentucky. Louis and Mary H. Renfro purchased four-hundred acres, which included the Great Falls of the Cumberland, in 1850 and built a small cabin on the land. They later built a two-room lean-to for visitors and fisherman to enjoy.

In 1927, the Cumberland River Power Company had started devising plans to dam the river. Later that year, in November, T. Coleman DuPont made an offer to buy the falls and all the surrounding land and hand it over to the commonwealth so it could be made into a state park. It wasn't until March 10th, 1930, after DuPont had already passed, that the state elected to accept the offer. DuPont's wife purchased five-hundred-and-ninety-three acres of the land for $400,000 and closed the deal her late husband had previously proposed. On August 31st, 1931, the area was added to the list of state parks. Over the ensuing years, many improvements were made to the park, and lodges and inns were built and burned down. Repairs and more improvements were made, but no matter what was erected and what fell, nothing ever stole the grandeur of the great falls.

The serenity of the Cumberland Falls can only be matched by the unique beauty of the moonbow that appears on moonlit evenings. When the moon is full, its glow refracts off the water, creating a nighttime bow of colors. It is truly one of the most captivating sights in the entire world. The only other moonbow known to exist is at Victoria Falls in Africa. This is one of the main attractions of Cumberland Falls.

Many visitors are attracted to the falls every year. One evening in the 1950s, two of those guests happen to be a newlywed couple enjoying the falls on their honeymoon. They had come to stay at the DuPont Lodge and were so eager to explore that they went out immediately after checking in, not even changing out of their wedding attire. They went for a walk and stopped near the Pillars overlooking the falls. The groom wanted to take a picture of his wife with the breathtaking falls in the background. The bride, in her excitement to be there, began dancing around and slipped off the drop and into the waters below where she died and was carried away by the falls. This tragic accident earned the area the ominous nickname, "Lover's Leap."

Ever since this accident, visitors have claimed to see her ghost lingering around the cliff. People who have spotted her describe her as being a woman in a long wedding gown. Many have reported her spirit standing on a bridge near where she died.

Drivers who are coming up the bend in the road that heads to the falls have claimed to witness her wandering out into the road to be hit by the car. When the drivers get out, she is nowhere to be found. It has also been said that she often trips people up and messes up rooms in the DuPont Lodge.

Allegedly, on the nights of the moonbow, her spirit will appear in the water. Some tourists who came out to see the famous moonbow reported spotting a woman in a long white gown appear in the water, only to rise up from below like a ghost. Others have said that she will float so high she will hover before them and beckon them to come closer, perhaps enticing them to step off the cliff and join her in the murky depths below.

The moonbow manifestation of the fallen bride may or may not be just a wild tale told at night around Cumberland Falls to get a good scare out of people, but there have been numerous reports of her ghost—enough to give the claims a worthy consideration. But, whether or not her spirit still exists in Cumberland Falls State Park, or whether you believe it or not, the beauty of the falls cannot be denied, and neither can the attraction of the glorious moonbow.

BIG BONE LICK PARK

Big Bone Lick Park in Union, KY is a park with prehistoric ties. The name comes from the Pleistocene megafauna fossils discovered there. Paleontologists that have studied the area believe that the salt licks by the sulphur springs once drew mammoths to the area, as well as bison, oxen, mastodon, moose, musk, peccary, caribou, elk, and other animals. The land was once a swampland and many of the animals were stuck and died there. Over the millennia, the bones accumulated and were discovered by archeologists.

These impressive fossils became part of local lore told by the Native Americans in the area. In 1739, French-Canadian explorer Charles LeMoyne discovered the site. An Indian trader by the name of Robert Smith took some fossils from the area in 1744. Robert McAfee gave a detailed account of the lick in his journal in 1773, describing the land and the obvious effect the prehistoric creatures had on the area.

Once word spread about the lick, scientists around the world wanted to study the remains. During the 1800s, accounts of tusks, massive skulls, and large teeth being excavated from the land were recorded. One skull was said to weigh more than 5,000lbs. Academic interest in the land continued throughout the century.

In 1960, the land officially became a state park. Throughout the decade, the state bought as much of the land as it could, and by 1968, the park had expanded to 250 acres. It has since grown to over 800 acres.

Across the street from the Big Bone Lick State Historic Site stands the Big Bone Lick Methodist Church. This Greek Revival, Queen Anne style structure was built in 1888 to house the Big Bone church congregation. The church's first reverend was a German Civil War solider named George Froh.

The church is said to house the spirit of a former reverend who allegedly worked there by the name of Elmer K. Kidwell. Kidwell was a pastor at the Hughes Chapel Methodist Church who took his own life in December of 1967. His wife discovered his body on December 6th. He had sat down in the bathtub at his home on U.S. 42, four miles west of Union, pulled the curtain closed, placed a small caliber rifle in his mouth and pulled the trigger. No one knows for sure why he did it, but some think his spirit haunts the old church.

Investigators and those visiting the church have seen the apparition of a reverend walking along the aisles. They have seen him standing near the pulpit and looking out windows. Others outside have seen a man standing in the doorway and have heard voices coming from inside the church. Some have even described it as sounding as if a sermon was taking place.

The death of Rev. Kidwell is a documented death. Why some think it is he who haunts the church, we don't know. They say he worked there, but we found no record of that. Of course, that doesn't mean the accounts of his employment there are inaccurate.

The park itself is said to be haunted as well. Disembodied voices have been heard whispering in areas where no people were. People have reported dark figures walking through the fields and among the trees.

Some say there is an evil spirit that tries to deceive visitors into following it so that it can cause them harm somehow. One person reported this spirit led them into the woods, making them believe it was one of the friends they had traveled with, but soon disappeared. The person was then lost and started to call for their friend, only to be led further in by the spirit's voice. When the visitor found their way out, their friends had been looking for them. The person they believed they were following said they were never in the woods alone. There have been other reports of a strange person in the woods trying to talk to people and get them to come into the woods. But who can be sure that is necessarily a paranormal occurrence?

Big Bone Lick State Historic Site is a fascinating place. They have allowed ghost hunts in the church before. While there are some real creepy stories coming out of the area, it's a place to visit for the historic implications above all else.

THE HAINTIN' HOLLER

Located past Gray Gap Road near the end of Turner Branch Road in Marrowbone is a clearing of land known to locals as the Haintin' Holler, which is home to several ghost stories and legends. Many of these stories have travelled through the years, giving the holler a creepy reputation as a place of spirits and monsters. The kids in town would often speak of the area in hushed tones, daring each other to visit. Some who have braved the dark and desolate Haintin' Holler at night have returned with chilling tales to tell.

Some folks have reported tales of a Headless Horsemen that rides through the holler at night, chasing down intruders. His presence begins as the sound of hooves on the grass, followed by the snorting of a horse. Whenever someone turns to face the sound, they find themselves staring at the mounted, headless apparition. When they run, the spirit will chase them to the hollow's edge before retreating into the night.

Mysterious floating lights have been seen in the holler as well. They have been described as large orbs flying through the night. While some suggest that these are automobile headlights from the nearby roads, others claim that the proximity suggests that they are nowhere near the road and their movement is too erratic to be headlights, often moving up and down as if bouncing. There are those who believe these lights could be related to alien craft, but no other evidence has been found to support this.

Strange sounds and sudden temperature drops have been reported in the Haintin' Holler. Naturally, such evidence can be rationally explained, but the temperature drops have been described as being drastic, dropping more than ten degrees upon entering and returning to the normal temperature on exiting.

The sounds that come from the holler have been compared to that of a woman shrieking. When the area has been investigated, no one has ever been found.

There are also stories of creatures lurking in the holler that look like polar bears. These "White Thangs" have been described as close to ten feet, broad, and all white. Some believe them to be Bigfoot creatures. There have been large tracks and toppled trees found in the area, but one can't say for certain that it is the Missing Link who is responsible.

Locals have also reported seeing a Native American couple passing through the holler at certain points of the day. This couple has been seen on several occasions, but no one knows who they are. Those who have attempted to follow them have been unsuccessful in keeping track. Some suggest they are spirits tied to the land.

If these legends have any truth to them, it seems as if the Haintin' Holler is quite the hot bed for strange phenomena.

THE DEVIL'S GARDEN

On a warm summer night, many years ago, a group of teenagers in the town of Hutch decided to have a late night party down at the local swimming hole. More than swimming, the teens began drinking and horsing around. At one point, one of the partygoers might have had a bit too much to drink and got himself into a dire situation.

Wobbly and drunk, the teen decided to jump from the edge of the swimming hole into the water, but he could not maintain his balance properly. As he went to jump into the hole, his foot slipped on the edge and he fell hard, smashing his head against a large rock that was located in the shallow end of the hole. The blow knocked him cold and he lay there unconscious.

At the time, Bell County, where the swimming hole is located, was a dry county. Fearful of the repercussions if their parents and law enforcement found out about their drinking, they all decided to hide the body of their friend. So, they tied a heavy rock to him and left him under the water.

The next day, they decided to return to the swimming hole. The police were already on the scene and had uncovered the body. It turns out the drunk teen was not killed by the blow to the head, but by drowning. Mortified by what they had done, they all took a vow to never speak of this incident to anyone.

Fifteen years later, now adults, the group began to disappear one by one. Finally, when it came down to only two of them left, they decided to confess to what they'd done. According to the story, they were both sentenced to serve ten years in prison.

Now, anyone who visits the swimming hole during a full moon will see the moonlight unveil the reflection of a skull upon the water. This is believed to be the residual energy left behind by the teen who had drowned. Ever since this legend began to circulate, the swimming hole has been called the Devil's Garden.

That's the legend that was told around the area for a long time. But it seems that's not a true story. The swimming hole was built in 1947 by a man named Oscar who was on the swim team at Berea College. Oscar's idea was to build a swimming pool identical to the one at Berea and charge people to swim there. The swimming area began as a concrete pool with a concession counter and a shallower pool for children. In 1972, he built a new pool with a safer sand bottom a few hundred feet from the original. The new pool had to cease operations in 2003 because chlorine gas was outlawed after the 9/11 attacks, so there was no way to clean the pool.

The reason it became known as Devil's Garden is actually because of the area of the Cumberland Falls called Devil's Garden not far from the pool. The children that used to swim there liked the name so it stuck. That's the true story behind the name.

But the other story is better suited for the campfire.

BOONE CREEK WOODS

S pread out over Stanton, the Boone Creek Woods is a vast, rolling wilderness of trees that turns into a captivating prism of autumn colors come fall. With rocky hills jutting up from the sea of nature's greenery, the woods make for quite a breathtaking sight. It is a favorite for hunters and outdoors types. Deep inside there is an abandoned bridge that people like to frequent – those who are always up for a creepy piece of history.

As legend has it, the Boone Creek Woods actually is a good place to go to find something spooky. In certain locations deep within the woods, hunters have reported seeing a very disturbing sight among the trees. It seems there is a rather scary woman who lurks in the woods.

Some hunters describe her as pale and graceful, with long, flowing black hair. From a distance, she appears to be rather beautiful, but as she draws nearer, she becomes grim and withered, and her eye sockets are black and hollow. Her choked voice will often gurgle as she approaches. Before reaching you, she will lift her arm and reach a bony, death-like hand for you.

Other stories say that when the woman of the woods appears, any dogs that have been brought along for the hunt will immediately begin barking, snarling, and growling at the woman. Many times they have taken off after her. On one occasion, a pack of hunting dogs trapped the woman by a tree. But she appeared up top, standing on a branch, and began shrieking at the hunter and his dogs.

Who is this woman wandering the woods? This has never been speculated upon, as far as we could find. The woods are so large, it could be any poor soul who may have lost her way, or found herself on the receiving end of a deadly animal attack.

X CAVE

The Carter Caves State Resort Park located in Olive Hill has a unique cave with a poignant story to tell. The X Cave, so named because of the four separate entry points that form the shape of an X, is said to be the spot of a romantic tragedy. That tragedy, legend tells, still haunts the cave to this day.

European settlers discovered the cave in the 1700s, but before that, it was said to have been inhabited by a Cherokee Indian tribe. One of their warriors, a tribesman by the name of Huraken, discovered a silver vein not far from the cave. Instead of reporting this magnificent find to this tribe, he kept it a secret with the intentions of using the riches to win the hand of Manuita, the chief's daughter. Huraken had longed for Manuita for some time, but was afraid to pursue her because he was a warrior that had not earned himself a great standing among the tribe, yet. This, he was sure, would be the way.

When Huraken divulged his secret finding to Manuita, she was quite impressed with his abilities as a hunter to make such a find. When he told her of his intentions, she was receptive and reciprocated his desire. From there, it is said, their romance bloomed in secrecy as they waited for the right time to tell her father.

One day, a rival tribe had entered their territory. With a battle imminent, the Cherokee warriors rode off to meet the threat. It is said that this was a fierce battle that lasted through the day and into the night. Many men returned wounded, many did not return at all. As the night wore on, Manuita began to worry as Huraken had yet to come back. When most of the warriors were back, Manuita assumed her lover dead, and threw herself from a cliff, down to her death.

But Huraken was not dead. In fact, he had stopped by the silver vein on his way back from the tribe's victorious battle. He had decided it was time to unveil his discovery, as well as his love for Manuita, to the chief. He took some of the silver and headed home.

When he arrived, he found his people in a state of unrest. When he discovered the commotion was due to the death of his beloved Manuita, he lifted her broken body and took her to the X Cave so he could watch over her. When the chief found Huraken with her body, the young warrior told him everything. The chief was enraged and blamed Huraken for his daughter's untimely death. He ordered Huraken to be pulled from the cave and tried. The chief's vengeance was swift as he sentenced Huraken to death.

Before his execution, Huraken had one last wish: to look upon the body of Manuita once more. The chief granted him his dying request and had him walked back into the cave for one final viewing. He would never walk out of the cave again, as he was executed in the darkness and left to lie next to his love. Many years later, the bones were supposedly found with silver treasures lying around them.

According to some reports, Manuita and Huraken may still be down in the cave, forever together just as the warrior had wished. People have reported seeing firelights in the distance, but never able to make it directly to these fires. Some say they have gotten close without actually reaching the source. But, they claim to have gotten close enough to witness the couple gathered at the fire, embracing one another before they and the fire fade away.

Some have reported shadow people coming and going in large numbers, dancing about the cave, and whispering in the darkness. Some even venture so far to say that the cave may be a gateway to another dimension or a spirit world, with the portal located at the very center of the cave. This, some say, is why so many apparitions and shadows are seen near the center, and why many unexplained temperature changes happen there, too.

Though we believe this story of Manuita and Huraken could be nothing more than a romantic legend passed around over the years, it is quite possible Native Americans settled near X Cave. It is even likely that such a tale could have unfolded there or at least something similar to it. Maybe Manuita and Huraken did exist and their tragedy did transpire, and if so, we certainly hope they have found their eternal love in the afterlife.

PERRYVILLE BATTLEFIELD

Perryville Battlefield State Historic Site near Perryville is the site where the bloodiest battle in the history of the Bluegrass State took place. On October 8th, 1862, more than 7,600 soldiers were either slain or seriously wounded during the epic struggle in Chaplin Hills. It was the south's last effort to take the state, and from a tactical standpoint, they were victorious, but with a mass of Union reinforcements coming in, Gen. Bragg was forced to retreat to Tennessee, giving the north the victory and the state. Because of this, it has also been known as the "Battle for Kentucky."

The plan was for Bragg's army to distract the north from the south's Virginia and Chattanooga strongholds with an invasion of Kentucky, which was considered a key border state. Federal forces from Alabama and middle Tennessee took the bait and marched to the crossroads of Perryville to do battle with a Confederate cavalry at Springfield Pike. When the rebel infantry arrived, the battle moved to Peters Hill. A Union band, led by Major General Don Carlos Bell, marched on the hill and put up a valiant fight, but too many Confederate forces converged upon them, forcing them to fall back.

The battle went back and forth long after nightfall. The south had the upper hand, but had suffered severely, losing many men and resources. Word soon came in that the Union reinforcements were on their way, and that's when Bragg fell back to the Cumberland Gap, leaving Kentucky to the Union. The north tended to their dead, giving them proper burials along Springfield Pike before their bodies were moved to Union cemeteries in Lebanon, Kentucky and at Camp Nelson in Jessamine County. The rebels, however, had no one around to honor them, and the corpses of the Confederacy were left to rot in the sun before being thrown unceremoniously into a mass grave at the Bottom's family farm,

172

which is now the site of the park. In 1902, the Perryville Commission erected a monument to the Confederate soldiers who died there.

With so much death and bloodshed, and with so many emotions running high, it's no wonder people have reported ghostly activity all over the park. Full-body apparitions of soldiers from both sides wander the grounds, whether in daylight or after dark, walking through the grassy hills rolling along the land. Investigators have captured their voices on EVPs there with responses that allegedly were intelligent. Visitors have also claimed to hear disembodied voices chattering in places where no people can be seen. Glowing lights are said to float around the field late in the night, and it is believed these are the spirits of some of the roaming ghosts from the bloody battle.

The heavy thuds of cannon fire have been heard echoing in the night. Rapid gunfire and screams of dying men have often accompanied these sounds. Perryville does conduct reenactments of the infamous battle, but these sounds have been heard when there are no reenactments taking place.

During the battle, a building onsite known as the Dye House, which was home to the Dye family, was the headquarters of Confederate General Simon B. Buckner, and later transformed into a makeshift hospital. Many amputations and deaths occurred there. So much blood flowed onto the floors of the house that some of it could not be removed, and the stains are still there. Because of this mayhem, spirits of the dead are believed to be present in the house. Voices of men claiming to be Civil War doctors have been recorded. People have reported hearing loud, distinct footsteps stomping along the stairs. Doors will suddenly fling open and others will mysteriously slam shut. The confusion of the battle still seems to exist in the energy of that war-weathered building.

An employee there reported being in their office and hearing someone talking to them, but finding no one present when looking around. The museum is often disturbed, with items moved and knocked over. The same employee said that she can't explain why she would sometimes find the head of one of the mannequins lying in the middle of the floor.

Brigadier General Patrick Cleburne's horse was said to have been shot out from under him as he charged the enemy. Not long after the battle, people reported hearing a horse galloping hard across the grounds when no horses were present. In more recent years, an employee there said she was camping out at the site with some of the actors from the reenactments when they all heard the sound of heavy hooves thundering along the pavement close to where they camped. Fearing that one of the horses on site had escaped, they all got up to search for the animal. As they walked along the darkened park, shining their flashlights, trying to spot any escaped horses on the run, they were stumped that they did not see any. To be sure, they went to the stables to count the horses and come to find out they were all present. That was when the lady realized that they had all just witnessed the ghost of Cleburne's horse.

Two reenactors who were camping out were suddenly woken by an unidentifiable Civil War solider who asked them about the whereabouts of another soldier. This puzzled them because they did not recognize the man. After they inquired as to whom he was, the man said his name and rank and then rushed from the tent. The reenactors followed the soldier, saw him go into the neighboring tent and went in after him. When they went to the tent, he was gone. They then decided to look up the man's name and that of the soldier he was asking for and were chilled to find that both names were listed among the casualties of Perryville.

We did visit Perryville Battlefield ourselves, and as we walked along the rolling hills, listening to the breeze whisper among the trees, we turned on the spirit box in various places to try and get some responses. There wasn't much there for us that day, but Jenny did get a strange feeling inside the museum. Often, when she feels something strong in some place, we come to find out that there is a ghost story tied to the area. While we don't know if there are ghosts in the museum, she did feel a presence by a certain display case. When we checked that case, we found it was where they kept all the operation tools, particularly the crude, primitive bone saw used to amputate serious injuries. She had seen the image of a young soldier sitting near the case, and we wonder if this was a man who had possibly had something cut off during the battle, or maybe the medic that had the unfortunate duty of wielding that cruel but necessary device.

Most believe this historic battlefield is haunted, and we tend to agree with that notion. You can find out for yourself if the spirits of the slain do still linger there. The site does allow paranormal investigations for a fee of about $250 per person as of the date we wrote this. To make a reservation or find out more, you can visit their website at Perryvillebattlefield.org. Haunted or not, there are sections where a sense of serenity washes over the quiet park, but there are also feelings of unrest. It is a place worth visiting, if not for the paranormal claims, for the historic significance.

DEVIL'S CREEK

Near the back roads between Sawyer and Corbin, Kentucky lies Devil's Creek, a place with a chilling legend about darkness and evil.

Located near Cumberland Falls, Devil's Creek is also the site of Wolfpit Cemetery, also known as C.W. Ridener Cemetery. Local stories speak of a church that once stood near Wolfpit Cemetery in the mid-1900s. This church did not host your average small town congregation, however. It is said that those who gathered there to worship did so in the name of Satan.

In the 1980s, at the height of the Satanic Panic, people who went to Ridener Cemetery would find inverted crosses and pentagrams drawn on the ground and on the stones. Stories of animal bones being found in piles circulated as well. Frightened that nefarious people with ill intentions were lurking in the graveyard, locals stayed away and demanded their children do the same.

An array of terrifying tales has been told about the area around Devil's Creek. Naturally, teenagers, hearing these tales, liked to frequent the alleged cursed location. Most went there thinking it was some kind of joke, but some had experiences they would never forget. Even adults who heard these tales began to check them out, thinking they were less demonic or paranormal and more likely the work of dangerous individuals. Many of them, too, would be in for a surprise – or so the story goes.

Some visitors have been frightened off by the sound of intense growling all around them, but with no animals present. Others have been frozen in fear as they heard sinister laughter, and even the sounds of screaming. But sounds are not the only experiences people have had there. There are those who went in search of something scary and found themselves witness to bright lights dancing in the middle of the darkness – lights that were unexplainable, lights that did not come from anywhere beyond the land. Allegedly, large, shiny orbs have floated and flown across the cemetery, hovering over graves before disappearing in the ground. Some believe these might be the spirits of people buried in the graveyard.

Many believe that a force of cruelty and unfathomable evil stalks the grounds around Devil's Creek. A dark figure, void of all details except for its form, has been spotted standing at distances and walking through the wooded areas around there. Others claim that an abomination lives in the area – a half-bird, half-man hybrid standing more than seven feet tall will pursue you if it sees you. Before it takes off after you, it will let out a heart-stopping shriek, continuing to scream during the chase. None have said what happens if it catches you.

This sinister force could be the man buried in Wolfpit that people say is so evil he was buried upside down for fear that he would have crawled from his grave. They say a sick feeling of fear surrounds his horizontal grave, and when it snows, the flakes do not stick to his stone. Ghost hunters have supposedly caught strange voices on their recorders near his grave. Could he be the dark figure or bird-man hybrid people claim stalk the land?

Of course, much of this sounds like sensationalism. These are some wild stories that most logical folk would not believe. Though we do not know where the story of the birdman comes from, we do have an idea who this horribly evil man is supposed to be.

Though there is no man buried upside down in Wolfpit Cemetery, there is a man who was buried standing up. His name was Henry W. Barton, born in 1901 and died in 1974. According to the legend, he is age appropriate to have been part of the alleged Satanic church in the area. However, there is no evidence of such a church having existed, nor any reason to believe this man was involved in anything like that.

The truth is, we do not know why he was buried standing up. But we do know that there is a Henry Barton Road in Corbin. Perhaps this could be the man after which the road was named. We do not know exactly who he was, but Barton seems to be a popular name in that area, so he was likely part of a prominent family, and perhaps that prominence is why he was buried standing up, not because he was some malicious minster of the Devil.

If you visit the area, be aware that it is a bit treacherous and secluded. Be wary of your surroundings. There is an old abandoned house not far from the cemetery, and any sort of person can be hiding back there. Maybe that was the old "church."

HEADLESS ANNIE OF BIG BLACK MOUNTAIN

As most people who know anything about Kentucky's history are aware, the Bluegrass State was once coal country. Coal was among the most abundant natural resources of the state, and coal mining was one of the biggest occupations. Mining camps were spread out along the counties covering the eastern hills, and none had more camps than Harlan County. The extremely high demand for coal practically guaranteed that any able-bodied man in the county would have a job in the mines. The downside to this was that the owners of the mines did not want to pay the workers properly for their hard labor, and so many of the miners went on strike. The owners, refusing to allow their coal production to be halted, killed many of the miners on the picket lines. Because of this heinous act, the county became known as Bloody Harlan.

There was one man in particular who really found himself on the bad side of his boss. He was very outspoken against the pay and working conditions, urging the miners to form a union and strike. This boss decided he would make an example of the man, so he hired some hoodlums to invade the man's home and drag him and his family out to the woods on Big Black Mountain, which is the highest peak in the entire commonwealth. From thereon, the story becomes a bit gruesome, so be warned.

Once in the woods, the men made the man's wife and daughter watch as they cut off his legs and then tied him up to a tree to allow him to bleed to death. Next, they inflicted the same gory punishment upon the mother, leaving the daughter to watch the horrific display.

Then it was the young daughter's turn. She was only twelve years old, and her name was Annie. The sadistic brutes proceeded to decapitate Annie and throw her body off a nearby cliff. They left her there and let the animals feast on her remains. The murderers were never apprehended and were likely never sought out.

Ever since that night, people say Annie has wandered the roadways near where she was brutally murdered. If you are driving past there around the time she was killed, you will find her headless ghost drifting along the roadside, dressed in her white nightgown and with a green ethereal glow surrounding her. Some believe this glow protects her soul from harm and also guides her sightless spirit through the darkness. But Annie is not a particularly benevolent spirit. On the contrary, for in death she is angry, wants revenge – and more than anything else, wants her head.

If you encounter Annie, she will fling herself onto your car. No matter how far you are from her and no matter how fast you go, you will not escape her. Once she lands upon your vehicle, your engine will stall and your car will die. If this happens, lock your door and, most importantly, roll your window up, for Annie will try to enter your car. If she succeeds, she will attempt to take your head, and if you are caught in the aura around her, you will find yourself without a head, which will have been absorbed by the ghost of Headless Annie.

We don't know if the story of Annie is true or not. It very well could be a complete fabrication. However, the conditions the miners were subjected to were notoriously bad. These were likely in the days before the Labor Movement, or at least the movement had yet to reach such a small town. Companies were known to have men who opposed them killed, and most of the governments sided with the companies. So, it is certainly possible something like this happened. No doubt the men are long dead, but perhaps Headless Annie will have her vengeance in the next life.

JACOB FLOYD & JENNY FLOYD

THE BARDO HOLLOW LIGHT

In the area around Catron Creek in Harlan, there is a hollow known as Bardo Hollow. By all appearances, it's just one of many ordinary hollows in the state of Kentucky. But, there is an eerie mystery that takes place there every spring.

Whenever spring first rolls around and the weather warms and darkness comes a little later in the evening, those who wander into the hollow might find the mysterious light of Bardo Hollow waiting for them. This light, which is said to glow rather bright, like a hovering flood light, will begin to shine from the far end of the hollow. It's not a star, as it hangs low enough to cast a glowing radius on the ground around it. Some have mistaken it for someone else in the graveyard with a spotlight. But as the witnesses stay to watch the light, they will see it move. It will bounce and drift, as if floating on air, and bring its light with it. Normally, one of two things will happen: the light will either drift all the way to the bottom of the hollow, or it will disappear.

This light has been seen for a few decades and no one is sure what it is. Some believe it is a spirit of someone who may have died near or in the hollow. Others think it's a guiding spirit for anyone lost in the dark. It's been suggested this light could be alien in some fashion. Whatever it is, it has left many locals baffled.

THE MUSHROOM MINES

The Mushroom Mines of Carter County in eastern Kentucky have drawn a lot of attention from those fascinated with creepy locations and supposed haunted spots. Located in the ghost town of Lawton, filled with dilapidated houses, drooping power lines, overgrown foliage, cluttered vacant back roads, boarded up buildings, and stairs that lead to nothing, the mines are burrowed into the nearby hills.

The Mushroom Mines were originally tunneled in an attempt to dig for limestone, which ended in the 1950s. After sitting abandoned for a time, someone purchased the land in 1967 and turned the mines into a mushroom farm. That endeavor only lasted until the 70s. After that, there were apparently talks of turning the mines into a fallout shelter. Given that the United States was still locked in the Cold War with Russia at the time, that's not surprising. The entire construct is a winding warren of twisting tunnels and mazes pushing back deep into the hills. It could make for a very good place to ride out a nuclear war, though there might not be anything to climb out to. There is a lake located in the farther reaches of the mines, so maybe that could provide water. In the late 2000s, the mines were targeted for a new project that involved storing a lot of digital ware, such as tapes, hard drives, and items of that nature. Sounds like a rather odd transformation. But it didn't happen. The plan fell through and the abandoned project left behind a few buildings that were built in preparation.

Of course, it is only natural that spooky legends surround the dark and ominous mines. Among them are tales about occultist groups gathering in the blackened passages to hold Satanic masses and conduct demonic rituals. If these tales possess any validity, it would likely have been events that had taken place many years ago, as Satanism seems to have lost its appeal in eastern Kentucky these days.

Though such accounts are not impossible, those that are more probable are stories of drug deals and other illicit activities taking place in the Mushroom Mines. The eastern portion of the state has been known for drug production and distribution, and a location as secluded as the Mushroom Mines would be prime for anyone looking to conduct shady business far from prying eyes.

Outside of devilish priests and drug dealing gangsters, the mines are also known for hosting the spirits of the dead, making it a "rite of passage" for teenagers in the area. But before they can enter the mines, they must pass through the fields near the woods, where an angry Bigfoot supposedly resides. Some of those who have traveled through the area have reported monstrous howls and growls rising from the woods. Others have described a massive red-eyed creature with bulging arms and shaggy fur emerging from the shade of the trees and chasing them. With that water source within the mines, if such a creature were to choose a place to live while hiding, that would be an excellent choice.

Once you make it into the mines, you have to contend with the specter the Satanists unleashed. They say the entity screams like a woman, but is a tall, pale, masculine wraith that wanders the murky corridors in search of trespassers in its lair. As it draws near you, you will hear the chilling scrape of its bony feet traveling along the stone. An intense fear will settle over you as the air freezes all around you. As the frightening white form comes into view, you must leave. If you are touched by the creature's cold hands of death, you will not leave the mines. You must avert its gaze as well, for if you peer into its darkened eye sockets, you will be rendered paralyzed and the creature will surely claim you.

Silly legends, of course, but they are nonetheless fun. The bit about the cryptid primate isn't as silly. It's quite possible such a creature exists. But a life-sucking wraith with the ability to paralyze? Well, that's a hard yarn to tie. Undoubtedly though, the Mushroom Mines sound like a very interesting place to explore.

THE PHANTOMS OF BUGGER MOUNTAIN

S tanding between the small rural towns of Barbourville and Corbin is Gilliam Hill, also known as Bugger Mountain. Back in the 1950s, before the freeways were built, the only passage from one of those towns to the next was the narrow, serpentine Highway 25. During the drive, travelers would be introduced to one unfriendly track, twisting and turning its way up the hill. After reaching the apex, the descent becomes more dangerous as the curves in the road turn sharper, making it more difficult for the driver to maintain control without drastically slowing down.

One night sometime in the 1950s, a rig was making its way along Highway 25 through Bugger Mountain. After it crested the hill, it began to weave on its way down. Whether or not the truck lost its brakes or was going too fast is not specified in this legend. What is told is that the rig veered off the highway, sped over the edge, and tumbled to the bottom of the hill, killing the driver in the crash.

Though the truck was smashed and the driver dead, it is believed that he still drives that eighteen-wheeler along the deadly Highway 25. Legend says that if you find yourself driving over the hill on a Saturday night, you might find yourself staring down the bright lights of the phantom truck. When the bright lights burst through the darkness, you will realize they are headed right for you. You might try to turn, dodge, or move over to evade the oncoming monster, but it will do you no good. The semi will turn your way, appearing to be ready to collide with you. In the second right before the crash, the lights will turn away from you and head for the hill. If you watch you will see them drive past off the side and plunge into the darkness below.

But this is not the only legend that people tell of Bugger Mountain. Allegedly, there was once a serial killer roaming the desolate hills. The story does not specify when this killer was on the loose, but he is said to have targeted young redheaded women. He would abduct them, take them into the hills, and slaughter them. Rumor has it that he left a couple of the bodies out in the open, and their bloody remains were discovered by passersby. No one ever caught the man that they know of, and no one knows what became of him. Some believe the spirit of one of his victims still lingers on Gilliam Hill. People have reported seeing a large ball of light hovering in the darkness, and as it grew brighter and they drew nearer, they could discern the dark shape of a human inside of it. While it is believed this is one of the killer's victims, some think it could be the killer himself, and others theorize that this is the ghost of the truck driver who died in the crash. Whoever the figure inside the ball of light is, people say if you are up there in the hills and you feel the presence of someone watching you, or you get goosebumps and your hair tingles, then the spirits are very near.

Whether or not there is a phantom truck or a serial killer's victim encapsulated in a ball of light, Bugger Mountain is a scary place to be at night. Coming down that hill, apparently, can be a real nightmare. So, be careful.

WITCH HILL

A little ways south of Cincinnati in the town of Alexandria, Kentucky is a forested area of grassland with a bumpy road running down the middle called Witch Hill. This place was once home to what many people called the Witches' Tree. It is a tree where legend tells three notorious witches were hanged.

These witches, who remain unnamed, were said to often terrorize the town. They would sweep in, make mischief, cause bad things to happen, and frighten children. Some even say these witches cursed the townsfolk just for fun, and many accidents and ailments would befall the people. After they'd had their fun, the witches would vanish into the night to return to their home in the woods.

After a time, the town got sick of living in fear of these witches, so a lynch mob formed. The men of the town went into the woods and found the witches, dragged them to the large tree, and strung them up. Once the witches were dead, they were then buried in a line in three separate unmarked graves. The road passing through the area was said to have been built over their graves and the angry, restless spirits of the witches have caused the three bumps that are now present.

It is said before they hanged, the witches cursed the land saying that anyone who cuts down their tree would suffer, and evil forces would roam the land around it. Since then, those fascinated with the tale of the witches have reported strange occurrences in the area. A strange hollow whistle can sometimes be heard in the trees, along with voices chanting and whispering in the dark. Those who used to touch the tree would be plagued with nightmares. It is also said that any attempt at taking pictures of the area will fail. The latter isn't true as pictures of the place exist.

Of course, it is likely this entire story was something made up to scare kids, or something rooted in a small amount of truth that has grown into the sensational tale that is written here upon these pages. Either way, it's an interesting tale.

Of the curse – the tree has since been cut down and no catastrophes have befallen the area.

CHILD'S CREEK

In Closplint, near Child's Creek, there's a story about a miner who got into a dispute with one of his bosses and struck him while on the job. The man was fired and sent home. Now, desperate and angry, he came back and attempted to unionize some other miners. Several joined him, as they were sick of the boss's actions, as well as the low wages and unsafe working conditions. So, the crew threw down their tools and went on strike.

After a couple days of the strike, the boss reached out to the miner and told him that he could have his job back if he got the other men to end the strike. The miner then asked if the other workers' demands would be met, to which the boss replied that they would not. The miner then refused to call off the strike.

That night, or perhaps the next, the boss sent a few of the miners who were on his side over to the man's house. They called him outside under the pretense that they were going to join the strike, then beat him senseless and dragged him out to Child's Creek. There, they held him down and cut off his head then threw it in the water. After that, the other miners returned to work.

Now, it is said that the man's headless ghost stalks the grounds near Child's Creek, searching for his lost head. He also seems to be seeking out the men who decapitated him, but since he cannot see, he believes anyone he comes into contact with is one of his assailants, so he will try to strangle anyone he touches.

PINE MOUNTAIN

A man named Martin was driving through Pine Mountain on a cold rainy night when he came across a woman in a wedding gown hitchhiking along the side of the road. When he picked her up, seeing that she was soaked and shivering, he offered her his coat. She thanked him, put it on, and then warned him that bridge they needed to cross ahead had collapsed. Martin then turned and went around another way.

Once he dropped the woman off at home, he watched her go around to the back of the house to make sure she made it in alright. He then resumed his drive home. About halfway home, he realized the young lady still had his coat. Instead of going back on such a messy night, and since it was too late to disturb anyone, he decided he would wait until the following day to retrieve his coat.

When Martin knocked on the door of the house, the woman's mother answered. He informed her he had dropped the young lady off there last night and that she was still in possession of his coat. Looking sad, the woman explained to him that the young lady he was speaking of was her daughter and she was dead.

To make matters even stranger, it turned out that the lady had been buried in her wedding dress. Also, the bridge really had collapsed the night before thanks to the floodwaters.

This particular story is one told often about the ghost of a young lady hitchhiking on a dark road during a rainy night. Different variations of this story – the man offering his coat, dropping her off and realizing she still had it, then going back only to have her mother tell him she died some time ago – are told in different towns, cities, and states. As you may recall, it has already appeared once in this book – on Meshack Road.

Though we doubt the validity of this story, what we want to know is where it originated. Somewhere, sometime, this story was first told, and we want to know when, where, and about whom.

While we don't discount the possible existence of hitchhiking ghosts, we don't believe this story keeps happening repeatedly in different towns. So, did the first telling, wherever it was, have merit? Was there truth to the historic part of the legend? Did someone really claim this paranormal incident happened to them? If so, whom? Of course, it's always possible that the entire story was fabricated and it just managed to travel, hitchhiking its way from town to town. But if this story does truly belong to someone, finding out that pertinent information could be paramount to unraveling the metaphysical mystery within it.

MAMMOTH CAVE

It is said that there have been more than 150 reports of alleged spiritual activity in the many subterranean passages of Mammoth Cave, located in the Green River Valley of south-central Kentucky. These reports have come not only from tourists, but also from park rangers and scientists over a number of years, with many stories lining up and corroborating one another. There have been books written about the location, most notably *Scary Stories of Mammoth Cave*, by park rangers Colleen O'Conner Olson and Charles Hanion, as well as a seemingly endless string of articles and accounts posted on numerous blogs and websites all over the Internet. Beyond that, there are several word-of-mouth tales people who've been to Mammoth Cave or worked somewhere within the compound will tell you they've experienced. Some have even speculated that the cave itself may be some sort of passage between the physical realm and the spiritual world beyond.

The sheer size of the world's largest known cave system is astounding; the interconnected passages twist some thirty stories down into the darkness and run around four-hundred miles long—and that's only what has been discovered. It is believed that there is a lot of uncharted territory, as more mileage is discovered almost weekly. None have yet to tell just how massive this underground world really is. No doubt, though, that the place is certainly creepy. In 1905, it inspired the short story, "The Beast in the Cave," by famous horror author, H.P. Lovecraft.

A comprehensive history of the paranormal legends of Mammoth Cave—if indeed someone could manage to track down and document everyone one of them—would no doubt fill an entire volume set of encyclopedias, which is why the system has been dubbed the most haunted natural wonder in the world. Just digging through online reports is a chore, but we have managed to compile a concise and abbreviated account of some of the most well-known stories coming from the depth of the world beneath the Bluegrass State.

Being that Mammoth Cave is a natural landmark, determining how long ago man began to delve into the system is difficult to do. But, it has been decided that the earliest evidence of human exploration dates back 6,000 years where it is believed pre-historic Native Americans used to mine for minerals in the walls by torchlight. Primitive stone tools have been found down in the darkness, and four bodies were excavated from the cave since the 1800s. No one yet knows why the Natives vacated the caves, but they do believe that they mined there for nearly 2,000 years.

Sometime in the late 1700s, a bear hunter discovered the cave, which was later used as a saltpeter mine for gun powder production. After the Revolutionary War ended, the cave became the first tourist attraction at Mammoth Cave. It was during this time that the bodies were first discovered. Initially, they were believed to be the corpses of an unknown race of people, but were later concluded to be early Native Americans.

Since the area was dry and rich in mineral, the bodies were well-preserved, practically mummified. For some time, they were on display in the caves. Rumor has it that the spirits remained around the bodies, often appearing as shadows and silhouettes lingering nearby.

In 1843, a young Southern woman named Melissa, who grew up around Mammoth Cave, fell in love with her tutor, a man from Boston by the name of Mr. Beverleigh. Now, accounts differ from this point. Some say she brought him down to an area known as Purgatory Point near the Echo River and left him there as a prank. Another account claims that Mr. Beverleigh didn't return her affection and so she decided to give him a tour of the cave and left him down there as an act of revenge. But this revenge was not meant to be permanent. Melissa lost Mr. Beverleigh and he was never seen again. Heavy with remorse over her cruel and fatal joke, Melissa returned to the cave every day to try to find him, but never did. Melissa later died of tuberculosis. Though there is no actual record of Melissa, it is said that she haunts Purgatory Point, wandering along the Echo River calling for Mr. Beverleigh. Her apparition has been seen in the area, and her frantic cries have been heard there in the darkness. It is even said that the sounds of her coughing, as if suffering from TB, can be heard near the river.

In 1839, a man by the name of Dr. John Croghan bought the cave from Glasgow attorney Frank Gorin for $10,000. Along with the property, he received a slave by the name of Stephan Bishop, who was possibly the first man to give the cave tours there, and has also gone down in history as one of the greatest cave explorers in the history of Mammoth Cave. His physical abilities and vast knowledge of the cave led to him discovering more than twenty miles of passages, as well as the blind albino fish occupying the Echo River underground; he was also the first man to cross the cave's "Bottomless Pit," a 150-foot drop down into the darkness, by laying a ladder across it and crawling to the other side while holding his lantern in his teeth.

But, Dr. Croghan's plans were not simply to give tours. He believed that the constant moderate temperature of the cave could cure tuberculosis, which was called consumption back then. So, he decided to turn Mammoth Cave into an underground hospital, building eleven huts in the darkness and moving in fifteen patients. This plan did not go well, however, as all patients got worse. Two of them died, as did Dr. Croghan in 1849.

The huts still remain and can be visited on the tours. Out front of the huts—also known as "Consumption Cabins"—lies "Corpse Rock," the slab of stone where the TB patients' bodies had been laid after their deaths. This is one of the many areas in the cave that is believed to be haunted. Some say that you can still hear the sounds of patients coughing and gagging as they breathed their final breaths in the darkness of the failed, makeshift hospital. One of them might even be the doctor himself.

Bishop died in 1856. He is buried in the Old Guide Cemetery nearby, alongside several other slaves who had been used as guides. It is believed that some of them, especially Mr. Bishop, often return to the warren they knew so well, as they have been seen, heard, and felt moving in the shadows down below. Allegedly, a ghost fitting Bishop's description has been seen many times during the lantern-lit tours.

During the tours, rangers will turn out the lights to show the tourists just how dark it is down there. During these blackouts, rangers have reported being shoved, grabbed, and touched by someone unseen, and have heard footsteps nearby only to turn and find no one is near them.

We will point out the glaring hole in these accounts by stating that during the blackouts, they're not likely to see anyone nearby because it is pitch black inside the cave. We have been in there. Anyone can do anything without being seen. It is a state of total blindness. Also, inside a cave, the sound will be altered, so footsteps can sound like they are coming from anywhere. While we don't doubt the cave has spiritual energy, these particular occurrences can be easily explained. However, as we always say, just because someone can offer an explanation, it doesn't mean the explanation is accurate. You also need proof your theory is real in order to truly debunk any paranormal claim.

But, there is one story from these blackouts that does raise some eyebrows. One ranger reported seeing a family at the back of the crowd during a tour. The adult male wore a white Panama hat and was listening very intently to what the guide was saying. The guide found this to be odd because he didn't recall seeing this family any time prior to this. When it came time for the blackout, the other ranger shut out the light. When the lights came back on, the family was gone and was never seen again on the tour.

Perhaps the most famous spirit said to dwell in Mammoth Cave is that of the local cave explorer, Floyd Collins. Floyd lived during what was known as the Kentucky Cave Wars, where the various private owners of different caves in the area were competing over the increasing tourist traffic of the time. Floyd owned a section called the Crystal Cave, which he discovered in 1917, and it was losing the war due to no lodging and difficulty reaching the entrance. So, on January 30th, 1925, he decided to begin excavating an entrance into the Sand Cave nearby to make his own cave more accessible and appealing to the affluent tourists. But, he broke one of the most fundamental rules of cave exploration: he went alone and didn't tell anyone where he was going. While navigating his way through a very tight squeeze, Floyd found himself pinned by a boulder and trapped in the cave.

He was later discovered stuck down in the hole. A media frenzy then ensued as radio stations and newspapers were keeping listeners and readers updated on Floyd's condition. The more morbid-minded people gathered at the cave to watch the drama unfold, setting up food stands and selling souvenirs in the process. Meanwhile, Floyd was slipping further away beneath the soil of Central Kentucky. Rescuers attempted to move the massive boulder from Floyd's leg, but could not. Then there was a cave-in that blocked him off from all help. Two weeks later, Floyd died of exposure.

Due to the difficulty rescuers had reaching his body Floyd was left where he died as funeral services were held on the surface. His family was not pleased with his body being left in the Sand Cave, so his brother Homer managed to reach the corpse two months later and pull him out. He was then buried in a grave at the family farm near Crystal Cave, now known as Floyd Collins's Crystal Cave.

In 1927, Floyd's father Lee sold the cave and property to a man who is said to have been a dentist named Thomas. Thomas managed to get permission to have Floyd's body exhumed and moved to the entrance of Sand Cave, where it lay in a glass-lidded coffin for all the tourists to see.

As if this isn't bizarre enough, Floyd's body ended up being stolen in 1929 and later found in a field, missing a leg. Most people figured this to be the act of rival cave owners who were angered by the amount of tourist attention the corpse was getting. The leg was later recovered and the entire body placed back in the coffin, but without the viewing lid—though it has been said that a lot of tourists took a peek anyway.

The National Cave Systems purchased the Sand Cave in 1961 and closed it to tourism. One would think that an organization such as this would not only remove the body of Floyd Collins and give it a proper burial, but would make it high on the priority list. However, for whatever reason, that did not transpire until 1989, leaving Floyd to decay in the Sand Cave for almost thirty more years. It took a team of fifteen men to remove the casket and the tombstone, but when it was all said and done, Floyd Collins was put to a proper rest at Mammoth Cave Baptist Church Cemetery, at the request of his family.

If ever a spirit had a reason to be in a state of unrest and haunt an area and its people, it would be that of Floyd Collins. To say his death was unfortunate, and to say it was poorly handled, would be an understatement. So, it really comes as no surprise to learn that there have been numerous witnesses to ghostly goings-on near where Floyd lost his life.

In the past, people have reported hearing a man's voice calling for help when near the spot where Floyd died. It's been said the phrase, "Help me, Johnny, I'm trapped!" has been heard—or some variation of that. Others have even described the sounds as "wailing cries for help." When looking around after these occurrences, people have found no one near, but still continued to hear the sounds.

There have also been accounts of rocks being thrown through the darkness, at an angle that suggests it had not fallen from above, but had come in from the side. Could this be Floyd showing his anger about his body being abused?

If it is him, we don't know if he's very angry. Colleen O'Conner Olson had an experience while exploring in one of Floyd's old spots. She told Wave 3 news in Kentucky that she had started to fall and felt someone grab her and pull her back up. Naturally, she thought it was her caving partner. But, when she turned to thank him, she found that he was on the other side of the cave. She then said, "Thanks Floyd."

But, the cave system isn't the only part of the park that is supposed to be haunted. People have reported strange occurrences along the Heritage Trail. Misty apparitions and transparent shadow-like images supposedly move along and around the trail; disembodied voices from nearby have been heard when it was clear no one else was around. The most chilling incident reported from the Heritage Trail is a pair of legs with no upper-body walking down the path. It has been claimed that this pair of legs has been seen walking both towards and away from people in plain view at distances close enough for witnesses to be able to tell with certainty that these legs are without a body. Undoubtedly, this is the most sensational of all the claims that we have uncovered at Mammoth Cave National Park. Nonetheless, if we are willing to believe a full body ghost can manifest, why not a spirit only capable of partial manifestation?

Mammoth Cave—as old as the Earth itself—there's no telling what all has happened there, or who has died, and by what means, in that lightless labyrinth beneath the hardened dirt of Cave City. With so much uncharted territory that most believe still snakes its way through the underground, there might be even more historic evidence and frightening ghosts waiting down there for someone to discover. If it is indeed a passage between our world and theirs, maybe one day some brave explorers will dig deep enough and find some answers waiting in the beyond.

It's an interesting thought, at least.

OTHER BUILDINGS

BOBBY MACKEY'S MUSIC WORLD

Perhaps the most notorious haunted location in the Bluegrass State, with its only rival being Waverly Hills Sanatorium, is the secluded music bar in Wilder, Kentucky known as Bobby Mackey's Music World. Located just south of Cincinnati, and only open on Friday and Saturday nights from 7pm to 2:15am, Bobby Mackey's has long been a stop for ghost hunters and paranormal enthusiasts. The building has a very dark history and a very demonic present, according to those who have both worked at and visited the bar, as well as various teams and individuals who have investigated the paranormal reports coming from within. There is even a sign on the wall warning patrons of the possibility of ghosts, and it tells them that the establishment is not responsible for any hauntings experienced therein.

The legends and lore that are often told about the bar have never been substantiated, and there are those who believe the history of murder, Satanism, and suicide are nothing more than sensational tales and myths that have grown from generations of campfire storytelling. Despite that, there are those who insist that the sinister forces, both past and present, attributed to the place are indeed very real.

The professed tale of Bobby Mackey's begins in 1850 (some versions say late 1840s), when a large slaughterhouse and meatpacking facility was built on the land where the bar now stands. Allegedly, there was a "well" dug below the building where workers would dispose of the blood, viscera, and remains of the slaughtered livestock. This "well" was actually a drain that carried these remains to the nearby Licking River. For whatever reason, the slaughterhouse closed in the 1890s.

But, this did not leave the building abandoned, according to legend. After the slaughterhouse ceased operations, a local group of theist Satanists began gathering in the facility, and they supposedly conducted satanic rituals in the basement, sacrificing small animals (and some claim even children, to further sensationalize the tale) and dumping the remains of the offerings into the old drain.

During this time, a tragedy struck the small town of Fort Thomas, about five miles to the northeast of Wilder, when the headless corpse of a young pregnant woman from Greencastle, Indiana was discovered on John Locke's farm. The day was February 1st, 1896, the woman was named Pearl Bryan, and the tragedy rocked northern Kentucky.

Bryan's body was identified by a Newport shoe store owner, L.D. Poock, who solved the mystery of the body's identity when he took an interest in the boots worn by the victim. They were an uncommon size three. After examining them, he found an imprint of a shoe store in Greencastle, IN inside, along with the manufacturer's lot number. After contacting the manufacturer and giving them the number, they were able to trace the boots back to Pearl Bryan. Her parents indentified the clothing on the corpse as being that of Pearl Bryan's shortly after.

Scott Jackson, who was much older than Bryan, became the prime suspect because he was, at the time, studying dentistry in Cincinnati and many believed the two were having a secret affair. After he was arrested, he confessed that he had arranged for Bryan to come to Cincinnati to have an abortion. Only it wasn't his child. He claimed that it was actually Bryan's second cousin, Will Wood—who had lived next door to Jackson in Greencastle and some had believed to have been having an affair with Bryan, as well—but Wood denied this claim and told the police that it was Jackson who had seduced and impregnated the victim.

While testifying, Jackson admitted to having lain with Bryan, but said she was already pregnant with Wood's child. Wood denied having ever had relations with his cousin, though several witnesses gave testimonies that were quite the opposite, saying that Wood had often bragged about his affair with Bryan. Nonetheless, it was never officially determined who the father actually was.

After being arrested, Jackson told authorities that he had left Bryan in the care of his roommate Alonzo Walling, and that he was to ensure the abortion took place. When Walling was arrested several hours after Jackson, he claimed he had never made the appointment and that Jackson had actually killed the woman. He went on in greater detail that Jackson had confided in him that he was going to lure Pearl to Cincinnati, poison her to death, and then cut her body into pieces and leave them in various vault toilets around the city.

Though each man denied his involvement and tried to pin the murder on the other, a thorough investigation led to a coach driver by the name of George Jackson. His testimony was said to have confirmed many others, and tied the story together. It seems that George, with Walling sitting next to him, drove Walling's carriage across a bridge to Kentucky after being paid ten dollars by Walling. During the drive, he heard the woman moaning in the back and tried to stop the ride. Walling then threatened him with a pistol, so he drove on. Once the journey was complete, George saw another man emerge with the woman, and the two of them, along with Walling, ventured off into the woods. After that, he left the scene on foot.

However, this story has been questioned on several occasions as small details don't match up. Some accounts mixed up the days that Jackson and Walling had been spotted about town with Bryan, some saying Friday while Jackson said it was Tuesday. Others stated that Jackson had a full beard, which he'd been wearing for several months. But, he had claimed that he had shaved it off before the night in question—a claim that was corroborated by both his barber and landlady. This new piece of evidence makes it impossible that he could have been seen about town with a full beard on the night he was with Walling and Bryan.

Many who challenge the story point to the testimony of George Jackson as being the most questionable of all. First off, it didn't make sense that Jackson and Walling, both having been very capable horsemen, would have hired someone else to drive the coach, especially while Walling sat next to him. To do so would do nothing more than create a witness to the men's illicit activities. The driver came forward about two weeks after the murder, but had difficulty identifying Jackson and Walling. To make him seem even less credible, he was convicted of perjury, regarding an unrelated case, in Springfield, Ohio after testifying against Jackson and Walling. It was said that he was known in Springfield as an attention-seeking conman.

In the end both men, despite their insistence that they knew nothing of the murder, were convicted and sentenced to hang on March 20th, 1897. As was the procedure in those days, lawyers sought both men's confessions as a way to justify their executions. But neither admitted guilt, and their stories matched. Not only had Bryan come to Cincinnati for an abortion, but now it seemed a well-known physician had agreed to perform it. A man by the name of Dr. George Wagner from Bellevue, Kentucky had been the man who agreed to carry out the procedure. As the story goes, there were heavy complications and, despite the doctor's best efforts, Bryan died from those complications. To cover the incident up, Wagner severed Bryan's head with a dissecting knife then dropped Jackson and Walling off at the bridge and they all went their separate ways.

This report was validated by Walling's girlfriend, who convinced Dr. Wagner to attempt the abortion. The druggist who was said to have prescribed Wagner ergot for the procedure confirmed that he did indeed fill that prescription. He went on to corroborate a claim of correspondence between Scott Jackson and the doctor's daughter, Maude Wagner. The story involving the prescription changed once he took the stand; he went on to say he never received any prescriptions from Wagner. When it was discovered that he had a feud with Wagner, his entire confession was then in question.

Nonetheless, it led to subpoenas for Wagner's wife and two daughters, but not Wagner himself, since he was committed to the Eastern Kentucky Asylum for the Insane shortly after. Wagner's family, after hearing Jackson's and Walling's confessions, were vexed by these claims and sent telegrams stating that Dr. Wagner was in Nicholasville at his father-in-law's home on the night Bryan was supposed to have been murdered.

When all of the confessions were sent to Governor Bradley, he determined that there were too many holes in the story, and would not overturn the sentence. Scott Jackson and Alonzo Walling were then hanged together on their scheduled execution date of March 20th, 1897.

Pearl Bryan's head was never found and her body was buried without its head. In the course of these accounts, there is no mention of the slaughterhouse, Satanism, or the men's vow to return as spirits and haunt the land. That does not mean that there were not satanic cults in the area using the building for rituals, nor does it necessarily mean these claims about Jackson and Walling were not true, it just means those claims have no supporting evidence. But, if there were anonymous Satanists using the building, it very well could be that some dark energy was unleashed.

Despite the dubious nature of the claim that the two men sacrificed Bryan's head to the Devil (which they did not), it does not mean the land did not experience other tragedies, or that there are no ghosts there. It is believed that there was once a small community nearby called Finchtown, where several illegal lynchings occurred after the Civil War. In June of 1892, a bridge that was being built over the Licking River not far from the property collapsed and killed forty workers.

A well-known distillery in the area, the Old '76 Distillery, caught fire in January of 1907, causing many of the barrels inside to explode, and the inferno spread, burning away a chunk of the town. Prior to this, in 1876, the man who owned the distillery, George Robson, Jr., had three tunnels dug under the distillery. One of these three tunnels is the alleged Gate to Hell people claim exists under the bar. The conflict in this claim is that while the ghost stories of Bobby Mackey's claim this tunnel used to carry waste out to the Licking, it was supposed to have initially pumped water in from the river, instead. Additionally, maps of Finchtown show that the slaughterhouse was actually several hundred feet to the southwest of where Bobby Mackey's is located. It appears that the distillery would have been there and not the slaughterhouse.

When you juxtapose the two stories (the story told today about Bobby Mackey's and the history that has been accounted for), you find that the distillery was in full operation, so there's almost no way Jackson and Walling could have stuck Bryan's head down the "Gate to Hell." Even if they could have, the head would not have gone to the river considering the tunnels flowed into the building as opposed to out towards the Licking River. Nothing about this case ever led investigators to the distillery or the slaughterhouse, according to documented history.

But, there are claims that the building became a roadhouse that turned into a speakeasy in the 1920s, after the "slaughterhouse" was torn down. It is said that the speakeasy would turn rather violent and that many gamblers and gangsters had been killed there. Their bodies were allegedly disposed of, probably in the river. If this is true, then there would be reason to believe angry spirits remain. Many former illegal casinos and speakeasies have been known to house the departed souls of mobsters. So, this claim could stand to reason.

Once prohibition ended, E.A. "Buck" Brady purchased the building and turned it into a legal casino and tavern known as the Primrose. It was quite a successful joint in the 1930s, and that drew the attention of a local crime syndicate known as the Cleveland Four Syndicate. They came to Brady and tried to force him out, even going as far as to put a hit on him. He eventually gave in and sold to them, an act that allegedly caused him to commit suicide. Legend says that he vowed the establishment would never find success as a casino ever again before killing himself in 1965.

In the 40s, it became a dance hall known as the Latin Quarter. The mob still controlled it and illegal operations are said to have persisted. So, there's no telling what might have gone on if this were true. But, there is a story of forbidden love that supposedly transpired sometime during those years, and it led to a tragedy that is believed to have caused some of the ghostly activity encountered at the bar.

In the 1950s, Johanna Jewels, the daughter of the Latin Quarter's owner, who was said to have always worn rose-scented perfume, fell in love with a singer who had performed there by the name of Robert Randall. Johanna became pregnant with Randall's child and intended to runaway with him. Once her father found out about it, he used his criminal connections to have the man killed. Once Johanna found out, she poisoned her father and hanged herself in the basement. At least that is how the story goes. How true it is, we cannot say. There is no record of a Johanna having committed suicide in the basement, but there is a record of a Johanna committing suicide down the road at another location, only her name was Johanna Ragan.

There are no actual records to support most of this story. It came about as a result of a caretaker supposedly finding Johanna's diary in the basement. This diary was said to have told the entire story. When some of the entries were examined, their authenticity was questioned. Combined with the inconsistencies in whether or not Mackey's Johanna was actually the daughter of the night club owner, this story is shaky. One fact to keep in mind is that Bobby Mackey's full name is Robert Randal Mackey.

The police busted the Quarter up in 1955 and removed all the gambling machines. After that, the building changed businesses quite often due to all the violence that happened there through the years. This excessive string of violence earned the building the nickname, the "Bloody Bucket." At one point, someone was able to buy it for one dollar.

In 1973, the place became known as the Hard Rock Café Biker Bar (not affiliated with the popular restaurant franchise). Staying true to the building's history, the bar was known for violence and is reported to have had numerous shootings on the premises. After a triple shooting in 1977, the bar was shut down.

Now, here we see some more questions cast upon the historic accounts about Bobby Mackey's. Again, the stories may not be entirely accurate, but that is not to say there is no truth to them. Not to mention the history of violence in the area. Even if everything doesn't completely add up, that doesn't necessarily mean no paranormal activity exists. So, what is that activity? Apparently, there is quite a bit.

Bobby Mackey bought the joint in 1978 and has run it as Bobby Mackey's Music World ever since. Aside from the country music flowing from the honky tonk, a long list of paranormal encounters has been compiled, as well.

The drain beneath the building is what many have called the Gateway to Hell. It is essentially a semi-covered hole in the floor. Some believe dark spirits arise from this portal to haunt the bar. People have heard deep growling coming from the ragged mouth of the portal. A lot of people refuse to even go near it due to the feeling of dread they develop in its presence. Could this be the gateway from where the spirits come?

Despite all the questionable claims surrounding the Pearl Bryan murder, the entities of Scott Jackson, Alonzo Walling, and Pearl Bryan are all believed to haunt Bobby Mackey's. Mackey's wife will not come in the bar anymore after being picked up, thrown down, and pushed down the stairs by an apparition that looks like sketches of Walling. Witnesses have reported seeing a headless ghost dressed in apparel that matches clothes worn by Pearl Bryan in some of her photos. A psychic who visited there claimed to have seen the angry spirit of Scott Jackson yelling at Pearl Bryan as she clutches her severed head in her hands, sobbing and screaming, "My head!"

A dark spirit has been seen standing behind the bar in the form of a very angry-looking man. This may be the spirit that likes to start fights in the club by poking people and pulling their hair. Due to the history of rough characters frequenting, owning, and working at the place, it is hard to say with certainty who this mischievous ghost could be.

On top of being manhandled by the ghost of Alonzo Walling, another story says that Mackey's wife was picked up and tossed around by Johanna while she was pregnant. As Mackey's wife was leaving the building, she heard a woman's voice angrily yelling, "Get out!" at her.

This isn't the only account of Johanna making an appearance, though. Others claimed to have seen her appear behind Bobby while he is on stage performing. People have reported smelling her rose-scented perfume, as well. She has also been spotted in other places around the bar.

The apparition of a hostile little girl has appeared in the basement and thrown rocks at visitors. A little boy who was murdered by some of the past gangsters has been seen down there, as well. The entity of a man with a handlebar mustache has been seen in the men's bathroom saying "die game" over and over. This is said to be Spanish for "dying well." The sign on the wall about the hauntings was suggested by a lawyer after the spirit of a man in a cowboy hat ripped someone's clothing in the bathroom.

There is a flight of stairs down there close to the portal that have been dubbed the "Stairs to Hell" and have often had phantom footsteps walking up and down them. Other strange occurrences in the building include a flying trashcan, oppressive heat, and an endless pounding along the catwalk after someone dropped a chair nearby.

While a rather loud band was performing, the ghosts allegedly showed their displeasure by throwing various objects at them from the ceiling. During this time, a disembodied female voice was screaming at the band to leave. One of the men in the crowd started getting phantom text messages on his phone, which he later turned over to a paranormal investigation team.

A manager at the club claimed she would make her rounds, ensure all was locked up, and everything was turned off, only to find the bar wide open hours later. The lights would be on, the doors unlocked, and the unplugged juke box would be playing the "Anniversary Waltz."

More sinister incidents have occurred as well, such as investigators being scratched. But, the worst of all happened to former caretaker, Carl Lawson. While at the bar, he was possessed by what he believes was a demonic spirit. An exorcism that was performed on him seemingly cleansed his soul, but the event was quite frightening.

So, it is hard to say what has caused these incidents and reports. Some who have investigated Bobby Mackey's believe that conditions of the building, location, and high EMF readings—along with the legends of the place being haunted—have caused people to believe they have experienced such events. Others think that the long history of violence in the area may have left behind dark forces that are trapped there because they cannot cross the Licking River. No matter what you believe, it does seem there is something strange going on at Bobby Mackey's Music World. Even if the legends of sacrificed heads and Devil-worship aren't likely, too many people have witnessed some unexplainable things for there not to be something worth looking into.

A PERSONAL STORY

J enny has experienced paranormal occurrences most of her life. She grew up with strange things happening in her homes. Her mother Jeanie has also had some spooky moments as well. Once upon a time Jeanie used to work for a rather large antique dealer in Louisville named Joe Ley Antiques. In the twenty years she'd worked there, she had experienced some hard-to-explain events.

The building housing the antique store was built in 1890 and was once the Hiram Roberts Normal School. It stands three stories and has a tunnel running underneath. The room Jeanie worked in had a four-foot candelabrum, and just about every day a candle would fall out of it. Well, so you might say it could have just been faulty, which is a good point. But one day, when a customer came to Jeanie and asked her if the building was haunted, they both watched as the candle lifted from the candelabrum, moved to the side, and fell as if someone picked it up and dropped it. The customer's eyes went wide and she said, "Did you see that?" Jeanie replied that she had indeed and then addressed the spirit by saying, "We know you're here. Would you please not to do that anymore?"

That isn't the only strange incident to occur there. After coming back from a two-week-long winter break, during which no one was in the store, the employees found a bunch of chairs upstairs had been removed from their locations and placed in a circle. No one working there had an explanation for this. But gathering chairs wasn't the only activity the possible spirits liked to do during winter break. Another year, the employees returned to another unexplainable occurrence. One of the rooms upstairs was a sports room, with many sports-related items. Among these items were several basketballs that were kept in a wire basket. This time, when they returned, they found the basketballs had all rolled down the stairs. Again, no one had an explanation for this.

It wasn't only at the antique shop where Jeanie experienced possible paranormal happenings. When Jenny was a child, she and her mother were in the living room of a house they lived in. Jenny's remote control Barbie car was sitting in the room and it began moving back and forth across the room on its own. Jeanie took the batteries out of the car and it still moved back and forth across the room, and continued to do so until Jeanie put it away.

There was also an incident at an apartment during the Christmas season. She and her dog, Tinkerbell, were in the living room while Jeanie was decorating a four-foot Christmas tree. She suddenly had the feeling that something was in there with her. Then, the tree lifted and began shaking, as if someone had picked it up and started rattling it back and forth. She and Tinkerbell looked at each other and Jeanie then said to the spirit, "I'm glad you like my tree."

It's been said before that the paranormal has followed Jenny around her entire life. It looks as though it could have been an inherited trait, as her mother clearly has some ghost tales of her own.

MARY'S BOOKS

The building at 440 Main Street in Bowling Green has hosted a variety of establishments through the years. Built in 1871 for a man named John Getty, the building was used as a dry goods store and shoe store for many of its early decades. A skating rink was constructed up on the third floor in 1930 and still remains intact today. The rink also doubled as a dance hall for the town elite, as well as a practice room for the Southern Norman School basketball team. During World War II, a local USO utilized the first floor as a headquarters. After the war, the Bowling Green Business University called the first level home. In the 1940s, the original Parakeet Café was also at 440 Main. The Western Auto Parts store resided in the building until 1992. As you can see, there has been a variety of people passing through over the decades.

Though a number of businesses were operated from 440 Main, the most famous inhabitant has to be a woman named Mary who lives in a closet – or, should we say, "exists" in a closet. The second floor of the building is an apartment, and there have been reports of some very disturbing activity transpiring up there.

Mary, it seems, loves books, and we can all appreciate that. Legend tells that she had a tragic death of some kind, though none can specifically say what that death was. After her passing, her apartment was cleaned out, all except for a closet that held some of her most cherished books. The books are still there to this day because if anyone tries to move them out, they experience some hostile paranormal activity, such as items being hurled at them from across the room. Apparently, it is not just a one-time incident, either. It seems that until the books are returned to normal, whoever occupies Mary's old apartment will find a lot of their personal belongings shattered as Mary's spirit will continue to fling them about the place.

But, there does seem to be maybe one other way to curb Mary's tantrum. Once her outbursts become too much for the resident, if they yell, "Mary, go read your books!" she will cease her onslaught and remain quiet for a spell. But it will not last forever. So during the temporary ceasefire, it might be best for whoever lives in the apartment to gather Mary's books and place them back in the closet where they belong.

PARAMOUNT JOE

The Paramount Theatre opened in Ashland, Kentucky on September 5th, 1931. Initially, it was intended to show silent movies exclusive to Paramount Studios, but the emergence of talking pictures happened during the three years it took to plan and build the theatre. Ironically enough, the first movie showed at the Paramount was a talking film called *Silent*.

Despite the original plans for it to be a silent film theatre, the Paramount would become a model for the transitioning theatres, as it was among the first to view talkies. Unfortunately, the Great Depression took its toll and Paramount Studios wanted to pull out. An Ashland-based company then bought the building and took control of the project, with Paramount staying partially involved in terms of interior furnishings. Rapp and Rapp—the same company that designed the Chicago Theatre—drew up the Art Deco design. The Paramount Publix Corporation leased the building once the project was complete. Much of the original interior design has been preserved.

Prior to the onset of the Depression, Paramount had planned to build these theatres in every state of the union. Only a few, however, other than Ashland's, were completed: Abilene, Texas; Anderson, Indiana; Aurora, Illinois; Austin, Texas; Bristol, Tennessee; Cedar Rapids, Iowa; Charlottesville, Virginia; Denver, Colorado; Oakland, California; Seattle, Washington; and Springfield, Massachusetts are still operational today. One still stands in Boston but is vacant; the Paramount in Hollywood was restored and renamed El Capitan in 1991. The theatre in Ashland closed in 1971, but was reopened a year later by the Greater Ashland Foundation and used as a community theatre.

During the early days of its construction, the Paramount experienced a tragedy. All of the workers, except for a man named Joe, went on lunch. When they returned, they found Joe hanging by the neck from the rafters—some accounts say he was hanging from the curtain rigging. No one knows if this death was an accident or a suicide, but many believe Joe is still in the building.

People have reported strange and unexplained sounds throughout the theatre, often accompanied by inexplicable cold spots. Various items will be moved and even go missing without anyone knowing how it happened. The apparition of who people believe to be Joe has been seen throughout the Paramount, as well.

Popular opinion of Joe is good. Those who have encountered him insist he is a congenial ghost. Country music star and Kentucky native Billy Ray Cyrus had an incident with Joe when he was there to film the music video for his mega-hit "Achy Breaky Heart." It is said that during filming, Billy Ray was speaking with Joe, joking with him and asking him for help. Once the set was over, Billy Ray gave all the female staff—plus Joe—autographed posters. The ladies hung theirs by their desks and Joe's was hung in the box office alongside the other performers' autographed photos.

Over time, more autographed posters came to adorn the wall, so the staff was asked to remove their Billy Ray posters since they were all identical. None of the staff wanted to take their picture down, so they removed Joe's instead. The next day, the staff came in to find that all other Billy Ray posters had been knocked off the wall, strewn about the area, many with their frames broken. Another version of the story states that all pictures and Billy Ray posters were removed and neatly lined against the walls, with their frames and glass still intact. The latter would make more sense as it is more in line with Joe's gentle nature. Naturally, they believed this was Joe's retaliation for having his poster removed. Now, his poster hangs in a special spot located in Paramount Joe's Rising Star Café.

There is another story about two new employees who were taken to the basement by the marketing director. The path down into the basement is lined with many light switches. After the director turned the light on at the top of the stairs, he had to take a phone call. When he came back from the call, he met the employees as they were coming up. They thanked him for turning on the rest of the lights, but claimed they could not get the lights to turn back off. A confused director then informed them that he did not turn the other lights on for them. When they led him down into the basement to see what was going on, they were met by complete darkness.

Paramount Joe surely seems to enjoy his time at the Paramount Arts Center. If he's simply stuck there, at least he is making the most of it. He even got to make an impression on a celebrity in the process. Sounds like Joe really knows how to live it up.

WASHINGTON OPERA HOUSE

Washington, Kentucky is alleged to be the sight of the first stage performance west of the Allegheny Mountains, with records showing that a performance was held there in the very early 1800s at the Washington Court House. By 1817, a theater was erected in Maysville, not far from Washington and just across the river from Cincinnati, on the corner of Second and Fish Street, now known as Wall Street. In 1850, a fire raged across Second Street, razing most buildings to the ground, including the theatre and the Presbyterian Church. The congregation found a new home over on Third Street and the opera house was built on their old lot. In 1898, another fire hit Second Street and took this opera house down as well. That's when the current two-story brick building was built. Now, for more than a century, the Washington Opera House has brought fine arts and films to the people of Maysville and provided a place for the town to gather for community events.

Maysville is the home of George Clooney's father Nick Clooney and aunt Rosemary Clooney. The Washington Opera House has always held a special place in the hearts of the Clooney family. On March 24, 2008, along with Renee Zellweger, George went to Maysville and premiered his film *Leatherheads* at the opera house.

But it wasn't just the Clooneys that loved the Washington Opera House. The entire town of Maysville has always embraced their performing arts. Over the years, many performances of both stage and film have been shown there. As a result, many patrons and performers have passed through the building. It is believed that a number of spirits remain there, and even though most are unknown, they all leave an impression.

One ghost is thought to be that of Loretta Stambo, a former singer and dancer in a performance group that would stop in

Maysville once a year in the late 1800s. It is said that the Washington Opera House was Loretta's favorite place to dance. So, one night, even though she had pneumonia, she got on stage and attempted to dance her part. Before she could finish, she collapsed and had to be taken to her hotel room. Later that evening, Loretta passed away. Allegedly, her dying wish was to be buried in a dressing room located directly under the stage. Rumor has it that her wish was granted, but no proof exists. The second fire happened shortly after, and if there had been a grave marker, it most likely burned.

Many believe Loretta is present in the opera house. A few decades back, an actor left a glass cola bottle sitting on Loretta's grave and the bottle jumped up and shattered in the air. To honor Loretta, there was a mural of her painted on the wall in the lobby. Some felt the eyes in the painting looked out at them with feeling, watching them as they passed. Those who made this eerie eye contact with the picture left the opera house feeling a tad uneasy. The picture began to make so many people feel uncomfortable that staff finally painted over it. However, the paint later faded and the picture came through once again, with Loretta's eyes appearing angry. It is said that the picture was painted over a few more times, but each time the mural would bleed back through and Loretta's eyes would look angrier each time. They finally managed to paint over it for good...so they are hoping.

It seems the dancer's ghost is looking out for the opera house, too. Allegedly, a group of investors had visited the Washington Opera House to consider purchasing it. As they were discussing possible projects, they brought up the idea of tearing the building down and constructing something else in its place. This did not sit well with Loretta it would seem, as just seconds later, a light fixture had fallen from the ceiling and nearly landed on the investors.

Loretta doesn't mind helping people in the theater. A woman who was setting up some scenery asked her co-worker to hand her a piece of wood. Without warning, the piece of wood she needed began to slowly float down from the ceiling and land softly within her reach. After picking the wood up, the woman thanked Loretta for her assistance.

During a dress rehearsal, a wooden beam tied to a tier above one of the actresses came loose and began to fall. However, it slowed down in midair, as if being caught by invisible hands, and floated safely to the floor. The performers were unsure if it was Loretta alone who did this, but thought it could have been a combination of the many spirits who watch over the opera house.

It also seems that at least one of the spirits in there is a joker. As two workers there were closing up one night around midnight, they both got a bit of a scare as they passed through the stage area. There, dangling in the middle of the room was a long rope, not tied to any beams or rafters – it just hung there, as if someone were holding it in place. As the two workers approached the rope to investigate, they say the air around it became extremely cold.

Other scary incidents include disembodied voices saying people's names, footsteps walking across the stage, loud bangs at the far end of the auditorium, doors opening and closing on their own, and a misty apparition that drifts across the stage. These occurrences have become so frequent that most just take them as part of the daily fabric there in the Washington Opera House.

In truth, there is no record of Loretta Stambo even existing, at least none that ever visited or died in that area. The story about the painting is also unproven. No trace of that painting exists, so it could have been a completely fabricated tale. But with the long history, all the human energy passing through there over the years, and the fires, there's no telling what could be attached to the Washington Opera House.

Whether or not Loretta is a lone spirit in the opera house, it seems there is at least one entity there who likes to keep watch and play pranks. Even in death, you can't take the performer off stage.

EASTBROOK STATION APARTMENTS

It's not unusual to hear of someone's apartment being haunted. Apartments see many people over the years, and people die in them, tragedies happen, a lot of emotional energy could be left behind, so it should seem natural to anyone who believes in the paranormal that some form of haunt would remain in an apartment unit from time to time. But the thing about Eastbrook Station in Harlan is that the ghosts pop up all over the complex.

When we heard an entire apartment complex in Harlan was haunted, we were a little surprised and a lot interested. We already knew Harlan County was among the most haunted places in Kentucky, likely second only to Louisville, but hearing an entire apartment complex is haunted is the kind of topic we seek out. But we thought this would be some abandoned housing project or a compound so old that it was chalk full of town history. Well, it's not exactly that, but it is rather old, and it's not a full complex, but a high rise apartment building with years of memories.

We weren't able to get any legend or folkloric stories about Eastbrook Station, other than there had been people who lived there their entire lives, and even generations of people living in the building, but we did hear of some interesting paranormal incidents several different residents had.

In one apartment on one of the upper floors, there is a spirit that likes to knock on the walls. Those who have lived there have experienced strange rapping on the walls at night, taps that seem to travel along the wall. One man thought he had mice in the wall but realized no one else had any rodent problems. Thinking that whatever it was might go away eventually, he went about his business. But the noise never stopped. It kept going on randomly for years. Knocks on doors, in different rooms, and even on the ceiling would startle him at different points of the day. He moved out eventually, but never found out what was knocking on his walls.

On either the second or third floor, there is a voice that often cries for help in the hallways. This voice has been heard by a few different residents over the years. It most often happens late in the night, or very early in the morning before sunrise. Most have described it as a little girl's voice, while some said it sounded simply like a child. But the voice will cry up and down the hall for help, sometimes louder than others. But when people step into the hall to see who is calling out, no one is there. Is it a ghost, or someone playing a prank?

One resident had issues with hearing girls talking in their bathroom. The voices of two young girls could be heard talking about putting on makeup from time to time, even though no young lady's lived in the unit. It seems it was a harmless haunt, probably residual, or perhaps people in another unit.

On the first floor, there is a pesky spirit that likes to roam the halls banging on doors in the middle of the night. Most of the time, the paranormal prankster only hits three or four units, but there have been times when nearly every door along the floor experienced the banging. Naturally, no one has ever been caught doing this. Though it's quite possible this is a master mischief maker, most believe someone's playful—and annoying—ghost travels the hallway waking people up.

The top floor holds probably the creepiest haunt of them all. A couple once living up there said they had trouble with faces appearing in their unit. Not just normal, everyday human faces, but twisted, deformed, and even demonic faces. The first one was noticed as a mysterious stain on the wall. It was described as beastly, like an angry dog. It took some elbow grease, but they were eventually able to erase the face from the wall. The next one they saw appeared in the steam on a bathroom mirror. This time, they say it was an elongated face with large ears and lidless eyes. The woman saw it and showed it to her husband, who immediately wiped it away. Another face soon appeared on a window. They said it looked mostly average, only its mouth was wide open, as if in a scream. This one seemed to appear in condensation. The final straw came when they saw a face take shape from out of nowhere on their bedroom wall. They said it looked as though it looked right at them, had a pointed chin and a devilish grin. They called a priest and asked him to bless the unit. He did and the faces never came back.

These are some very interesting accounts from this building. Who knows what is causing all this. Perhaps the knocking is a problem with pipes or ventilation. The person crying for help could just be someone in another unit. As we said, the young lady's talking could actually be coming from another unit, and the resident just happened to hear it. The banging on the doors could be a prankster living on that floor. The creepy faces could be nothing more than pareidolia, even though we don't always like that explanation, it seems to fit here. But one never knows – there very well could be some strong spooky energy roaming Eastbrook Station.

JACOB FLOYD & JENNY FLOYD

IMMACULATE CONCEPTION CHURCH

A Catholic presence in the Kentucky counties of Bracken, Campbell, and Pendleton dates back to the 1840s. Irish, German, French, Swiss, and Bavarian immigrants had moved into the area near the mouth of Stepstone Creek, then known as Motier – the town would later become Carntown. Since there was no organized congregation or building to host religious gatherings, the children of these immigrants were baptized at the Church of the Trinity in Cincinnati, OH in the late 1840s. Mass was often held in the homes of the families until a log-structure church was erected in the 1850s and named the Immaculate Conception Church. The building that exists now was built in 1861. During the early 20th century, the congregation dwindled, as many began to go to Sts. Peter and Paul Church. The last wedding was held in the Immaculate Conception Church in 1941 and it eventually became that the only services held there were funeral services, which it is still occasionally used for, as well as Mass of the Feast of the Immaculate Conception during the warmer months, since there is no electricity or heating in the old building. The church and graveyard are both registered historic landmarks.

Along with that history comes a dark urban legend. According to local lore, a man hanged four teenage girls from a cross in the loft and then attempted to set the church on fire. What possessed the man to do such a thing the story does not say. But it is believed now that the four young girls haunt the place, and their screams and cries can sometimes be heard in the night by people passing by. The echo of sinister male laughter can also sometimes be heard. Witnesses also report seeing shadows flying around near the top inside the church.

We could find no records or accounts of these alleged deaths, nor of any murders in the area that would align with this tale. The tale of the murders is lore, even if people have reported paranormal activity within the church. It is possible the ghostly accounts have merit, but it is also possible this whole story is nothing more than a creepy tale about an abandoned old church.

ROHS OPERA HOUSE

The Rohs Opera House in Cynthiana is considered one of the most haunted locations in the state, behind Waverly and Bobby Mackey's, though outside of those two notoriously haunted locations, there are many places that lay claim to that distinction. While it is debatable as to whether or not Rohs is more haunted than anywhere else in the Bluegrass State, it is certainly a location with a lot of reported paranormal activity.

The building, located in downtown Cynthiana, twenty-miles north of Lexington, went up in 1871 as a live production theatre known as Aeolian Hall. In 1941, H.A. Rohs and his son Karle added the Rohs Opera House. Eventually, it was turned into a movie theatre, which it still is today. They also allow paranormal investigations due to the haunted reputation the building has gained over the years.

The most well-known spirit is a full-bodied apparition of a woman in a long, flowing white gown known as the White Lady. She is most often spotted walking around the second floor, hanging out near the balcony doors at the end of the hall. It seems no one knows who she might be, but many people have spotted her at and near that area.

The spirits of two children are said to run and play through the theatre in various locations. People have heard these kids laughing and talking, banging on things and running down aisles when no children were around. Though, like the White Lady, their identities are unknown, they have been heard numerous times.

The Angry Man is another ghost people have encountered. His loud hostile voice has been heard in corridors and corners, and even supposedly caught on EVPs. People have experienced hard tugs on their hair only to turn around and find no one there. It is believed this is the work of the Angry Man.

It seems as though there are a few ghosts hanging about the Rohs Opera House. We don't know if it's the third most haunted place in Kentucky, but it certainly sounds like it has some hard-to-explain occurrences. For the price of a ticket, you might get more than you bargained for.

C.C. COHEN BUILDING

The C.C. Cohen Building in Paducah has housed several different businesses. Built sometime around 1865, it has been used as various stores, a distilling company, and a few restaurants, including the most recent (as of this writing) called Shandies. But it wasn't always a commercial building. Actually, for quite some time it was a residential location.

From 1921 to 1980, the Cohen family resided in the building. The last member of the family to live there was a woman by the name of Stella Cohen Peine. After her husband was murdered in a nearby alley, Stella lived alone in the area just above the restaurant, her only companions being her two Doberman Pinschers. When Stella passed away in the building in 1980, she lay dead there for several days. Rumor has it that her dogs, having gone so long without food, started eating her corpse. Apparently, when the authorities finally discovered her body, it was a rather gruesome scene, and one of the responders rushed from the building sickened by the sight.

Since then, it is believed that Stella's presence has been keeping watch over the building. When the building changed ownership sometime in the 1990s, the strange activity began when the renovations started. Equipment that was not damaged or even that old would inexplicably stop working in the building, only to work somewhere else. Workers would discover that their tools were moved or missing altogether. Many of them often had the eerie sensation that someone was watching them.

Once the renovations were over, the ghostly activity did not stop. In the restaurants, chairs will suddenly fall over on their own, or be balanced on their back legs. Salt and peppershakers move on their own and have been seen falling from tables and found across the room. Glasses mysteriously fall off the bar. Blurry images have been seen reflected in mirrors and brass. Upstairs, lights will flicker, lamps and signs will often be found mysteriously unplugged, and cold spots have been known to dominate the rooms.

People passing by or standing outside the restaurant have reported seeing a pale, grayish woman in a window of the storage room on the second floor peering down at the street below. Some have even captured her image in photographs. Whenever she has been mentioned to employees at the building, none can account for who she is and most just believe her to be Stella keeping watch over the building.

Apparently, the Parlor on the second floor has been made into a recreation of the Cohen sisters' old bedroom and their picture still hangs in the room. Some evidence gathered by paranormal investigators leads some to believe that Stella's sister Goldie remains there as well. EVPs of multiple female voices have been captured, as well as images of a woman that looks more like Goldie than it does Stella.

There is still speculation about the nature of the strange incidents taking place at the building. Maybe time will tell which sister, if not both, remains there. Until then, enjoy the fine dining at the restaurant.

JAILHOUSE PIZZA

The rustic old pizza joint in Brandenburg, Kentucky that sits atop a hill overlooking the Ohio River was once the Meade County Jail. It was built in 1906 and ceased operations in the 70s. At one point, Hank Williams, Sr. spent some time in the jail.

The facility still remains in practically the same condition it was then, save for a little wear and tear. There is even an old deteriorated police car parked out front for show. Only now it is Jailhouse Pizza and is said to harbor some spirits somewhere in the cellblock.

As was the case often back in those days, this jail was built in close proximity to the courthouse to make it easier to convey the prisoners back and forth. This is also the reason that there is a gallows area with Plexiglas where the trap door used to be. Needless to say, many men met their last days in that jail.

Stories circulate that apparitions of those put to death there still roam the grounds, most often the cellblock. In particular is a former inmate by the name of Bigsby. Old Bigsby has been seen walking the cellblock, making noises, thumping along the floor, and making sounds on the iron cells. Bigsby's origin is mysterious, but it seems his ghost is not.

When we visited, we didn't see anything. But, there is a definitely a strange feeling when you stand on the gallows. A coldness, both physical and spiritual, seemed to settle into Jacob when he stood on the Plexiglas. He could almost feel something pulling at him. He got dizzy and felt peculiar. Jenny felt it, too. It was like a sadness pervading the area. When he stepped off, the feelings left. When he crossed over it once again, they returned. Jacob's not one given to sensationalism, and the fact that men had died there does not bother him. Perhaps it was just the novelty of standing on a gallows with only Plexiglas between him and the bottom floor, though that didn't really bother him, either. The sheet is pretty sturdy and the drop is not that far. Nonetheless, we can't rule it out. But, we also can't rule out the possibility of spiritual energy hovering there, especially since ghosts have been reported in the vicinity numerous times.

Jailhouse Pizza is a really cool place of historical significance. We recommend anyone in the Brandenburg area making a stop there to look around. They're pretty open to the paranormal topics, as they offer ghost hunts for a fee. That might be something you fellow paranormal enthusiasts should check out.

THE SHAKERS OF PLEASANT HILL

Led by a woman named Mother Anne Lee, the United Society of Believers in Christ's Second Appearing formed out of the Quakers (also known as the Society of Friends) and the French Camisards in England in 1747. Quakers believed that church was not necessary to worship God, as God lived in the individual, and their form of worship included violent trembling, which earned them the name, "Quaker." That style of worship changed however in the 1740s, all except for one sect who still adhered to the shaking and quaking fashion used to express your oneness with the Almighty. They were called the "Shaking Quakers," and split from the new brand of Quakerism.

Shakers lived communally, sharing everything equally. They believed in gender and race equality and encouraged intellectualism and artistic expression within their rural culture, even though they championed austerity. They remained celibate, prohibiting procreation, and relied on adopting and conversion to grow their community. They even purchased slaves, then freed them and welcomed them into their community.

Shaker villages relied on a number of businesses—such as farming, furnishing, basket-making, and architecture—as a way to grow. Utilitarianism was the method by which they lived, worked, and worshipped. Their products were workaday and practical, built only for functional purposes. Their daily lives were without decorations. Their worship services were very pragmatic, uncluttered, and straightforward.

The Shakers remained segregated from society, as they believed it to be filled with corruption. Upon reaching the age of 21, anyone adopted into the Shakers was given the choice to leave. Outsiders, referred to by the Shakers as "People from the World," were allowed to have contact with them. One man in particular who was permitted to observe their culture and practices was author Nathaniel Hawthorne.

There were nineteen communities total in the United States, between Kentucky, Ohio, and the northeast. The third largest Shaker village in the United States sat atop Pleasant Hill, southeast of Lexington. Pleasant Hill was settled by three missionaries and grew to about 500 people. Goods which came from Pleasant Hill were reputed to be among the best of Shaker quality, and sold for as much as a third more than the items from many other Shaker settlements. Pleasant Hill was also known for its robust livestock and innovative engineering. It was a strong community until the end of the 19th century when the membership began to dwindle. By 1910, Pleasant Hill was disbanded.

Thanks to a renewed interest in the Shaker lifestyle, people began to take notice of Pleasant Hill again after many decades. This led to a preservation effort visited upon the village. Today, thirty-four of the original buildings still remain, and you can visit the farm, the historic centre, the stable, the preserve, and the river. You can even stay overnight at this historic settlement and enjoy the 3,000-plus acres it covers.

The Shakers were at the forefront of the Spiritual Movement of the early to mid 1800s. It was believed by many that Mother Anne possessed spiritual powers, such as the ability to heal with her hands, receive visions, and read prophecies. It was said that the power of God resided in her touch, and these traditions were carried into their style of worship. From 1837 to sometime in the 1850s, the Shakers were in what came to be known as the Era of Manifestation, when they believed they received visions from the souls of the deceased. They expressed their otherworldly experiences in song and dance.

With that kind of spirituality, it's no wonder visitors and employees alike have reported that the peaceful spirits of the Shakers remain at the village. For years, people have experienced many unexplained phenomena, which is not surprising. Shakers believed that all spirits remained on Earth until the Day of Judgment, so it should come as no surprise that they may still be drifting about Pleasant Hill.

Visitors and staff have reported seeing Shakers walking the streets, the fields, and through the restored buildings around

Pleasant Hill. Many have thought them to be re-enactors at first glance, and were surprised to find that no re-enactors were there that day. One woman woke in the morning to a knock on the door, followed by the turning of a key in the lock. The door came open and a woman in full Shaker attire entered the room with some towels and set them down. After the Shaker woman left, the guest later found that a towel she had previously used to wipe off her makeup had been replaced by a clean one. When she spoke of the incident to a staff member later, she was informed that only the re-enactors wear Shaker clothing.

A former re-enactor by the name of Thomas Freese wrote a book about his unexplained experiences around Kentucky's famous Shakertown called *Shaker Ghost Stories from Pleasant Hill, Kentucky*. In it, he discusses the Meeting House, where residual sounds of singing and clapping have been heard by many. It seems Freese had entered the house with another re-enactor, and while she had gone upstairs, Freese stayed downstairs and began singing. During his song, a human form materialized on one of the benches from out of nowhere. This frightened Freese into leaving the house. Later, he found out that the song he was singing was a tune used to call meetings.

Guess someone heard his call.

THE HIESTAND HOUSE

The Hiestand House is a stone cottage built in 1823 on the Hiestand family plantation in Campbellsville, Kentucky. Jacob Hiestand was born in York County, Pennsylvania, and his wife, Eve Landis, was born in Botetourt County, Virginia. They moved to Kentucky from Highland County in Ohio around 1816. The plantation expanded to over a thousand acres, including several barns and outbuildings, a servant quarters, a spring house, meat house, schoolhouse, and distillery. With its Scot-Irish floor plan and traditional German colors, the house is considered to be among the best examples of homes during the Kentucky settlement period.

Hiestand ran a tannery in Campbellsville and though he was raised as a pacifist, he joined the 99th Regiment of the Kentucky Militia and became a colonel. After building the stone cottage, he sold the tannery business and became a distiller. He and Eve had ten children. Three sons became physicians; another became a sheriff of the county.

Their daughter, Araminta, married Senator Joseph H. Chandler and inherited the home in 1849. They were living in the house when John Hunt Morgan's army raided it on July 4th, 1863 during the Great Raid. Joseph was a Union Democrat and Kentucky State Representative who often spoke of rallies in support of the Union. On the day of the raid, he was scheduled to be on the courthouse lawn for a speech by Congressman Aaron Harding. But John Hunt Morgan and his raiders rode into town from the south, following their defeat at the Battle of Tebbs Bend at Green River. They came in search of food for themselves and their horses and rode through Chandler's fields, destroying cornstalks and wheat. They robbed the corn crib and stopped at the house in hopes that Araminta would cook their dinner. Araminta refused, and since she was home alone with her children, she stood in the doorway with a rifle and warned the cavalry men that any who dared to invade her home would be shot. The raiders decided not to test the woman's resolve and moved on. There is a marker nearby telling of this historic moment. The Chandlers remained in the house until 1873, and over the next hundred years that followed it was owned by the Gilmore family.

Another son, Josiah, settled a town in Grayson County, Texas in 1851, called Annaliza—after his daughter, Ann Eliza—but those who lived there decided to start calling it Kentuckians' Town, or Kentucky Town, and the name stuck. As the railroads were built in the late 1800s, none were laid to pass Kentucky Town, and the small community slowly died. In 1883, all that remained was a store and a post office; the post office closed in the 1920s. Today, the population of Kentucky Town is about twenty people and all that remain are the Kentucky Town Baptist Church, its cemetery, and a few crumbling homes.

The Hiestand House faced demolition in 1988 when the Green River Plaza was in development. But it and the family plot were saved by relocating about a half-mile north to where it and the graveyard are now. But despite the move, it seems the spirits of the Hiestand family remain in the home. Accounts of paranormal encounters have occurred in both the house and graveyard over the last few decades.

The building is a museum now, but it is said that one family who moved in beforehand, long after the home had been abandoned, left the home after seeing apparitions of the Hiestand family. Obviously, this would not have been the Gilmores, for they remained there for a century or more, but a family that would have taken up residence after the Gilmores left the property. But, it is believed that the ghost of James I. Gilmore can be seen wandering about the Hiestand Chandler-Gilmore cemetery at night. It is believed to be Mr. Gilmore because he has supposedly vanished after stopping at the grave of James Gilmore. People also believe that Araminta walks the graveyard at night, checking up on the plots of her husband and sons.

Ghostly footsteps have been reported numerous times. But, the most peculiar of the paranormal activity revolves around the oil lamps in the home. People have seen these lamps ignite on their own, burn for a short while, and then flicker out.

Though the cottage is small, it carries a large history with it. If you want to hear more about that history, you can contact them and reserve a tour. Admission is only three dollars. You might as well check it out, but we don't know if they talk about the ghosts.

HILLVIEW LAUNDROMAT

The Hillview Laundromat is located in a shopping center at the edge of the small town of Hillview. The Laundromat has been in operation since before we were born. Now, there are no ghost stories we ever heard about the place, and we don't know much about its history. All we know is it's been there for a long time and Jacob had a weird experience there once.

When you walk into the Laundromat, there is a seating area to the left and the washers make up two rows straight ahead and to the left. To the right, the wall is lined with dryers. All the way in the back is a bathroom. One time, we were doing our laundry there and Jacob walked in to put the clothes in the dryer. No one else was in there at the time. The bathroom door, which had been open, slammed shut. Thinking he had been in there alone, Jacob walked back to the bathroom and knocked on the door. There was no answer, so he opened the door to find no one in there. When he went back to putting the clothes in the dryer, he heard a scraping sound like a chair over by the washers had moved, then one of the dryer doors a few spots down from him popped open. He finished putting the clothes in the dryer and left.

That was the only occurrence he had there, and Jenny never experienced anything. We've never dug around and asked any questions about the place and have decided to just leave it be. But we thought it might be a fun little incident to share in this book.

MR. GATTI'S PIZZA IN MOREHEAD

Other than Morehead State University being haunted, it also seems Mr. Gatti's Pizza across the street has its resident specter as well. They call him Carl, and those who have experienced him believe he is the ghost of a man who once lived in that building.

The legend says that several decades back, the building was once a saloon with apartments above it. Carl was one of the residents in the apartments. Carl took up an affair with a married woman who was trying to hide her unfaithfulness from her husband. She didn't do a very good job, however, as her husband found out and, in a jealous rage, stormed into the apartment and shot Carl in the head, killing him instantly.

Now, employees and customers at Mr. Gatti's have had some very chilling experiences while in the building. Workers have reported seeing apparitions moving around the store after close. Strange noises and disembodied voices have been heard coming from the manager's office. Also, employees have gone into the game room long after the final customer has moved on and found that some of the games hand been recently played. Could Carl be a gamer by nature?

CHEYENNE

Located on US-421, the building that houses Cardinal Financial Services, Inc. is alleged to be haunted by a noisy spirit named Cheyenne. Cheyenne isn't mischievous, but neither is she shy about her presence. Cheyenne exists there as if she is carrying on her everyday life, unperturbed by the presence of the living. It is said there have been many encounters with the brazen specter by several people.

Whenever someone hears the unexplained jangling of keys, they know Cheyenne is near. She will also open and close doors as if she is merely passing from one room to the next, sometimes flicking lights off on her way out. She has also been heard humming in the hallways. Whenever items mysteriously end up in places they were not left, most just attribute this to Cheyenne moving things around.

The ghost woman doesn't completely ignore her living building mates. People have reported feeling her presence coming up behind them, as if a living person was standing at their back. People have reported feeling her breathing on their necks, as well. Whenever they turn around, no one is there.

We couldn't find out who Cheyenne is. We don't know if she is a former employee, someone else who used to frequent the location, or someone attached to the land itself. We're not even sure why she is called "Cheyenne." Whoever she is, she is not afraid to let people know she's haunting the halls around them.

HAZARD APPALACHIAN REGIONAL
HEALTHCARE BUILDING

The Hazard ARH is a pretty normal place by day. Workers are there milling about, patients coming and going; nothing out of the ordinary seems to occur. But according to staff, once night comes, strange things begin to happen.

Workers there throughout the years have openly discussed having paranormal encounters when the building has gone mostly quiet. Rolling tables have moved on their own, people have watched items move from one end of a desk or table to the other, chairs have been mysteriously overturned, and footsteps have been heard walking down empty hallways.

One man who had worked there for fifteen years said he experienced a number of creepy incidents. Among them was a time he was in his office, which wasn't that far from the stairwell, and he heard footsteps coming up the steps. Thinking he was alone in the building, he got up from his desk and headed towards the door to see who was coming. Before he made it to the hall, he heard the heavy door to the stairwell slam shut. Assuming the maintenance crew was still working in the building, he returned to his desk to resume his work. The next day, however, he found out the maintenance crew had the night off and he had been alone in the building.

Another former employee saw someone nobody else had seen. A man standing near the elevator looked at her when she looked his way, nodded his head, and then boarded the elevator. She turned away briefly, then looked back and he was not there. You say he got on the elevator, correct? Well, he shouldn't have, not if he was a living human being, because the elevator hadn't worked in more than two decades and the door didn't open.

Apparently, there are a lot of other incidents involving disembodied voices, doors opening and closing, lights turning on

238

and off – all the usual ingredients in haunted locations. No one knows for certain who these spirits are, but they have no doubt that they are there.

THE LITTLE GIRL ON MAIN STREET, LA GRANGE

Historic Main Street in La Grange consists of a few commercial row buildings standing on each side of the CSX Transportation Mainline that runs right through the heart of town. The city itself was settled in 1827 when the Oldham County seat moved there from Westport and was named after the French country estate belonging to the Marquis de Lafayette, who had visited the area just three years earlier. The county seat returned to Westport in 1828, but returned to La Grange in 1838, and the town was officially incorporated by the state legislature in January of 1840.

The buildings along Main Street consist mostly of small shops and eateries, all of which have a perfect view of the train as it passes through. It also seems that these buildings consist of lingering spirits, as well. There are tales told of many buildings along Main Street being haunted. In fact, these stories can be heard on the Spirits of La Grange Ghost Tour that takes place during the fall each year.

Among the many haunted locations, there is 117 East Main, which has been several businesses since being built. As we write this, it is a Latin cuisine restaurant known as the Mayan. Prior to that, it was the Rails Restaurant, and the Irish Rover Too before that. If you go even further back than that, there is a legend of an eight-year-old girl named Jennie who allegedly died of typhoid fever in that building in the 1800s. The accuracy of this story we cannot confirm, because a property records site we visited lists this building as being built in 1910, though we do not know the reliability of this site. Seeing as the nearby city of Louisville had many disease outbreaks, including typhoid, cholera, influenza, and tuberculosis, throughout the late 1800s and early 1900s, it is not difficult to believe a young girl died in that building from one of these diseases that proved so fatal in those times.

This young girl, who appears in a white dress with a bow in her hair, is said to be the mischievous sort—not dangerous, but the type who likes to pester the staff and play little jokes. One night, after a cook had locked up for the night, he was getting in his car and saw the little girl peering out at him from a window out back. Wondering how this odd little girl got into the building, he went back in to tell her to leave. After searching the entire restaurant, he did not find her anywhere.

The back room of the restaurant seems to be her favorite, as she has often been spotted hiding in there and seen looking out the window. She has also been heard laughing, running, and carrying on in there. Staff members have claimed items seem to mysteriously vanish and somehow move on their own in that room. Maybe this was her old room, or perhaps the room she died in.

Waiters who have returned to open in the mornings after closing the night before have found the chairs they had left stacked on the table pulled down. Dishes that had been put up or left to dry have been found sitting on counters and tables. Waiters and cooks have also reported feeling hands touch them, tugging on their cloths, and even pushing them lightly.

Jennie's presence does not seem to be confined to 117 East Main, however. Her pale apparition has been spotted playing with her toys in the parking areas. She has been seen out front of the building, frolicking about, smiling to herself.

If Jennie does remain behind, it could be due to a discovery made by some workers during renovations. As they were moving stuff around, changing the interior décor, they found some very old toys tucked away in spots that were previously inaccessible. It seems like Jennie just likes to play.

The ghost has been called Typhoid Jennie, but we prefer to just call her Jennie. It sounds to us like she's an exuberant spirit still full of life who just wants to spend her time in limbo playing with her dolls.

EARLE C. CLEMENTS JOB CORPS CENTER

Camp Breckenridge was a WWII infantry camp and prisoner-of-war camp built in 1942 and located near Morganfield. It was named after General John C. Breckinridge of the Confederate Army, former Kentucky Senator, and the youngest Vice President in American history, at the age of thirty-six.

At one time, more than 40,000 soldiers stayed there as they prepared themselves for war. There was also about 3000 German POWs held there prior to the camp's deactivation around 1949. After some renovations, the old camp became the Breckenridge Job Corps Center in 1965. In 1980, it was renamed the Earle C. Clements Job Corps Center after Kentucky politician Earle Clements, who was born in Morganfield.

There are some wild tales about men supposedly being killed in the camp, by falling on a live grenade, by being disemboweled after sneaking off to see a girlfriend (don't know how that happened), or by murder. There is no proof of any of these accounts, but having been a POW camp as well, it's not hard to imagine some bad energy hanging around there.

Although we couldn't find any detailed information regarding the alleged deaths, we did find out about some interesting paranormal encounters that have been reported at the facility. Some students there have waked in the middle of the night to find men in green Army suits standing over their bed. Others have been roused by the sound of the men moving through the room, only to look around and see them hovering over someone else's bed. It is said these men don't do anything other than stare at the person in bed, but that's unsettling enough.

One student reported choking in their sleep, and when they woke up they felt pressure around their neck as if someone were strangling them. They tried to move but something kept their head down. The force around their neck began to squeeze tighter, blocking any air from their lungs. The student struggled to break free from the unseen assailant for several seconds but to no avail. They thought they were going to die, but as suddenly as it started, the pressure was gone and they were able to breathe again. Could it have been a dark or angry entity attacking the student? Could it have been a former guard at the POW camp just doing what he knew to do? Or, maybe it was just an odd occurrence or some health condition that caused this. Well, the latter explanation might be easier to accept if other students hadn't reported similar experiences. More than one has claimed to feel unseen fingers pressing at their throat, closing it off from oxygen while they tried to sleep. It leaves one guessing if there was once a man there who used to go about strangling the POWs.

That is not the only physicality felt from the supposed ghosts. Although nothing else is as severe as the nighttime strangler, others have reported feeling a hand clamp down on their shoulder, or a light touch going down their arm. This experience has actually caused people to turn and look behind them, expecting someone to be there, but finding no one. The touch, they say, feels so real that they were sure it had to be someone. But the emptiness that they find behind them speaks to the possibility of paranormal activity.

The other typical activities also occur at the center: cold drafts from nowhere, disembodied footsteps, lights flickering, doors opening and closing. What haunted location would be complete without any of those? However, there is one more claim to talk about.

There are those who have said they've seen the ghost of General Breckinridge walking the grounds. He passes through doors, travels down hallways, and wanders through rooms. Some have seen him standing in different locations looking out windows. He never acknowledges anyone, just goes about his business. If these accounts are accurate, it would seem the general is a residual residence there.

LEESTOWN DIVISION VA HOSPITAL

L exington, much like Louisville, is known for having its haunts. In our book, *Kentucky's Haunted Mansions,* we discuss four of the historic Lexington homes purported to be haunted: Ashland Estate, the Loudoun House, the Hunt-Morgan House, and the Mansion at Griffin Gate. But, the haunts don't stop there. There are a few other places around the city of thoroughbreds known to be haunted, and one of them is the Leestown Division VA Hospital.

Made up of several different buildings spread across 135 acres of dense wooded area, the center opened in 1931 just one year after President Franklin D. Roosevelt created the Department of Veterans Affairs. The Main Building is a multi-bay revivalist structure that stands four stories high and sits atop a raised basement. The design is symmetrical, and at the center is the three-bay projecting pavilion. On top of that pavilion is the oculus overlooking the entire grounds, supported by four pilasters beneath a pediment.

In 1934, the facility transitioned into a neuropsychiatric hospital for veterans. This led to the creation of a miniature golf course, softball field, and horseshoe pits on the campus. The wood and brick cupola that was once above the pediment was removed completely in 1950 after having been severely damaged by two lightning strikes. This building is one of the eleven original buildings erected on the campus. Once construction ceased in 1950, there stood forty-one buildings total, and the monumental Main remains the most decorative.

The hospital has been the site of some very frightening occurrences through the years. Phantom moans and screams coming from empty rooms and hallways have frightened visitors and occupants. Numerous apparitions have been spotted wandering the halls day and night, sometimes lingering in doorways before vanishing entirely. Doors have slammed shut on their own right in front of people, and the loud thuds have been heard reverberating down the halls when no one was around the have closed the door. The unnerving clacking of disembodied footsteps tapping along the corridors when no one is there has sent chills up the spines of many witnesses. Electronics in the hospital frequently malfunction for no known reason, and are often physically turned off and on when no one is near them. It is also said that the power in some of the older buildings goes off completely at random, but perhaps that is faulty wiring. These unexplainable events happen daily and have led people to believe that the Leestown Division VA Hospital is one of the most haunted places in Lexington.

THE GREENWOOD SLEEPER

In 1996, a shopper walking through the parking lot of the Greenwood Mall in Bowling Green spotted a truck sitting at the far edge of the lot. From where they stood, they thought they saw a man sleeping in the front seat, so they decided to check on him to see if he was okay. When they approached the vehicle to investigate, they discovered that the man was not sleeping – he was dead.

Alarmed by such a strange discovery, the shopper notified the authorities. When the police arrived and searched the vehicle, it was discovered that the truck had been stolen. Assuming the man in the truck was the thief, police tried to find out his identity. However, he had no identification on him. It is said they never found out who the man was, nor could they determine a cause of death. This unexplained occurrence resulted in a few theories.

The most common conclusion is that the man stole the truck and died in it. It is believed authorities determined this to be the answer and left the case at that. Another is the truck wasn't actually stolen and the man found dead inside was the owner. This deduction makes sense because nowhere in this legend does it say if they ever found the owner of the truck, which wouldn't have been a difficult task.

Another theory is the dead man was neither the thief nor the owner, but the victim of murder. Those who believe this suggestion think the truck was stolen by someone else specifically for the purpose of murdering this man. After killing him, they removed his identification and left his corpse in the vehicle. The logic behind this answer is sound because why would the man have no ID?

In other versions of the story, the vehicle was a van and not a pickup truck. The man was also supposedly removed from the van and buried in a nearby cemetery. After the burial, the van mysteriously vanished from the parking lot. Did the killer, or former owner, return for the vehicle, stealthily removing it from the scene of the alleged crime before any worthwhile evidence could be gathered? Or did mall management simply have it towed? It is also quite possible the police had it towed to their compound for investigation.

Whatever the answer to this mystery, it is believed this death has left a specter in its wake. In the spot where the van once sat, some say there is an oil stain that is shaped like a face. Time, weather, nor extensive cleaning have been able to remove the disturbing stain, as it allegedly still remains there to this day.

Even more chilling than that, if one parks their own car there overnight they might come face to face with the sleeper himself. If you leave your vehicle in the spot where the sleeper died, he will appear in the driver's seat at dawn, only to quickly fade away.

This is a very interesting legend indeed. Our biggest question is where is the parking spot? Apparently, one simply needs to seek out the face-shaped oil stain that won't go away.

SHELL GAS STATION IN PAINTSVILLE

The Shell gas station at 506 South Mayo Trail in Paintsville is reportedly haunted by the spirits of Native Americans. Many former employees have reported frightening occurrences in the store when they were alone. Objects have been thrown across the store, even towards the counter where the employees are. Items have also jumped off shelves and landed quite a ways down the aisles. The cooler doors often open by themselves and lights have been known to flicker.

While these events are pretty unsettling, the disembodied sounds of footsteps and murmurs have really disturbed past employees. But what gives them the idea that these spirits are those of Native Americans are the apparitions that have been witnessed by a few former employees. Allegedly, the ghosts have been seen in full form, looking as though they are dressed for a war party, passing through the store. That's enough to make anyone quit...and it has. It seems it is hard for this particular Shell to keep employees because of this.

These are not the only Native American spirits reported in Paintsville. According to rumors, the entire city was built over a Native American battleground and burial mounds still exist there. This is believed to be the cause for much paranormal activity throughout the town, including the many sightings of Native American spirits.

WAVERLY HILLS SANITORIUM

One can't write a book about Kentucky haunts without including the largest paranormal shadow looming over the city of Louisville: Waverly Hills Sanatorium. Often afforded the distinction of being one of the world's most haunted places, Waverly has quite a collection of ghost stories and gruesome tales reaching up from its history. Reports about a dark shadowy entity lurking the halls to a crawling specter known as the Creeper, to a little boy who supposedly rolls a ball around the hallway, this abandoned tuberculosis hospital has rightfully taken its place among the world's best known super-haunts, right alongside Dracula's Castle and the infamous Winchester Mansion, and has been featured on every credible paranormal show on radio and television. It has also been written about numerous times and been the subject of several television specials. It is a ghost hunter's dream.

Most people know the history and haunts of the ominous structure that sits atop a dark hill overlooking East Pages Lane near Dixie Highway, so a thoroughly detailed account will not be necessary; a brief summarization should suffice.

In the late 1800s, the land was purchased by Major Thomas Hays as a place to raise his family. Since there were no schools nearby, he had a one-room schoolhouse erected and hired a teacher, Leslie Lee Harris, to run it. Since Mrs. Harris was a fan of the Waverley novels by Walter Scott, she called the school the Waverley Schoolhouse, and the name was applied to the entire land by Major Hayes.

After Major Hays died in 1909, the land was purchased by the Board of Tuberculosis Hospital. Due to the catastrophic outbreak of tuberculosis that ravaged the Louisville wetlands along the Ohio River in the early 1900s, the original two-story wooden sanatorium was opened in 1910. It was not the mighty complex it is today. The hospital merely consisted of an office building and two open-air pavilions that housed about fifty patients. The old schoolhouse remained but collapsed over time.

Once the Louisville City Hospital project got underway in 1912, many patients were brought in and kept in tents raised on the property. After more money was granted to the project, a few more wings were added to the building – including a children's pavilion (both for child patients and children of patients who had nowhere else to go) – and Waverly's capacity increased to approximately 130 beds.

The rapid spread of the disease created a greater demand for care. That, along with the constant need for repairs on the building, prompted the construction of the five-story titan that still stands today. Th e project began in 1924 and was completed in 1926, and when it was done the medical sanctuary could hold more than 400 patients.

For the next couple of decades, Waverly Hills Sanatorium remained the refuge for those suffering from the horrid ailment sometimes known as the White Plague. The amount of suffering and death that must have taken place there is immeasurable, and the place kept on filling up. But, when the antibiotic known as streptomycin was introduced in the early 1940s, the spread of tuberculosis was halted and the number of cases began to lower. Eventually, the remaining patients were moved to the Hazelwood Sanatorium and Waverly Hills ceased operations in 1961.

The following year the building was converted into a nursing home that dealt primarily with elderly patients suffering from dementia, as well as those who were severely mentally handicapped. It operated as Woodhaven Geriatric Center for about twenty years before being shut down for patient neglect. After that, in 1983, there were plans to turn it into a minimum security prison, but those plans fell through thanks to neighborhood protestors not wanting that element near their homes. The next project that was slated for the land came in the 90s when the purchaser planned to erect the largest statue of Jesus Chris the world had ever seen, as well as opening an arts and worship center in the building. The money could not be raised and the project was cancelled in 1997.

Enter the current owners. They bought the property in 2001 and have turned it into quite the attraction. With the help of a local paranormal investigative team, they have made Waverly famous for its haunts. Now, they offer overnight paranormal investigations, ghost and historical mini-tours, and a really spooky haunted house attraction during Halloween. There are plans in place to convert the building into a four-star hotel and conference center, which is sure to be a complete success, as the waiting list is said to already be at three years and the project hasn't even begun. With the notoriety Waverly now has, it's safe to say that these folks have helped save the landmark from obscurity, and perhaps even eventual demolition.

It has been reported that nearly 9000 deaths occurred in that building through the decades. Though there has never been an official death toll issued, it is known that many people did meet their end within those walls, and the energy that has been left behind, and the souls that are said to linger there, have often made themselves known in many different forms: shadows, mists, orbs, loud bangs, glowing eyes, rotten stenches, disembodied voices, and even outright manifestations and physical encounters. There are countless videos and photos in circulation that allegedly contain paranormal evidence at Waverly, and various accounts written about people's personal encounters there.

Room 502 on the fifth floor is said to be haunted by the ghost of a nurse who found out she had gotten pregnant out of wedlock and hanged herself. People have reported hearing a woman's voice tell them to get out. When we were in that room, we heard a woman's voice say something from the bathroom area, but could not quite make out the words. A soft humming sound issued from there, as well.

The spirit of a young boy, about six or seven, named Timmy is said to wander the halls of Waverly rolling a ball around. Many visitors will bring balls for the boy to play with and some have reported, and even recorded, the ball seeming to move on its own. As we walked through the place, we saw several balls randomly lying about in different areas, but never got to witness any move on their own. On the fifth floor, we did stand our spirit box up by a ball and we did hear a voice say "Timmy" on the box. Whether or not it was him or something mimicking a child, we could not tell. Timmy's history is unknown, so we didn't have much to go on.

The Death Tunnel, or Body Chute, is rumored to be haunted, which doesn't come as much of a surprise considering this is where the corpses of the deceased were taken so the other patients wouldn't be disturbed by seeing the corpses conveyed through the building. It was also a delivery area for supplies.

It is a long, sloping trip of about five-hundred feet to the bottom, and then a long, steady crawl back to the entrance. To say it is an eerie adventure traveling down that rounded, cold, concrete passage would be putting it mildly. In the dim light of just our lantern and our companions' phones, the trip did come with a sense of uneasiness. Unexplained echoed footsteps, disembodied voices, and moving shadows have been reported in this tunnel by some investigators and visitors, as well as the capturing of some very curious EVPs.

A woman by the name of Lois Higgs is said to still be hanging around Waverly in her old room near the second-floor breezeway where she passed away. She has reportedly been heard talking and been seen wandering in and around her old room. Inside the closet of the room, an old photograph of Lois sitting on the ledge of the breezeway stands with a short bio about her.

Not only did we have spirit box issues in that room, but so did one of the employees who walked with us through the building for a while. We experienced the same thing: our spirit boxes randomly shutting down. They didn't go off or stop working altogether; they were just silenced. The volume was turned low as the lights kept blinking on the devices. Though we all wanted to chalk it up to battery issues or technical problems, the devices worked just fine when we went into other areas. Maybe someone didn't want us communicating with Lois.

There is an area on the fourth floor where it was reported that trespassers became trapped behind a door and couldn't get out, screaming for help until one of the security guards had to open the door for them, after which they bolted from the area as fast as they could. This is also the floor where the notorious shadow people are said to be seen moving around a certain section of the hallway.

One of the most distressing creatures that is said to be in Waverly is a black shadowy form that crawls along the floors, up the walls, and across the ceilings. This entity has been called the Creeper. People who have encountered this nightmarish fiend have expressed a sense of dread and foreboding while in its presence, which has led some to conclude the monster is inhuman, not of this world, and possibly demonic.

There is a theory that the Creeper is the creature that protected a young boy from being tortured with electro-shock therapy many years ago by swooping into the room and warning the doctors to leave the lad be. The description of the being was large, misty, and black with something that appeared to be wings on its back. It was never reported to have crawled, but some believe the Creeper's origins may stem from this specter.

However, another ghost hunter caught a picture of a shadowy form with what looked like wings on its back inside Waverly many years ago. As we were examining our own photographs, we came across one that was taken in a storage area and it shows, in the right corner of the picture, cast along the wall, the same form with wing-shaped protrusions on its shoulders. We think maybe there are good spirits watching over the place, as well, and this may be one of them.

At one point, as we wandered the floors, we kept getting words over the ghost box that we interpreted as warnings. Two words in particular kept clearly ringing out: "Hustle" and "Hurry." Given the events that followed, we think maybe this was someone telling us to leave as soon as we could because something malevolent was on our heels.

Recently, we joined a group of people who decided to partake in the overnight that they offer. For a somewhat hefty admission fee, if one can gather the required group of ten people needed to even be able to enter the place, you can have pretty much free run of the facility from 10pm to 6am, save for a few areas they keep sectioned off for operational and safety purposes. But, if you're a ghost hunter and/or a paranormal enthusiast, it is worth the price of admission.

Not long after we first arrived, Jacob and another man were out on the breezeway – the open air corridor where patients used to soak up the wind and sun as part of their treatment – and saw on the floor above us, through the windows in the center section of the building about a hundred or more feet away, a shadow moving in a doorway. We stood and watched it for a minute. It appeared to move in and out of view a few times before disappearing altogether. While we never discovered the actual source of this shape, the odd occurrences did not end there.

A few minutes later, as the entire group was led around by the employee that was with us, Jacob and the other man heard what sounded either like a sharp hiss or a long scrape of feet along dusty concrete. Both halted and listened, then tried to follow the sound to its source. After they split from the group and ventured down the hallway on the second floor, they heard a loud bang, like a door being slammed. They started wandering the corridor further looking for the cause, but were eventually called back to the group.

While retracing their earlier path down the second floor hallway, they came across a door that had been closed when we passed that way before. They pushed open the door and tried to close it to recreate the sound, but decided it was not the same sound and went on.

Next, they came to the corroded elevator shaft with the rusty door. The other man thought maybe the sound they'd heard earlier could have been something banging against the door, so they both started hitting it, but were never able to make the same bang, so they determined this was not the source of the sound, either.

They decided to walk a little further down the hall to see what they could find. Eventually, they came across an out-of-place, slim door, much lighter and less rusted than the others, with the number 8 spray-painted on it. Since the door looked out of place, they thought they'd inspect it. The other man pushed the door open then Jacob stepped inside the room and slammed it – and perfectly recreated the sound. The man then pushed the door open harder, making it bang against the wall, and Jacob slammed it shut again for a second examination. This, they decided, was what they heard earlier.

Though there was no proof that door 8 slamming shut was the loud bang initially heard, nor could they explain what slammed it if it was, there had been a loud bang in the hallway and it sounded just like that door slamming shut. Seeing as the door is both marked and very different in appearance, it made Jacob suspicious of the reasons why. A trick door somehow, maybe? Or, is it known to have a lot of paranormal activity around it?

At one point, as Jenny and Jacob walked along the breezeway alone, doing a spirit box session, different words came across the frequency, but one in particular disturbed her. Just as she looked up and caught a glimpse of a shadow figure trailing behind Jacob in the dark, the box said, "I'm watching you." Was this perhaps the figure Jacob and the other man had seen previously?

Outside of all other knocks, bangs, scuffles, and voices we picked up throughout the night, one instance really changed Jacob's perspective on the energy that rests inside the historical tomb of Waverly Hills.

It happened when we came across the employee again. Apparently, she is both a history buff and paranormal enthusiast, and she has quite an impressive ghost box, which we will discuss in a bit. But, after the group had gathered once again in full, she joined the party for a little while and we found ourselves gathered on a makeshift stage on the first floor that they had used for their recent Halloween haunted house attraction. She informed us that she believes she has encountered something otherworldly, something that has never been human, a few times while she's been walking the halls alone at night, and also while using her ghost box. She told us that this male entity had cussed her out over the box and often said her name. At the time, her box was back in the office on the second floor, but we had our box ready in our backpack.

Jenny got it out and the employee adjusted it to the settings she preferred and began trying to make contact. A few possible responses came through, though hard to fully interpret, but something peculiar did take place. She and Jacob were sitting on the stage as the rest of the group stood in front of them. She was talking and Jacob was filming. She asked, "How many spirits are in here?" and the box answered, "Seven."

A few seconds after that, Jacob felt a heavy presence standing on the stage behind him. It felt as if someone had risen and began standing right between them. Jacob looked over to see if she had stood up, and she was looking in the direction where he felt the presence. When they began discussing it, it felt like they were talking from somewhere far away, like something had encircled Jacob, muffling his voice. When she replied, it sounded like she was talking with someone standing in front of her, their body making her voice hard to hear.

After a while, the box experienced that sudden drain of energy discussed earlier, so she grabbed her own box and we took it to the second floor into Lois's room. This is when she couldn't get her own box to work. It was doing the same thing ours was: lights were on but the sound was so low and intermittent that it sounded like it was about to die.

After a break, we decided to go up to the roof, and this is where the night got interesting, and it is also when we think we might have figured out why voices on the spirit box had been telling us to "hustle" and "hurry," earlier, as well as another voice that said to Jenny, "Boo! You got to go."

On our way up, when we came to the stairway on the second floor, a sudden foul odor rose up in the hallway right about the same time Jenny began to feel an oppressive presence on top of us. The smell was like sulfur, or methane, or maybe rotted meat, and it followed us up the next two floors. On the fourth floor, Jacob stepped from the stairwell into the hallway and the smell briefly followed him out there and then seemed to dissipate. The others had stopped by the stairs because the employee was beginning to feel sick and develop a headache, so she waited for a minute. When he rejoined them, the smell was gone, and everyone went up to the fifth floor.

When we climbed the last flight of stairs, the smell was still not with us, but Jenny could still feel the energy, like someone was about to talk to her. We crossed the fifth floor towards the roof and, suddenly, the stench returned. The employee then put her ghost box on a window ledge and turned it on—and it worked just fine.

Her ghost box works differently from ours. While the one we have, the SB-11, scans through radio frequencies, picking up static, hers has no static, and the voices that come through speak full sentences and phrases. Ours often do too, but the sound is distorted due to the static, making it sometimes hard to decipher. Not so much the case with her box. The voices will often come out garbled and sometimes broken, as well as tangled with other voices, making it hard to always interpret, but there is no static to mistake it for.

Not long after Jenny heard the humming in Room 502, the box started getting active. A woman's voice seemed to mingle with a rough-sounding male's voice, and it almost sounded as if they were talking back and forth. Intrigued by what was taking place, Jacob knelt beside the box to get a better listen, and began hearing some disturbing stuff.

The female voice began what sounded like a rhythmic chanting, repeating the same thing multiple times. He couldn't make out all of it, but he did hear the phrase "Kingdom come" and the word "light" quite a few times, as well as "Go away."

The male voice was far different. It began to sound agitated, and outright angry. It repeated the word "three" several times, and Jacob also heard it say some horrible things. He heard it issue expletives that were derogatory towards females, and the employee got nervous and started pacing around on the roof. She said it was "him" and did not seem pleased about it.

The voice continued, and Jacob began to hear it say raunchy things. We don't know if the acts it was describing were aimed at the employee or at the female voice chanting against him, but they were pretty explicit in bits, and we don't imagine them being uttered on any radio station.

The energy got pretty intense, and the smell kept wafting about the area. Jenny was ready to go, and there even came a point when Jacob decided we needed to leave. We called that session quits and went back downstairs.

On our way down, despite being shaken up by the session on the roof, Jenny felt at ease when we came across a graffiti warning scrawled on the wall. It read: "King Enubis was hers so prepare to have fear." We wonder if "hers" was actually supposed to be "here." Nonetheless, despite that, and the fact that Anubis was spelled incorrectly, it gave Jenny comfort as she considered it a sign that someone was watching out for us, as if it was telling the bad spirits they'd better beware.

After passing the fourth floor and descending the stairs to the landing, Jacob stopped upon hearing a soft thud in the darkness behind him. When he looked up towards the floor, he saw two yellow lights that looked like eyes peering at him from the darkened floor above. He raised his lantern to see if he could cast enough light to see if someone else was in the building, but saw nothing. Jenny then called for him so he moved on.

We passed the next floor and came down to the first. Everyone else was ahead of Jacob because he kept stopping to see if he could glimpse anything strange in the dark, maybe the eyes again, or a shadowy figure, but he didn't. Just as he was exiting the doorway, the other man from earlier said a quick prayer and told any entities that might have been following us to stay upstairs. Just after that, Jacob heard what sounded like a small rock or pebble tumbling down the steps, like someone had kicked it while walking behind him. He halted and raised the lantern again, saw nothing, and continued. He then heard the thump of footsteps behind him. So, he turned again with the lantern and still didn't see anything. He then told the man that his prayer was probably just making the thing mad, and laughed it off with a chuckle.

Once we got onto the last stretch of the first floor hallway, far away from the last doorway leading away from the stairs, Jacob turned and looked back and saw a form standing in the doorway everyone had passed through. It stood there for a second then passed out of view. He then told the other man to shine his flashlight down there, and when he did, he, Jenny, and Jacob all saw a form standing there in the doorway. It was so far away that we could not discern any details, but it was clearly a form that was moving. That's when everyone decided to leave.

The employee went to the bathroom and got sick and Jenny was too shaken to stay there. She insisted that it was time to leave and, after experiencing her accurate empathic abilities, Jacob did not argue. We stood out on the back porch with the employee and the other man for a little bit, then left.

As we were getting into our car, the employee went to get her golf cart and meet us at the gate, and we heard a strange tapping against the wall across from where we parked. Jacob figured it was merely water coming off the gutter, but as soon as Jenny got in the car, it stopped. Jacob stood outside the car and surveyed the length of the wall and didn't see anything at first. But, just before he turned to get in the car, he saw a quick shadow rise on the wall. It looked like the shape of a man standing there looking at him. It was about twenty feet away, so it could have been anything, or it could have even been someone lurking outside the building. In case it was the latter, Jacob got in the car and drove to the gate where the employee had opened the gate.

As Jenny was looking through the pictures we took, she came across one that was taken on the roof while the male voice on the ghost box was spewing obscenities and innuendoes, and the rotten aroma was antagonizing us. She discovered she had photographed something dreadful towards the edge of the roof. The image was most noticeable by two round lights, set apart like eyes and located in a spot beneath where no streetlights were shining, and below those glowing orbs there appeared to be something like a torso, or arms, gray and thick. It looked as if the creature was hunched over, resting on its knuckles, like a gorilla. When Jacob saw that picture, he decided he had to admit that the two yellow lights he saw could not be explained away as a trick of lights reflecting off something from outside. He went over the picture several times and just could not debunk it. Then he realized: Waverly really is haunted.

Did we encounter something sinister, even demonic, which tailed us all the way up to the roof to keep an eye on us? Is this why voices were telling us to hustle and hurry? Was there a feminine spirit trying to keep the creature at bay? Who knows? Firm believers in the supernatural would say yes. Hardcore skeptics would say no. Those in the middle would conclude that anything is possible, but it could also be explained. Then, those of us who were there, who felt its presence, smelled its stink, and heard its words, would say that we absolutely believe something was creeping through the darkness with us on top of Waverly Hills Sanatorium.

ABOUT THE AUTHORS

Jenny and Jacob Floyd, known as the Frightening Floyds, live in Louisville with their two dogs (Tarzan and Pegasus) and four cats (Baloo, Narnia, Pandy – full name, Pandora Opossum – and Maleficent, whom they call Baby Bat because she looks like a baby bat, and somehow that name has evolved into Bat-Bat, or just simply, The Bat). They enjoy ghosts, aliens, cryptids, Disney, horror, and a bunch of strange and unusual things.

BIBLIOGRAPHY

As always, when investigating stories of ghosts and allegedly haunted locations, we visit some of the same online sites. While we might use these sites, as well as Wikipedia, as reference points, we never solely rely on them. With Wikipedia especially, we are always careful to check all sources listed at the bottom of the page, as well as researching topics further to find them on other sites. We also try to find people to talk to personally who may have information on said haunts. Naturally, given how many stories we find and/or receive, it is impossible to visit all locations and find people to interview for every one of them. Though we make every attempt to do our best research, we cannot claim that everything is one-hundred percent accurate. For many of these locations we did find people to talk to, or had people tell us about them at book signings or during tours. Some of them we researched and found a fair amount of information, others we did not. However, as we stated previously, this book is meant for entertainment purposes only and is not to be considered a historic reference guide (despite our every attempt to provide accurate historical information), nor is it to be considered paranormal evidence. Though we are ghost hunters and paranormal enthusiasts, our work is not dedicated to scientific research and we do not claim to be scientists. This book is more of a collection of stories and legends centered on the paranormal for those who enjoy such things. Below are the many sites and articles we found pertaining to the histories and ghost stories.

As always, we thank those who took the time out of their days to provide us with more information.

Bullittcountyhistory.org

"Fire Ravages Whiskey Row Buildings," by Phillip M. Bailey, Sheldon S. Schafer, Gina Kim, and Janica Kaneshiro, published at

Courier-Journal.com at 5:16pm on July 6th, 2015 and updated at 8:27am on July 7th, 2015

"Whiskey Row" by Tim Talbott at explorekyhistory.ky.gov

"Ghosts and Spirits of Bourbon Distilleries" by Maggie Kimberl at flaviar.com

"The Assassination of Bull Nelson; The Firing and Rehiring of Don Carlos Buell," published by *The Civil War Daily Gazette* on September 29th, 2012 at civilwardailygazette.com. ***This site credits *All for the Regiment* by Gerald Prokopowicz; *Days of Glory* by Larry J. Daniel; *War in Kentucky* by James Lee McDonough; *Perryville* by Kenneth W. Noe as sources.

"Actors Theatre's Top 5 Haunted Louisville Sites," published October 13th, 2016 at actorstheatre.org

"Spirits at the Heart of American Theatre—Actors Theatre of Louisville," by Lewis Powell IV, published April 23rd, 2013 at southernspiritguide.org

"The History of Actors Theatre" at actorstheatre.org

"Get into the Spirit of the Season with Four Haunted Louisville Bars," by Lauren O'Neill, published October 28th, 2014 at 1:55pm at Louisville.com

"Let's All Drink with Ghosts in Louisville's Most Haunted Bars," by Michelle Eigenheer, published on October 17th, 2016 at thrillist.com

"The Classiest Dive: Hilltop Tavern" by Elizabeth Myers, published October 31st, 2014 at Louisville.com

"The Silver Dollar, Louisville" at hipstorical.com

Scary Stories of Mammoth Cave by Colleen O'Conner Olson and Charles Hanion, published by Cave Books on October 29th, 2009; ISBN-10: 0939748541; ISBN-13: 978-0939748549

"Mammoth Cave National Parks Harbors More Than a Few Ghost Stories," posted by Haunted Hitchhiker, published on October 30th, 2009 at nationalparkstraveler.org.

"Ghosts in Mammoth Cave," posted by J. Nathan Couch on August 7th, 2013 at cultofweird.com
"Is Kentucky's Mammoth Cave Haunted," by Ghostghoul, published on November 27th, 2012 at ghostsnghouls.com

"Two of American's Most Haunted Caves," by Christy Gordon, published on August 20th, 2013 at myertiousuniverse.org

"Haunted Mammoth Cave," by Virginia Lamkin, published on April 6th, 2014 at seeksghosts.blogspot.com

"Mammoth Caves" by Andrea Edwards, published January 22nd, 2016 at werewoofs.com

"Black History: Slaves Found Unique Work as Mammoth Cave Guides," posted February 29th, 2004 at bgdailynews.com

Jailhousepizza.com

"The History of the Meade County Jail" by Gerald W. Fischer, posted on June 8th, 2016, at visitmeadecounty.org

Roadsideamerica.com

"50 Most Haunted Colleges and Campuses," by Linda Weems, posted at onlineschoolscenter.com

"The Haunting of Transylvania—Happy Halloween!" by Peter Brackney, posted at kaintuckeean.com Transy.edu

"Constantine Samuel Rafinesque (1783-1840); naturalist" at faculty.evansville.edu

"Spirits of Old Morrison and the Gratz Park Historic District," posted October 11th, 2010 by Lewis Powell IV at southernspiritguide.com

"Kentucky's Cumberland Falls," posted by Virginia Lamkin at 12:07pm on Tuesday, December 15h, 2015 at seeksghosts.blogspot.com

"Cumberland Falls History," at parks.ky.gov

"The Beautiful and Mysterious Cumberland Falls," posted on Thursday, May 9th, 2013 at thecryptocrew.com

Rohsoperahouse.com

"Rohs Opera House, Kentucky," at theresashauntedhistoryofthetri-state.blogspot.com, posted Monday, February 6th, 2012

Hauntedplaces.org

"Paramount Joe—Paramount Arts Center" at hauntedplaces.org

"Paramount Arts Center, Ashland," at hauntedhovel.com

"Billy Ray Cyrus Meets a Ghost…at the Paramount Arts Center in Ashland, KY!" posted Saturday, May 21st, 2011 at theresashauntedhistoryofthetri-state.blogspot.com

Paramountartscenter.com
Benhaminn.com

"Ky.'s Benham Schoolhouse Inn," posted Wednesday, March 5th, 2014 at Theresashauntedhistoryofthetri-state.blogspot.com

"The 11 Most Haunted Hotels in Kentucky," at hauntedrooms.com

"Haunted States: Kentucky," posted October 8th, 2015 at inwanderlust.weebly.com

"Cold Spots: The Ghost of Octavia Hatcher," published on December 15th, 2009 by Scott A. Johnson at dreadcentral.com

"The Story of Octavia Hatcher," by David Tabler, posted April 3rd, 2012 at appalachianhistory.net

"The True Story of Octavia Hatcher - History vs. Myth," by J'aime Rubio, posted Tuesday, January 13th, 2015 at dreamingcasuallypoetry.blogspot.com; this site also credits the following resources: familysearch.com; findagrave.com; 1870 Consensus, Pike, Kentucky; *Daily Review*, Decatur, Ill. (09/28/1892); prairieghosts.com; *Milwaukee Sentinel* (08/03/1959); *The History of Kentucky*, by William Elsey Connelly, (1922); *A Fever in Salem* by Laurie Winn Carlson; *Framing Tropical Disease in London* by Patrick Manson (1891-1902); "A Wake-up Call About Sleeping Sickness" by Peter G.E. Kennedy, M.D., posted October 1st, 2003 at dana.org; *Mysteries at the Museum*, aired on Travel Channel on December 20th, 2012 (Season 3, Episode 6); *Pike County News* (10/05/1939); "Add to the Legends of Ivy Creek," by Henry P. Scalf, published on June 21st, 1956 in the *Floyd County Times*; *The Man Behind the Monument* and *The Case of the Missing Memorial Arch* by Robert Perry

"Weird Happenings at the Baxter Avenue Morgue," by Brandon Vigliarolo, published September 5th, 2014 at Louisville.com

Louisvilleparanormalinvestigations.net

"10 Creepy Houses in Kentucky That Could Be Haunted," by Jenn Shockley, posted October 7th, 2015 at onlyinyourstate.com

Baxter Avenue Morgue Facebook page: @BaxterAveMorgue

The highlandsoflouisville.com

"Wikipedia: Articles for Deletion/The Vanderdark Morgue" at knowpia.com

"Baxter Avenue Morgue" at louisvillehalloween.com

"Bobby Mackey's Haunted History," posted at travelchannel.com

"Bobby Mackey's: Wilder, Kentucky", at trytoscareme.com

"Gambling, Gangsters, and Girls," at newportcityofsin.wordspress.com

"Bobby Mackey's Music World," at creepycincinnati.com

"Who Killed Pearl Bryan and Where is Her Head?" by Shannon Byers at Americas-most-haunted.com

"The Mysteries of Pearl Bryan," by Robert Wilhelm at murderbygaslight.com; originally published as "Pearl Bryan: Headless Corpse Found on Northern Ky. Farm" by Robert Wilhelm in Kentucky Explorer, Volume 26, No. 6, November 2011; others sources listed from this article are: Cincinnati Enquirer, February 1896 – June 1896, January 1897 – March 1897; Cincinnati Tribune, February 1896 – April 1896; Cincinnati Post, March 1897; Greencastle Banner Times, January 1897 – February 1897; Greencastle Democrat, February 1896, January 1897 – March 1897; Indianapolis Sun, February 1896; and Poock, L. D. *Headless Yet Identified; A Story of the Solution of the Pearl Bryan or Fort Thomas Mystery, Through the Shoes*, Cincinnati, OH: Hann & Adair, Printers, 1897. Also posted at *Northern Kentucky Views*

Wilder, Kentucky at kyatlas.com

"The Robsons' Old '76 Distillery – Plague of Finchtown," by Jack Sullivan, posted at pre-prowhiskeymen.blogspot.com

"Covington & Bridgeport, KY Bridge Construction Collapse, June 1892," at gendisasters.com, from *The Salem Daily News Ohio,* June 16th, 1892

"Haunted Honky-Tonk," by Larry Nager, posted at cincinnatimagazine.com

"Bobby Mackey's Music World," at hauntedhouses.com

"Haunted History of Bobby Mackey's Music World Fails to Stand Up to Scrutiny," at doubtfulnews.com

"Bobby Mackey's: America's Terrifying Portal to Hell," by Dana Newkirk at roadtrippers.com

"Top 8 Most Haunted Places in Kentucky," by Jenn Shockley at kyforky.com

"Stories of the Castle on the Cumberland," by Mycheala Bruner at wpsdlocal6.com

"Talking *HAUNTINGS OF THE KENTUCKY STATE PENITENTIARY* with Author Steve E. Asher on After Hours AM/America's Most Haunted Radio and paranormal news with Joel and Eric, your real ghost stories with Kirsten Klang" by Eric Olsen at Americas-most-haunted.com

"Haunted Kentucky State Penitentiary," by Tony Brueski, at thegravetalks.com

"Caged in at the Castle," by Benjamin Joubert, at kentuckynewera.com

"Corrections Officers Attacked by Inmates at Kentucky State Penitentiary," by Ellen Miller at wkrn.com

"Inmates Attack Corrections Officers at Kentucky State Penitentiary," by Greg Kocher at Kentucky.com

"2 Corrections Officers Attacked by Inmates at Kentucky State Penitentiary," by Kara Apel and Marion Kirkpatrick at wsmv.com

Kentucky index at deathpenaltyusa.com

Kentucky State Penitentiary, Ep. 220" at historygoesbump.com

"Top 8 Most Haunted Places in Kentucky," by Jenn Shockley at kyforky.com

Camptaylorhistorical.org

Fort Knox, Kentucky at kyatlas.com

Influenzaarchive.org

"The History of Camp Taylor – from WWI Military Camp to Working Class Neighborhood," by Cameron Aubernon, at insiderlouisville.com

"Maintenance Barn at Joe Creason Park to be Removed and Replaced; Historic Elements to be Documented and Salvaged for Possible Future Re-use," at louisvilleky.gov

"Preservationists Ask City to Reconsider Demolishing Old Camp Taylor Building," by Rick Howlett at wfpl.org

"The Creepy Small Town in Kentucky with Insane Paranormal Activity," by Andrea Limke at onlyinyourstate.com

"Top Haunted Places in Kentucky 2018," at kantuckee.com

"Hiestand House – Real Haunt in Campbellsville, KY," at kentuckyhauntedhouses.com

"The Heart of it All: Campbellsville-Taylor County KY," at taylorcounty.us

"Kentucky Town, Texas," at texasescapes.com

"Hiestand House – Taylor County Museum," at campbellsvilleky.com

"Campbellsville, KY – the Hiestand House," by Tyler Cooper at realhauntedplaces.blogspot.com

"John Hunt Morgan," at trailsrus.com: 27d – "Raid on Hiestand-Chandler House"

"Raid on the Hiestand-Chandler House," at hmdb.org

"Bernson's Corner: The Mystery Woman of Harrodsburg Springs," at wdrb.com

"Parks," at harrodsburgcith.org

"Unknown Grave in Harrodsburg Tied to Ghost Story" by Marvin Bartlett at foxlexington.com

"Molly "the Dancing Lady" *Black* Sewell" at findagrave.com

"Graham Springs Hotel," at theclio.com

Hometownforums.com

"Ordinary Looking Cover…to the Lady who "Danced Herself to Death?" by Patricia Kaufman at americanstampdealer.com

"The Haunting on Meshack Road," by James Donahue at perdurabo10.net

"Phantom Hitchhikers: Unnerving Tales of Ghostly Hitchhikers Who Vanish into the Air," by Stephen Wagner at thoughtco.com

"Tompkinsville, KY – Dancing Ghost on Meshack Road," by Tyler Cooper at realhauntedplaces.blogspot.com

"Guide to US Ghosts Finds Several in Kentucky," by Associated Press for *The Courier Journal*, published October 31st, 1996; clipping found at newspapers.com

"Roadside Ghosts," at profilingtheunexplained.com

"Spurlington Tunnel – Campbellsville, KY," at hauntedhovel.com

"Campbellsville, KY – Spurlington Tunnel," by Tyler Cooper at realhauntedplaces.blogspot.com

"Small Towns Can Be Spooky to, You Know…" at itsasmalltownlife.blogspot.com

"Haunted Places in Kentucky," at shadowlands.net

"Tip #983 – The Iron Horse Caused Many Deaths and Injuries from 1882-1935," at ancestry.com

"Timeline of the James Gang," at legendsofamerica.com

"James-Younger Gang," at Wikipedia.com

"The Members of the James-Younger Gang," at angelfire.com

"George Shepherd 'Killed' Jesse James, 1879 Lore" by Evelyn Flood at genealogy.com

"The Allendale Train Tunnel," at creepycincinnti.com

"12 Creepy Urban Legends Around Kentucky," by Jenn Shockley at onlyinyourstate.com

"Haunted Places: Grandview Cemetery's 'Gates of Hell," by Carly Garcia at Louisville.com

"Gates of Hell – Grandview Cemetery – Kasey's Cemetery," at hauntedplaces.org

"Enter the Gates of Hell," by Chad Benefield at wbkr.com; cites source at Kentucky Unknown on Facebook
*Also checked Google Maps to determine exact location of the cemetery since there is some misleading information out there. You will find its location under Grandview Cemetery.

"Grisly Finds at Hardin County Cemetery Prompt Investigation," by William Wilczewski at stithvalley.com, taken from the *Hardin County News Enterprise*, published on April 08th, 2003

"Top 5 Most Haunted Places in Kentucky," at kyforky.com

"Haunted Places in Kentucky," by Karen Frazier at paranormal.lovetoknow.com

"Investigate Perryville, Kentucky: Where the Ghosts of the Civil War Haunt the Blood-Stained Battlefield," by Greg Newkirk at weekinweird.com

"Perryville Battlefield" at parks.ky.gov

"The Haunting of Perryville Battlefield," at jdrhawkins.com

"Perryville: Battle of Chaplin Hills," at battlefields.org

Perryvillebattlefield.org

"The Ghosts of Perryville Battlefield," at americashauntedroadtrip.com

"Ghost Soldiers," by Pam Windsor at kentuckyliving.com

"Perryville Battlefield – Real Haunt in Perryville KY," at kentuckyhauntedhouses.com

"Top 9 Most Haunted Places in Lexington, KY," at hauntedrooms.com

"The Ultimate Terrifying Northern Kentucky Road Trip is Right Here – and It'll Haunt Your Dreams," by Jenn Shockley at onlyinyourstate.com

"Lexington's Historic Veterans' Affairs Hospital," by Peter Brackney at kaintuckeean.com
"Hebron Lutheran Church," at bcpl.org

"Hopeful Lutheran Church (BE 171)," by bcpl.org

"A Brief History," PDF found at bcpl.org

"Hebron Lutheran Cemetery" at hauntedplaces.org

"Haunted Cemeteries in Kentucky," by Lori Gross at hubpages.com

"The Belle of Louisville, Louisville, Kentucky (Haunted Place)," at what-when-how.com
Belleoflouisville.org

"History of the Great Steamboat Race," at discover.kdf.org

"10 Most Haunted Places in Louisville, KY," at hauntedrooms.com

"Belle of the Boos—Louisville, Kentucky," at southernspiritguide.org

"Star-crossed Lovers of Carter Caves," at theresashauntedhistoryofthetri-state.blogspot.com

"The Haunted X Cave, Kentucky Cave, is Haunted by Native American Ghosts," at beforeitsnews.com

"In the Valley of Love and Delight"—the Simple Spirits of Pleasant Hill," by Lewis Powell IV at southernspiritguide.org

"History of the Shakers" at nps.gov; site also credits these sources: *The Shaker Experience in America* by Stephen J. Stein; *The American Soul Rediscovering the Wisdom of the Founders* by Jacob Needleman; Shakers Compendium of the origin, History, principles, Rules and Regulations, Government, and Doctrines of the United Society of Believers in Christ's Second Appearing with Biographies of Ann Lee, William Lee, Jas. Whittaker, J. Hocknell, J. meacham, and Lucy Wright by F.W. Evans; *Principles and Beliefs* by the Sabbathday Lake Shaker Village; *The Shaker Legacy Perspectives on an Enduring Furniture Style* by Christian Becksvoort; *The Architecture of the Shakers* by Julie Nicoletta

Shakervillageky.org

"Hair-Raising History," at blog.shakervillageky.org

"The Story Behind Kentucky's Most Haunted House Will Give You Nightmares," by Jenn Shockley at onlyinyourstate.com

Records of the Abraham Ditto House Inn via Historic Resources of Hardin County at npgallery.nps.gov

"11 Most Haunted Hotels in Kentucky" at hauntedrooms.com

Fortduffield.com

"Ditto House Inn, West Point, Kentucky," at innsite.com

"Louisville's Water Tower and Museum Offer a Glimpse into a Historical and Integral Process," by James Natsis at insiderlouisville.com

Louisvillewatertower.com

"Louisville Water Tower Park," at gotolouisville.com

"Water Tower & Pumping Station," at historiclouisville.com

"Hauntings in Gratz Park," by Jamie Millard at smileypete.com

"Lexington's Haunted Gratz Park Inn," at theresashauntedhistoryofthetri-state.blogspot.com

"Ghosts in the Hallway at Gratz Park Inn," by Keila Bender at bitoftheblugrass.com

"The History of the Gratz Park Inn," at cecentral.com

"The Sire Hotel," at tapestrycollection3.hilton.com

"Refurbished Downtown Hotel to Open Under New Eye-Catching Name," by Janet Patton, published in *The Herald Leader* at Kentucky.com

"Haunted Historic Houses," by Victoria Reitano at thisoldhouse.com

"Narrows Road" at creepycincinnati.com

"Stay Away from Kentucky's Most Haunted Street After Dark or You'll Be Sorry," by Andrea Limke at onlyinyourstate.com

"10 Most Haunted Places in Kentucky with Chilling Stories," at hauntedia.com

"Coral Hill Road – Real Glasgow Haunts" at kentuckyhauntedhouses.com

"The Axeman Cometh…" at urbanlegendsofbarren.wordpress.com

Theshadowlands.net

Hauntedplaces.org

"Barren Co. Historical Society 10-26-2017" at urbanlegendsofbarren.wordpress.com

"Lindsey Wilson College – Real Haunts in Columbia Kentucky" at kentuckyhauntedhouses.com

Lindsey.edu

"1930s Death at Lindsey Wilson" at topix.com

"La Grange, Kentucky: La Grange Ghost Tour: Jennie the Typhoid Girl," at roadsideamerica.com

"Rails Restaurant – La Grange KY Real Haunts" at kentuckyhauntedhouses.com
Hauntedplaces.org

"Don't Drive on These 10 Haunted Streets in Kentucky…or You'll Regret It," by Jenn Shockley at onlyinyourstate.com

Lagrangemainstreet.org

Rennick, Robert M. (1988). "Place Names". Kentucky Place Names. Lexington, Kentucky; The University Press of Kentucky. ISBN 0-8131-0179-4
Xome.com

Wku.edu

***All *College Heights Herald* articles found at wkuherald.com

"Spooky Tales from WKU's Residence Halls," by Andrew Critchelow at wkuherald.com

"Official Recount Stories of WKU's 'Haunted' Spots," by Aaron Frasier at wkuherald.com

Ellis, William E. (2011). A History of Education in Kentucky; Lexington, Kentucky: University Press of Kentucky. ISBN 0-8131-4023-4

"Western Kentucky University" at ghost.hauntedhouses.com

"Western Student Crushed to Death by Elevator," from the Courier-Journal, page 43, November 8th, 1967

"The Haunting of Western Kentucky University," by Josie Huffman in *The Daily Chomp* at gatornews.org

"The Haunting of the Western Kentucky University" at hauntsofamerica.blogspot.com

"Things That Go Bump on the Hill," by Dana Albrecht at the *College Heights Herald*, October 29th, 1997

"Haunted Hill," by Lindsay Sainlar, at the *College Heights Herald*, October 30th, 2003

Westernkentuckyuniversity.pastperfectonline.com

Digitalcommons.wku.edu

"Season for Shivers," by David Sutherland, *College Heights Herald*, February 23rd, 1971

"Greek Goblins," by Melissa Gagliardi, *College Heights Herald,* October 29th, 1992

"Tales of Terror," by Perry Hines, *College Heights Herald,* October 29th, 1981

Wkuphidelt.org

Delts.org

"Former WKU Fraternity, Delta Tau Delta, to Recharter," by Spencer Harsh, *College Heights Herald*, March 5th, 2018

"WKU Chapter of Delta Tau Delta Suspended," by Kae Holloway, *College Heights Herald,* August 27th, 2014

Lambdachialpha.org

"8 Haunted Places at Western Kentucky University," by Elisabeth Moore at theodysseyonline.com

Kappadelta.org

"Thrill on the Hill: Ghosts, Spooks Haunt Western," by Chris Hutchins, from *College Heights Herald*, published October 30th, 1997

"WKU's Haunted Halls," by Justin Story, published at bgdailynews.com

Sae.net

"SAE Fire Set," by Jim Gaines at bgdailynews.com

"Charles J. Vanmeter" at findagrave.com

"Boo! Van Meter Ghost Haunts Western's Actors," by Dolly Carlisle, *College Heights Herald,* May 3, 1973

Ghosts of Western Kentucky University by Lynn E. Niedermeier

Hauntedjourneys.com

Kentuckyhauntedhouses.com

"15 Haunted Places in Kentucky That Will Give You Nightmares Tonight," by Jenn Shockley at onlyinyourstate.com

"The Historic Sherman Tavern" by Xavier Blanco at spooksandstuff.weebly.com

"The Sherman Tavern" at nkyviews.com, article taken from *Kentucky Progress Magazine*, 1932

"Sherman Tavern" by Barbara Brown, from *Bulletin of the Kenton County Historical Society*, from January/February 2013

"Dry Ridge, Kentucky Ghost Sightings" at ghostsofamerica.com

"Mrs. Stella Cohen Peine – C.C. Cohen Building, the Ghost" by Jeanettestakeonlife.blogspot.com

"The Ghost at C.C. Cohen" at kentuckyghosts.blogspot.com

Dark Creepy Places: Uncovering the Mysteries of the Supernatural by Larry Wilson, excerpt found at lwilsonurbanparanormal.blogspot.com

"16 Disturbing Cemeteries in Kentucky That Will Give You Goosebumps" by Jenn Shockley at onlyinyourstate.com

"Haunted Places in Kentucky," posted by Bob Uehlein at beaver1003.com

"These 10 Haunted Cemeteries in Kentucky Are Not for the Faint of Heart," by Jenn Shockley at onlyinyourstate.com

"Don't Drive on These 10 Haunted Streets in Kentucky…Or You'll Regret It," by Jenn Shockley at onlyinyourstate.com

Ghostquest.net

"A Haunted Harlan Road" at maps.roadtrippers.com

"The Hell Hound of Baker Hollow Road Cemetery" at theresashauntedhistoryofthetri-state.blogspot.com

"Baker Hollow Road Cemetery" at hauntin.gs

"A Guide to Haunted Cemeteries in Kentucky" at sawpan.com

"Baker-Phillips Cemetery Explanation" at westernkyhistory.org

"These 10 Haunted Hotels in Kentucky Will Make Your Stay a Nightmare" by Jenn Shockley at onlyinyourstate.com

"11 Most Haunted Hotels in Kentucky" at hauntedrooms.com

"The Campbell House Curio, a Collection by Hilton" at historichotels.org

"Top 9 Most Haunted Places in Lexington, KY" at hauntedrooms.com

"Big Bone Lick History" at parks.ky.gov

Hunter, David (October 1, 2003). *Shifra Stein's Day Trips from Cincinnati: Getaways Less Than Two Hours Away*. Globe Pequot. p. 138. Retrieved 2013-04-25.

Vaccariello, Linda (November 2009). "And On the Sixth Day, God Created Paleontologists". *Cincinnati Magazine*. p. 86. Retrieved 2013-05-18.

Kenneth T. Gibbs (September 1986). "Kentucky Historic Resources Inventory: Big Bone Methodist Church". National Park Service. Retrieved December 24, 2017.

Rev. Elmer K. Kidwell obituary at *Boone County Recorder*, 12-14-1967

"Big Bone Lick State Park" by Xavier Blanco at spooksandstuff.weebly.com

Haunted History Facebook page: @historyhaunted

"Barbourville, KY – Warfield Cemetery" at realhauntedplaces.blogspot.com

"Haunted Halls" by Heather Cole at thetimestribune.com

"Pfeifer Room 131" by Chris Privett at yourghoststories.com

"Union College Pfeiffer Hall Room 245 – Barbourville, Kentucky" at hauntedplacesofusa.blogspot.com

Union College Campus map at unionky.edu

Eku.edu

"MADSOCIAL: EKU's Ghost Stories – Dodd Talks Supposed Hauntings on Campus" by Sara Kuhl at richmondregister.com

"Haunting of Sullivan Hall" by Taylor Lainhart and Whitney Ferrell for *Upward Branch,* at upwardbound.eku.edu

"5 of the Most Haunted Places in Kentucky" at theodysseyonline.com

"Ghosts of E.K.U." at bitofthebluegrass.com

"Greenwood Mall" at ghosts.fandom.com

"Murder at the Mall," from *Tales of Kentucky Ghosts* by William Montell, page 199

"Phantom Trucker of Booger Mountain - between Barbourville and Corbin, Kentucky" at southeasternghosts.blogspot.com

"Brandenburg, KY - Meade County High School" at realhauntedplaces.blogspot.com

"Meade County High School" at meade.ky.mch.schoolinsites.com

Ghostlyworld.org

"Three Tales Of A Haunted Williamsburg" by Danielle Lynn Hayes at theodysseyonline.com

Monster Spotters Guide to North America by Scott Francis

Kykinfolk.org

Creepycincinnati.com

"The Legend of Devil's Garden" at thecryptocrew.com

Paranormalstories.blogspot.com

"Most People Don't Know the Story Behind This Hidden Tunnel in Kentucky" by Rachel Shulhafer at onlyinyourstate.com

The Southwestern Reporter. West Publishing Company. 1915. p. 628

National Geographic Society (U.S.) (March 5, 2013). *National Geographic Guide to Scenic Highways and Byways*. National Geographic Books. p. 122.

Dow, Fred (January 1, 2005). *U. S. National Forest Campground Guide: Southern Region*. Moon Canyon Publishing. p. 137. Retrieved 2013-05-03

Cliffviewresort.com

"The Paranormal at Home: Hauntings in 50 States – Kentucky's Pilot's Knob Cemetery" by Shel Gatto, at fringeparanormal.wordpress.com

"Myth of the 'Witch Girl' Next Door" by Peggy Gilkey at timesleader.net

"Debunking a Kentucky Cemetery Legend" at theresashauntedhistoryofthetri-state.blogspot.com

"Caleb: Fact or Fiction" at thetimestribune.com

"The Ghost of Headless Annie" at coolinterestingstuff.com

"Kentucky Haunted" at kysenate.tripod.com

"GHOST MAP: We dare you to explore these 300+ haunted places in Kentucky and Indiana" by Emma Austin at courier-journal.com

"Ghost Bride of Pine Mountain" at unusualkentucky.com

"Haunted tales from the old Hazard ARH" by Connor James, at wymt.com

"Disturbing Things Happened In These 11 Small Towns In Kentucky" by Jenn Shockley at onlyinyourstate.com

"Elesewhere, Kentucky" at reddit.com

"There's A Town In Kentucky That You Won't Ever Be Able To Find On A Map, And For Good Reason" by Seamus Coffey at thoughtcatalog.com

"City In Kentucky Just Disappeared – Tristate Haunts and Legends" by Leslie Morgan at wkdq.com

"Elsewhere, or Not?" at wanderinginthewonderful.blogspot.com

"Man Appears Out of Nowhere at Twin Tunnels" at newsnky.com

"The Twin Train Tunnels" at creepycincinnati.com

"The Little Girl Who Fell" at yourghoststories.com

Findagrave.com

Breathitt County Museum Facebook page

"The Washington Opera House" at hauntedhouses.com

Maysville, Kentucky Opera House Fire page at GenDisasters.com

MaysvillePlayers.net

Washington Opera House page at Northern Kentucky Views

Cincinnati Ghosts, and Other Tri-State Haunts, by Karen Laven, Schiffer Publishing Limited, pages 67-72, 2008

"Does a Ghost Haunt Nunn Hall?" by Jessalyn Fulton at thetrailblazeronline.net

The Trail Blazer, Vol. 41, Issue 9

"Morehead State University History". Archived from the original on 2016-03-29. Retrieved 25 March 2016.

"Morehead State University Ghost(s) Story" at bitofthebluegrass.com

"Loretta's Spirit Lives at the Washington Opera House" by Sean McHugh and Katie McHugh Parker at thespiritlady.blogspot.com

"Washington Opera House" at unusualkentucky.blogspot.com

"Morehead, KY – Mr. Gatti's" at realhauntedplaces.blogspot.com

Stanton, Shelby L. (1991). *World War II Order of Battle.* *Galahad Books.* p. 598. ISBN 0-88365-775-9.

"Morganfield, KY - Earl C. Clements Job Corps Center" at realhauntedplaces.blogspot.com

"Asbury Cemetery: Unusual Sights & Ghostly Tales" at fourriversexplorer.com

"Asbury Cemetery" at kentuckyghosts.blogspot.com

"Haunted Houses in Nicholasville, Kentucky" by Susan DeFeo at traveltips.usatoday.com

"Ghost Stories Linked to Kentucky Covered Bridge" by Marvin Bartlett at foxlexington.com

"National Register Information System Application Form". National Register of Historic Places. National Park Service. 1975-08-22.

"Haunted Colville Covered Bridge" at americanantiquities.com

"Colville Covered Bridge" at explorehistory.ky.gov

"Not Many People Realize These 7 Little Known Haunted Places In Kentucky Exist" by Andrea Limke at onlyinyourstate.com

Haunted U.S.A, Charles Wentzel, page 27; ISBN: 978-1402737350; released October 7th, 2008 by Sterling

Haunted Places: The National Directory: Ghostly Abodes, Sacred Sites, UFO Landings and Other Supernatural Locations by Dennis William Hauck, page 190; ISBN: 978-0142002346; released August 27th, 2002 by Penguin Books

"Ghost Towns and Mushroom Mines" at the kyfiles.blogspot.com

"The Mushroom Mines of Kentucky" at thecliosociety.blogspot.com

"Stanton, KY – Boone Creek Woods" at realhauntedplaces.blogspot.com

"The Cody Road Bridge" at creepycincinnati.com

"Most Haunted Places in Lexington, KY" at hauntedrooms.com

"Lexington Cemetery Mausoleum" at
unusualkentucky.blogspot.com

"The Ultimate Terrifying Kentucky Road Trip is Right Here
– And It'll Haunt Your Dreams" by Jenn Shockley at
onlyinyourstate.com

"Historic Homes and Places" at visitlex.com

U.S. Geological Survey Geographic Names Information
System: Hi Hat, Kentucky

Rennick, Robert M. (1987). *Kentucky Place Names*.
University Press of Kentucky. p. 140. ISBN 0813126312.
Retrieved 2013-04-28.

Kentucky's Haunted Mansions by Jacob and Jenny Floyd

Doeruninn.com

"Doe Run Inn" at frightfind.com

440main.com

"History, Folklore and the Supernatural Clash in Unseen
Bowling Green" by Adam Sims, at wkuherald.com

Louisville's Strange and Unusual Haunts by Jacob and Jenny
Floyd

"Happy Hollow Rd" – Real Haunted Place at
kentuckyhauntedhouses.com

"Haunted Tunnels" – *The Kentucky Files* at
thekyfiles.blogspot.com

"Free Union Separate Baptist Church" – Real Haunted Place at kentuckyhauntedhouses.com

"Our Immaculate Conception Church" at parish.stspp.com

"The Kentucky Chronicles: Bethlehem Academy" by Alexa Smith at *The Central Times* at chhsnews.com

ALSO AVAILABLE
FROM
ANUBIS PRESS

STRANGE AND UNUSUAL MYSTERIES

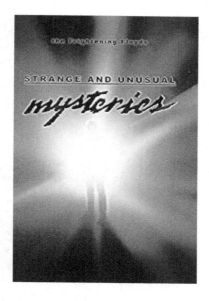

What you are about to read is not a news report; it is neither a bulletin nor an alert. Rather, it is a collection of accounts of strange and unusual occurrences – some solved, some unsolved, but all mysterious. These reports have circulated for decades; some so much that they have become the sources of legends and rumors, even theories involving deep conspiracies. Despite many investigations and countless hours of research, there remain many questions unanswered. However, for every mystery there is someone out there who knows the truth, who possesses the evidence to solve the riddle. Maybe that someone will open this book and find their report. That someone could even be you.

Ahead you will find tales of ghosts, missing persons, ancient legends, and extraterrestrial visitors. What are their stories, or, more importantly, where did their stories come from? Read the enclosed accounts and decide for yourself.

Please, join us – maybe you can help the Frightening Floyds solve a mystery.

AMERICAN CRYPTIC

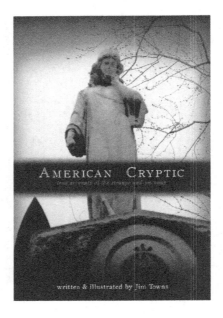

AMERICAN CRYPTIC is an open-minded cynic's take on the uncanny and sometimes frightening things which border our accepted reality. Through thirteen stories and essays, author and filmmaker Jim Towns examines several legends native to his own roots in Western Pennsylvania, and recalls some of his own unexplainable experiences as well. From legends of Native American giants buried under great earth mounds, to a haunted asylum, to a phantom trolley passenger, this work seeks not only to present the reader with new and fascinating supernatural tales, but also to deconstruct why our culture is so fascinated by their telling and re-telling.

HAUNTED SURRY TO SUFFOLK:
SPOOKY LOCATIONS ALONG ROUTES 10 AND 460

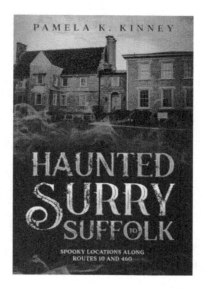

Take a journey along Virginia's scenic Routes 10 and 460 eastbound to enjoy the lovely countryside and metropolises that spread around these two roads. Most of all, discover that some historical houses, plantations, battlefields, parks, and even the modern cities, have more than touristy knickknacks, ham, and peanuts to offer. Many have ghosts!

Bacon's Castle has spirits haunting it since the 1600s. Stay in a cabin overnight at Chippokes Plantation State Park and you might find you have a spectral bedfellow. The city of Smithfield has more to offer than the world's oldest ham; it also has some very old phantoms still stalking its buildings. Take a ghost tour of Suffolk and see why the biggest little city is also one of the spookiest. Discover the myths and legends of the Great Dismal Swamp and see what phantoms are still haunting the wildlife refuge. And if that's not enough, Bigfoot and UFOs are part of the paranormal scenery. These and other areas of southeastern Virginia are teeming with ghosts, Sasquatch, UFOs, and monsters. See what awaits you along 460 south and 10. No matter which road you take, the phantoms can't wait to SCARE you a good time.

HANDBOOK FOR THE DEAD

DON'T FORGET YOUR HANDBOOK...

Welcome all spirits! The Frightening Floyds present to you, *Handbook for the Dead* – a guide to help all new manifestations realize their functional perimeters.

Within this anthology, you'll read paranormal accounts from individuals who have experienced phantoms and disturbances that have not only chilled them, but also left them with some new insight into the supernatural. Now, they want to share their stories and wisdom with you. That way, if you're feeling a little flat, or even if you're a lost soul, you won't have to draw a door and knock.

Handbook for the Dead is sure to please the strange and unusual in everyone, and we promise it doesn't read like stereo instructions.

ALIENS OVER KENTUCKY

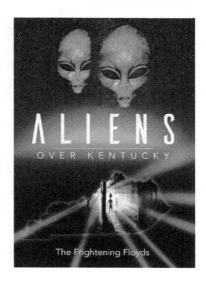

From the Frightening Floyds, the pair of paranormal enthusiasts who brought you *Be Our Ghost* and *Haunts of Hollywood Stars and Starlets* comes a new adventure into the realm of the unknown – *Aliens over Kentucky*.

This collection includes the most noted extraterrestrial encounters from the Bluegrass State, such as the Kelly Creatures Incident of 1955, the Stanford Abductions, the Dogfight above General Electric, and the tale of Capt. Thomas Mantell chasing a UFO through Kentucky skies. But that's not all. There are lesser known, but equally intriguing, reports herein, such as the train collision with the UFO, stories of unexplained crop circles and cattle mutilations, Spring-heeled Jack, the Meat Shower of 1876, and many eyewitness reports of various unidentified crafts. You'll also read a couple of personal experiences from the authors, and even Muhammad Ali gets involved in the alien action.

Join Jacob and Jenny Floyd as they dig into the mysterious cases and theories regarding Kentucky's "X-Files". Just be sure to keep one eye on the book and the other on the sky…

BE OUR GHOST

The Frightening Floyds invite you to be our ghost as we take you on a tour of the happiest haunted place on Earth! In this book, you will read about much of the alleged paranormal activity as well as urban legends spanning the various Disney theme parks around the world. From the haunted dolls of It's a Small World to the real ghosts of the Haunted Mansion, there are many spirits here to greet you. And make sure to say "Good morning" to George at Pirates of the Caribbean.

Enjoy the spooky and fascinating tales in *Be Our Ghost*! And don't worry, there are no hitchhiking ghosts ahead...or are there?

PARANORMAL ENCOUNTERS

The Frightening Floyds present *Paranormal Encounters*: a collection of 14 tales of true ghostly experiences. From a malevolent spirit remaining in an apartment, to a loving phone call from a lost relative; from a house with a sliding chair and slamming doors, to a snow globe moving across a bedroom; from a possible past-life experience to a ghostly stranger in a radio station, this anthology contains several strange and unusual stories that are sure to entertain fans of the paranormal.

HAUNTS OF HOLLYWOOD STARS AND STARLETS

Explore the dark side of Tinseltown in this collection of paranormal stories, conspiracy theories, curses, and legends about some of Hollywood's most iconic names: Marilyn Monroe, Rudolph Valentino, Charlie Chaplin, James Dean, Jean Harlow, Clark and Carole, Lucille Ball, Michael Jackson, Bela Lugosi, Lon Cheney, John Belushi, and the King himself—Elvis Presley—and many more. Join the Frightening Floyds as they take you on a terrifying journey through the city of glamour and glitz!

Thank you for reading! If you like the book, please leave a review on Amazon and Goodreads. Reviews help authors and publishers spread the word!

To keep up with more Anubis Press news, join the Anubis Press Dynasty on Facebook.

Made in the USA
Coppell, TX
21 September 2022

83394534R00174